# Creating
## Loving
## Attachments

*by the same author*

**Using Stories to Build Bridges with Traumatized Children**
Creative Ideas for Therapy, Life Story Work, Direct Work and Parenting
*Kim S. Golding*
*Foreword by Steve Killick*
*Foreword by Dan Hughes*
*Illustrated by Julia McConville*
ISBN 978 1 84905 540 6
eISBN 978 0 85700 961 6

**Observing Children with Attachment Difficulties in Preschool Settings**
A Tool for Identifying and Supporting Emotional and Social Difficulties
*Kim S. Golding, Jane Fain, Ann Frost, Sian Templeton and Eleanor Durrant*
ISBN 978 1 84905 337 2
eISBN 978 0 85700 676 9

**Observing Children with Attachment Difficulties in School**
A Tool for Identifying and Supporting Emotional and
Social Difficulties in Children Aged 5 11
*Kim S. Golding, Jane Fain, Ann Frost, Cathy Mills, Helen Worrall,*
*Netty Roberts, Eleanor Durrant and Sian Templeton*
ISBN 978 1 84905 336 5
eISBN 978 0 85700 675 2

**Nurturing Attachments Training Resource**
Running Parenting Groups for Adoptive Parents and Foster or Kinship Carers
*Kim Golding*
ISBN 978 1 84905 328 0
eISBN 978 0 85700 665 3

**Nurturing Attachments**
Supporting Children who are Fostered or Adopted
*Kim S. Golding*
ISBN 978 1 84310 614 2
eISBN 978 1 84642 750 3


*of related interest*

**Attaching in Adoption**
Practical Tools for Today's Parents
*Deborah D. Gray*
ISBN 978 1 84905 890 2
eISBN 978 0 85700 606 6

**Attaching Through Love, Hugs and Play**
Simple Strategies to Help Build Connections with Your Child
*Deborah D. Gray*
ISBN 978 1 84905 939 8
eISBN 978 0 85700 753 7

**Connecting with Kids through Stories**
Using Narratives to Facilitate Attachment in Adopted Children
Second Edition
Denise B. Lacher, Todd Nichols, Melissa Nichols and Joanne C. May
ISBN 978 1 84905 869 8
eISBN 978 0 85700 454 3

# Creating Loving Attachments

## Parenting with PACE to Nurture Confidence and Security in the Troubled Child

Kim S. Golding and Daniel A. Hughes

Jessica Kingsley *Publishers*
London and Philadelphia

Extract from *Harry Potter and the Order of the Phoenix* by J.K. Rowling (2003) on page 167 reproduced with kind permission from The Blair Partnership. Copyright © J.K. Rowling 2003.

First published in 2012
by Jessica Kingsley Publishers
73 Collier Street
London N1 9BE, UK
and
400 Market Street, Suite 400
Philadelphia, PA 19106, USA

*www.jkp.com*

**Library of Congress Cataloging in Publication Data**
Golding, Kim S.
  Creating loving attachments : parenting with PACE to nurture confidence and security in the troubled child / Kim S. Golding and Daniel A. Hughes.
       p. cm.
  Includes bibliographical references and index.
  ISBN 978-1-84905-227-6 (alk. paper)
  1. Problem children. 2. Parenting. 3. Attachment behavior in children. I. Hughes, Daniel A. II. Title.
  HQ773.G655 2012
  155.42'2241--dc23

                              2011042582

**British Library Cataloguing in Publication Data**
A CIP catalogue record for this book is available from the British Library

ISBN 978 1 84905 227 6
eISBN 978 0 85700 470 3

Kim and Dan would like to dedicate this book to our friends, colleagues and families across the world. We especially would like to acknowledge the many families we have had the privilege of helping and from whom we have learnt so much about PACE.

# Contents

# Acknowledgements

Kim acknowledges the support and friendship of many people: colleagues and parents, who are in her life and have accompanied her on her journey of discovery since starting to work with children looked after and adopted.

Applying PACE to my own life has been much easier with the sensitive support and kindness of friends, relatives and colleagues. Naming some of these always runs the risk of leaving others out, so I would like to say a big thank you to everyone who has taken such an interest in my work and given me kind words and helpful suggestions along the way. I would especially like to note the Dyadic Developmental Psychotherapy (DDP) Institute; it has been a rewarding experience making new friends and acquaintances from across the world, all sharing a common interest and enthusiasm. I would also like to mention the wonderfully welcoming people of Australia I met in Brisbane and Melbourne in August 2011. You gave me a wonderful sharing experience; thank you to Di, Chris and Jill for looking after me so well. Thank you also to Louise Bombér, whose work raising awareness of attachment in schools is such an essential complement to the support given to parents.

I reserve my personal acknowledgements for my close colleagues, friends and family. Colleagues within ISL and Team 2 are always kind and encouraging. Thank you especially to Debbie, Louise, Hannah and Hayley who read and commented on drafts of chapters. I would like to thank my close friends in my peer supervision group, Jane, Emily, Sue and Cas, for stimulating and thought-provoking discussions; all my supervisees, for teaching me as much as I teach them; Gina, Miriam and all at CPLAAC, so none of us feel alone; Joanne and the Adoption Plus team whose energy and commitment is inspiring; and my dear friend Julie, and all those who are working so hard to make DDP in the UK vibrant and stimulating.

Thank you to Steve at JKP for believing in me enough to suggest another book, and thank you to Dan for agreeing to write it with me and supporting my ideas, however whimsical.

And, of course, I have left the most important to last: my family – Chris who supports me, however busy I get; Alex and Lily who fill me with awe and pride; and a special thank you to Lily and Greg for literary ideas and contributions for this book, and to Alex for helping me with the diagrams. My mum, sister Cheryl and nieces Charlotte, Sophie and Olivia, whom I don't see as often as I should; and Chris's family who are in my thoughts especially as I write this.

Dan wishes to begin where Kim ended: with family. The unconditional love from my children, Meg, Kri and Maddie, carries the momentum of the joy that fills my days. And my granddaughter, Alice Rose, carries my merriment and bliss. A recent weekend in Pittsburgh captured the story of my life. My mother, Marie, had her arm around Alice Rose, while Meg and my sister, Kathleen, shared this moment. The warmth and contentment of that day left me experiencing what PACE has come to mean to me over the years.

Another deep thank you to Mairead, who journeyed to America years ago from Ireland, Dublin and Mount Errigal, and now is my most wonderful companion.

An ongoing expression of gratitude is for those who have used and taught PACE to others and now work with me on the Board of DDPI: Art, Deb, Mick, Pam and Robert from the US and Geraldine, Julie, Kim and Pam from the UK. Yes, the same Kim who has done the majority of the work on this book. Its strengths are gifts from her; where it wanders a bit, I am responsible.

And I must speak more of England and Scotland too (and more recently Ireland – North and South – and Wales). I have been welcomed with warmth and energy wherever I have travelled there. Wise, strong and caring people throughout. First in London, where I met Margot, Alan and Jay, who have become good friends and fellow travellers in our efforts to understand and aid troubled children and their families. And then through many of the other parts of England from Portsmouth to York and all the bits in between, many with names that I have forgotten and actually never could pronounce. And then up to Scotland, with Edwina, Ian and the wandering elephant. A heartfelt thank you to all.

Finally, I will end where Kim began. I must acknowledge all of the wonderful professionals and parents I have journeyed with over the years after I began to see the need – and the privilege – that is involved in offering aid to the many foster and adoptive families, some of whose stories may be found in these pages.

# Preface

## Meet the authors

Kim and Dan would like to welcome you to this book, which we hope you will enjoy reading as much as we enjoyed writing it. We would like to introduce ourselves to you here.

Kim is a clinical psychologist currently working in Worcestershire, England. Throughout her career Kim has always enjoyed collaborating with parents, working together to develop parenting skills tailored to the particular needs of the children being cared for. Over the last 12 years she has taken a special interest in supporting parents who have come to parenting via adoption, foster care or residential care. Kim and Chris are parents of two young people, both now in their 20s. They are enormously proud of what their young people have achieved, despite difficulties they have had to face. Kim wishes she had known much more about PACE when they were young. When Kim is not working or writing books, she loves to take her dogs for a walk. Their enthusiasm and freshness in the world reminds her of some of the other important things in life.

Dan is a clinical psychologist working in Annville, Pennsylvania, a very small town about ten miles east of Hershey, the chocolate capital of the US. Like Kim, Dan has spent much of his professional career working with those who care for the most vulnerable children – foster and adoptive parents and residential workers. He now spends much of his time working with the therapists who provide treatment for this very same group of families.

Dan is the proud father of three wonderful daughters, each unique, competent and caring, and one very incredible granddaughter. His time with them all is very special to him. He is also taking pleasure in seeing lovely parts of the world and writing a small book of poetry.

## The journey to this book

Kim remembers the day she saw a flyer for a professionals' day being run by a psychologist called Dan Hughes. This looked relevant to the work she was doing in a service for looked after children and she decided to go along. This decision changed her professional life, introducing her to an approach that transformed the way she worked with other professionals, parents and children. It also introduced her to someone who would become a mentor, colleague and dear friend.

Over the following 12 years, Dan has supported and encouraged Kim as she has developed as a psychologist, therapist and author. When Kim had the idea for writing this book, she asked Dan if he would like to join her. Dan happily accepted and quickly became amazed at Kim's enthusiasm, creative ideas, insights and editing skills, as well as her thorough knowledge of the many features of PACE. We can now share with you the fruits of our joint labours.

# Introduction

We have both sat with parents whilst they share with us how difficult it is caring for their children. Some are focused on the child, describing the frustration and hurt when a child rejects them, for example, or worrying about the implications of a child who will not stop stealing. These parents want answers to these behaviours, ways of producing different behaviours. Others are more focused on themselves: they are bad parents, or they are letting down those who placed their trust in them.

We are tempted to offer solutions to the first set of parents: try this and see if things improve. We are tempted to offer reassurance to the second set: you are a good parent; of course you are right for this child. We resist. If we offered solutions, we would all feel better but it is likely that the parents would return the following week, despairing that the behaviours are still there, or with a different set of behaviours concerning them. If we offered reassurance, we would feel better whilst leaving the parent in pain. Parents have told us, 'If you tell me that I am a good parent, I will know that you haven't been listening.'

And so what do we do? We listen; we stay with the pain of what we are hearing and we focus on our relationship with these parents. At some point, the time might be right to think about different ways of managing behaviour or of helping the parent to reach a different view of themselves, but the time is not yet. First, we must curiously explore the experience of the parents, accepting that this is their experience, providing empathy for how hard this can be, and at times interjecting a note of playfulness that allows us all to smile and laugh. Our relationship deepens, trust and respect builds on both sides, and we all feel stronger as a result.

The parents are different parents, and we are different therapists as a result of these interactions. Without judgement or evaluation, we are deeply influenced by each other. It is our belief that the child will have a different experience of being parented as a result. The parents will judge

13

and evaluate less; they will be more curious about and accepting of the child's experience, and their empathy will deepen. The relationship will strengthen and become more playful and enjoyable as a result.

This is the attitude of PACE. Through Playfulness, Acceptance, Curiosity and Empathy, our relationships will grow and thrive, to the benefit of the mental health and emotional well-being of all of us.

In this book we offer you an exploration of PACE. We especially consider the role of PACE within parenting, but this is not just a book about parenting children and young people. It is a broader journey into the realms of play, acceptance, curiosity and empathy. Journey with us and explore what these are, how they develop, the impact they have on us and on others, what happens when they are lacking, and, yes, how they can enrich us as parents so that we can nurture confident and secure children and young people.

As we go on this journey, there are two other 'ingredients' we meet along the way. We start the book with a consideration of love. This broadens into an exploration of two elements of a loving relationship that are central to parenting. The first is *attachment*, the offer of safety and security from parent to child. The second is *intersubjectivity*, the reciprocal sharing of a relationship where each influences the other.

Elsewhere, love has been placed within PACE as PLACE.[1] In this book, we have chosen to keep it separate in recognition that love is *more* than a part of the attitude. In our unconditional love of another, we bring PACE alive. We offer PACE as an attitude that can deepen our relationship with others. Love is the state of being that provides the unconditional acceptance at the root of healthy emotional development.

The final 'ingredient' we discuss is the role of therapy. In particular, we explore how the combination of therapy and parenting can be a potent mix when caring for children with attachment difficulties.

PACE as an attitude was developed by Dan more than 20 years ago, as a central part of attachment-focused family therapy (AFFT). It is familiar to many therapists and to parents of children adopted, fostered or living in residential care as dyadic developmental psychotherapy (DDP).[2]

This therapeutic approach is widely used as a therapeutic treatment for children with attachment- and trauma-related difficulties and their families. Dan has offered us more than a therapeutic approach, however. The principles are soundly based on our theoretical understanding of attachment and intersubjectivity. They are also informed by our knowledge of the impact of trauma, particularly the early experience from within the family of developmental trauma. These principles offer us a framework for building relationships, whether therapeutic, parenting or general.

Both Dan and Kim have previously explored PACE as part of a parenting approach for children with attachment difficulties.[3] In this book, we jointly turn the spotlight on to PACE. We are focusing on this element of the parenting approach because we recognize that it is at the heart of helping children with trauma and attachment difficulties, as well as being helpful for relationship strengthening generally. We hope we can bring PACE alive for you, not simply as a parenting strategy but also as a way of relating to others.

*Playfulness* brings fun and laughter to relationships. It provides reciprocal enjoyment and in the process helps a child to learn to experience and regulate positive affective states – in other words, to manage the arousal caused by the experience of emotions that accompany fun and laughter. A sad reality is that abused and neglected children have difficulty regulating positive emotions. Playfulness helps them with this process. Along the way, playfulness conveys a sense of confidence and hope for the future.

*Acceptance* creates psychological safety. The focus is on acceptance of internal experience – the thoughts, feelings, wishes, beliefs, desires and hopes that each person carries inside themselves. In accepting the internal experience of the other, we are communicating our understanding of this experience, that we are comfortable in knowing it and that we are not going to disregard or challenge it. Your experience is your experience. When parenting children, we may not tolerate particular behaviours, but we will accept the experience underneath this behaviour. Behaviours displayed by the child may be evaluated; the child himself is not.

*Curiosity* is directly connected to understanding. Who is this child we are accepting? When we curiously explore within a relationship, we are expressing interest in the other and a desire to know him more deeply. When we direct non-judgemental curiosity toward the experience of a child, he is likely to become responsive to understanding this experience of self, other or events in relationship with us. In sharing our experience, we know it more deeply. The child experiences with another rather than alone. The child becomes open to relationship and becomes stronger in the process.

*Empathy* communicates our curiosity and acceptance. We stand in the other's shoes and recognize and respond to his emotional experience. With the experience of empathy, a child is more able to experience a parent as being with him as he explores current and past experiences – experiences which might be positive, or the more challenging experience of trauma and shame.

This book is therefore very different from many other books that focus on parenting. Much parenting advice is focused on the behaviour of the child. We want our children to behave in a particular way; here is how to ensure this happens. On the internet are many websites devoted to parenting. Just a quick look at these can demonstrate how focused on behaviour we can be. For example, the home page of one site offers a source of advice on how to set house rules, how to get your child to do what you want him to do; how to get your child to help keep your house tidy; how to calm a crying baby.[4] We do not wish to criticize this website, as the advice is likely to be sound and helpful to parents struggling with such behaviours. We do, however, want to explore with you how parenting is much more than behaviour management.

We do have to manage behaviour, to teach our children what is acceptable and what is not. The boundaries and limits we provide give safety to the children until they are ready to place their own boundaries and limits on themselves. This is one hand of parenting, but parenting requires two hands. In the other hand, children need us to build relationship with them, to nurture them and to nourish their emotional development so that it flourishes. This second hand also wonders about the behaviour that we think we need to manage. What does it mean? Does it mean anything about our relationship with our child? In this book we pay attention to this side of parenting, providing a discussion of PACE as an attitude that can help us develop emotionally rich relationships with our children.

As we are writing this book, the BBC is reporting on the conclusions reached in studies carried out by UNICEF. The latest study compares British children with those from Sweden and Spain.[5] This qualitative study supports an earlier quantitative study which ranked 21 affluent countries for the well-being of their children. American and British children were amongst the least happy in the developed world. Two principal causes are identified: a lack of contact with parents and too much emphasis on material possessions. The latest study identifies that parents in the UK find it hard to spend enough time with their children, whereas family life, with parents and extended family, were better protected in Sweden and Spain. These studies identify time spent with family as essential to children's well-being, but also identify a culture of long working hours and material possessions, such as computers and televisions, reducing the time available. This is an important message. We need to find ways of placing relationships at the centre of families, and we need to do this urgently if we are to protect and enhance the emotional well-being of our children.

Nowhere is this need greater than when parenting children who have experienced trauma, abuse, neglect and loss within their early experience; children who, as a consequence, struggle with attachment difficulties. All children need relationships to thrive; traumatized children need relationships to heal. We hope that with a better understanding of PACE we can all find ways to offer this essential relationship experience for ourselves, each other, and our children and young people.

## Comments

1. It is always difficult to know how to refer to parents and children when using pronouns. If we keep to a consistent use of gender, we run the risk of appearing to be referring only to mothers and sons or fathers and daughters. Always using both, as in 'he or she', sounds clumsy and detracts from the reading experience. We have therefore decided to alternate usage of gender-specific pronouns between chapters.

2. In this book we have all parents in mind. Alongside biological and stepparents, some parents foster, some adopt, some look after children living in residential care, or they might be parenting children on behalf of friends or relatives. In all cases, the role they take is to parent the children, whether permanently, long term or short term; whether as legal parent or on behalf of family, friends or the state. In this spirit, we use the term 'parent' as a generic term to cover all forms of 'care'.

3. We have drawn on case examples, both fictional and real. All names and identifying details have been changed to ensure the confidentiality of any children and families who have inspired our examples.

4.  At the end of each section of this book, we have included short pieces of creative writing. These are short stories written for children, which can be read by us to change our experience of the topic, stimulating thinking through a different, lighter medium. We hope this gives you a pleasant change from the more academically stimulating chapters that precede them, as well as giving you ideas about how you can use stories with children.

# 1

# Love

## *The Essential Ingredient*

Love has been a focus of attention for poets, writers, philosophers and scientists throughout the ages. We all talk about love, sometimes glibly: 'I love your shoes'; but also with deeply felt intent: 'I'll love you for ever.' We fall 'in love' and we fall 'out of love'. We remember loved ones: 'in loving memory'. We rejoice in the highs of love: 'truly, madly, deeply'; whilst we plummet to the depths of despair as we experience that love hurts. We have symbols for love – Cupid's arrow, Eros, Romeo and Juliet – and we admire the sacrifice of love. Love really is all around us.

We all know and have experience of love, but knowing and understanding are different things. We rarely stop to think about what love is. Love is associated with the heart, not the brain. It is an emotional experience, not easy to put into words. In this chapter, we will explore love at a more cerebral level. Can we bring thought and understanding to love without diluting or weakening our sense of love? In thinking about love, will we lose the art of love? Will understanding reduce intuition? We hope not.

We wish to explore parental love and its power to bring health and happiness to parent and child. We hope that in combining brain and heart we can help you to enrich your loving to the benefit of both of you. In parenting a child who has experienced early difficulty, we believe you will love best if you combine intuition with understanding.

This book is about an attitude of parenting – PACE – that can foster healthy development and heal past traumas for children. As you increase and cultivate your ability to be playful, accepting, curious and empathic, we anticipate that you will have an enriched experience of parenting and a deeper connection with your child.

Whilst PACE is an attitude, love is a state of being. Love embraces PACE. It provides the strength for the journey and the courage to carry on when the present is difficult, challenging and relentless. In loving this child, you will have a relationship that will last for ever, whatever happens between you. The connections that you create will last, even if, at times of estrangement, this feels unlikely. Ultimately, you will have touched this child, and this touch will transmit through future generations. The child will be a healthier adult because of your love.

This can be a leap of faith, because the benefits of love are very long term and not always obvious in the present. We hope in this chapter to help you take that leap of faith by exploring what love is. In the sixth century BC, the philosopher Lao Tzu said that 'being deeply loved by someone gives you strength, while loving someone deeply gives you courage'.[1] Perhaps it is because it brings strength and courage that love is the essential ingredient that makes PACE work.

Eleanor Atkinson's story of *Greyfriars Bobby*[2] was first published in 1912. Bobby, the story goes, was a Skye terrier who lived in Edinburgh with his master, a shepherd called Auld Jock. Following the death of Auld Jock, the local people found a new home for Bobby, but he was having none of it. Neither locked door nor long distances kept him from Edinburgh. Each time he was removed, he returned to his master's grave in Greyfriars churchyard. So much did the local population take Bobby to their hearts that regulations were overturned and Bobby was allowed to live in the graveyard. The love of one Skye terrier gave the whole community a loving experience. There is a similar tale of a loyal dog in Australia. The story of *Red Dog*[3] is also one of commitment to a deceased master. The precursor to these modern-day loyal dogs is, of course, Argus, immortalized in Homer's *Odyssey*. Argus waited 20 years for his master Odysseus:

> The dog, whom fate had granted to behold
> His lord, when twenty tedious years had roll'd
> Takes a last look and having seen him, dies;
> So closed for ever faithful Argus' eyes![4]

It is hard to read these stories without thinking of the bond that developed between dogs and masters as being an expression of love. Argus, Bobby and Red Dog epitomize the words of the famous American psychologist Albert Ellis: 'The art of love is largely the art of persistence.'[5] We cannot know whether dogs form emotional attachments that in humans would be described as love. Perhaps such behaviours are no more than unusual expressions of a dog's instinct to form social bonds. The faithful dog, however, gives us a powerful symbol of love as commitment.

When we love, we will stick with the object of our love even through hard times. This can be a difficult task, taking courage and persistence. Fortunately, love is more than commitment; it is also enjoyment. Love reaps its own reward. Persist in love and caring for the child will be more than a job; it will also give you times of enjoyment. As relationships ebb and flow, enjoyment comes and goes. Love is the faith that if you commit to the relationship, caring for this child, moments of enjoyment will come back.

## What is love?

What is this emotional tie that we recognize so easily as love? This is a question that three psychiatrists from the University of California set out to answer in their optimistically titled book *A General Theory of Love*. Thomas Lewis, Fari Amini and Richard Lannon highlight the importance of relationship and connectedness. Love exists in the mutual attunement of two people, each influencing the other. These relationships are influential in our development. 'Love makes us who we are, and who we can become.'[6]

John Armstrong, an art historian in England, wrote a fascinating book on love which describes beautifully its multidimensional qualities.[7] He speaks in detail about how love is a behaviour, an act of knowledge, perception, imagination and desire. At times it may involve wanting good for the other, as well as passion, sexuality and romance. It can also lead to infatuation and the despair of separation. He also suggests the notion of love as charity, not just in action but also in judgement, perception and empathy.

These authors, all writing in this century, are very clear that love is an essential part of human relationships, none more so than the relationship between parent and child. This is not a new idea. Let us look back across the decades to child psychiatry in the 1950s and 1960s. The influential English paediatrician and psychoanalyst, Donald Winnicott wrote:

> If human babies are to develop eventually into healthy, independent, and society-minded adult individuals, they

absolutely depend on being given a good start, and this good
start is assured in nature by the existence of the bond between
the baby's mother and the baby, the thing called love.[8]

Winnicott described love as a bond that allows parent to be preoccupied
with child. This intense interest, he says, is 'like the sun coming out for
the baby'.[9] This preoccupation leads to a deep understanding of what
the child needs. In being loved, the child's capacity for relationship is
increased; if love is absent, Winnicott goes on to say, the child will be
disturbed in his emotional development, revealed in 'a personal difficulty
as the young person grows up'.[10]

The idea of love as an emotional attachment which provides
nurturance, caregiving and affection from parent to child reverberates
through the child psychology literature.[11] Margot Sunderland, a child
psychotherapist at the Centre of Child Mental Health in London,
equates love with aliveness and 'lighting up'.[12] She observes how the
child thrives on unconditional love, love that is present whatever the
behaviour of child or parent.

The experience of unconditional love is a central need for children
– love that does not get withdrawn as discipline, does not depend
on behaviour or achievement and does not impose the parents' own
needs on their child. If a child is not loved, or if a child cannot trust
in the continuity of love, he will be psychologically vulnerable. This
vulnerability is eloquently expressed by Margot Sunderland as 'loving
in torment', which she distinguishes from 'loving in peace'.[13] Instead of
getting the sense of well-being and contentment necessary for emotional
health, the child gets a sense of danger. Love feels fragile and emotional
health is jeopardized.

A parent's love for her child combines enjoyment and commitment.
Without enjoyment, love becomes a duty; it is a chore or obligation
that does not hold enough meaning for either child or parent. Mutual
enjoyment may not always be present for many reasons, involving
either parent or child or their relationship. In the absence of enjoyment,
the parent's commitment to her child needs always to be present. Only
then can love provide the security that the child needs to truly trust
that the parent will be with him when times are hard. The child needs
to know that no conflict will destroy the love that his parent has for
him. No conflict will destroy their relationship.

The challenge for parents parenting a child who has experienced 'love in torment' is to help him to believe in 'love in peace'. A child will anticipate a repeat of previous experience. In parenting with love and PACE, you will need mountains of patience and perseverance as you gently but persistently move the child to a belief that this love will last, unconditionally, whatever happens between you.

## Love as a biological process

Love as behaviour, feeling or need is something we have all experienced. What is more hidden is the importance of love as a physiological process. It is in understanding love at a biological level that we can really define the importance of the love of a parent for a child.

In the popular story of Harry Potter,[14] J. K. Rowling symbolically explores the importance of a parent's love. Under attack by a powerful wizard, Harry is saved from certain death by the love and sacrifice that his parents make. They die, and he becomes the child who lives and grows up to save the world from Voldemort's growing menace.

Fortunately, the biology of love does not require parental sacrifice, but replace magic, wizards and sacrifice with relationship, human connection and commitment and we have the ingredients that build emotional health and well-being. Your child may not grow up to save the world, but he will grow up able to relate to, connect with and commit to relationships. Voldemort's power came from separating people; distrust breeds distrust and evil can grow. Harry's power came from connecting with people. A mother's love allows a child's love to grow, and society is stronger as a result.

As J. K. Rowling does in literature, Thomas Lewis and his colleagues do academically.[15] They explore the essential need an infant has to be loved by a parent. Love builds the limbic structures of the developing brain, those parts of the brain associated with our emotional responses to things. These, therefore, are the areas of the brain that are especially connected with our emotional experience and its expression.

We are born with a mature 'reptilian brain'. This is essential for keeping us alive but is cold and unfeeling without the post-natally developing 'mammalian' brain that develops around it. This is the 'limbic' centre of our brain. It adds an *emotional* layer to our experience. Later still will develop the 'rational brain', the cortical structures which are involved in many complex brain functions such as memory and attention. These parts of the brain help us to understand and be fully aware of the world around us. They support our ability to think, use language and reason. René Descartes philosophized that 'I think therefore I am'[16] in recognition that consciousness – the human's unique ability to know that he knows – stems from this gradually maturing rational brain. Three brains in one – the triune brain, as American physician and neuroscientist Paul Maclean describes it – is an outcome of our genetics and our experience.[17]

The actions of parents have little influence on the already mature reptilian part of the brain, but their actions will exert an influence on the development of both the emotional limbic system and the rational, thinking cortex. Love and stimulation provide the essential experiences that allow healthy brain development, fostering the ability to feel and to think. Love is the necessary experience for emotional development.

As Kim writes this, her dog has sidled up to her, wanting some attention. She is distracted into stroking him. Their nervous systems relate as the emotional systems in their brains are activated. They are connected. She turns back to her computer, her dog still pressed up against her. She feels calmer and more fluent, a clear demonstration of the need for mammals to connect to each other, brain to brain, heart to heart – 'a collaborative dance of love,' as Lewis and his colleagues describe it.[18]

Kim enjoys connection; a child requires this: 'Feed and clothe a human infant but deprive him of emotional contact and he will die.'[19] Lewis and colleagues describe how the relationship between parent and child is a physiological bond which provides for 'limbic resonance'. Think of Harry Potter's mystical connection with his mother, providing protection when he needs it. When the emotional centres of two brains connect, each influences the other and both are stronger as a result.

This connection provides emotional regulation for the child, and this in turn develops the growing capacity for self-regulation. In other words, the child first experiences emotional regulation by the parent; he then learns to regulate with his parent before being able to do this by himself. The love of the parent shapes the brain of the child, and the parent's own brain is enriched in turn. As Lewis and colleagues put it: 'Who we are and who we become depends, in part, on whom we love.'[20]

The story does not end there; emotional regulation is only a starting point for the child. With increasing maturity, cognitive structures of the brain develop around the limbic centres. The child comes to know what he is feeling. As he knows himself better, the child also learns to look outward and to know the emotional world of others. He is ready to form relationships, to connect with others, to influence and be influenced on the wider stage that exists outside of his home.

At several points in this book we will meet the work of Jaak Panksepp, a distinguished American neuroscientist. He offers a rich theory of emotional development.[21] His theory will help us to understand the different elements of PACE and their importance in parenting. Two aspects of his theory of brain functioning are particularly important for understanding the importance of love. These are the process of social bonding and the instinctive drive to care for our young. Both of these explain the importance of the biological need for connection and relatedness within mammals, and its particular importance for bringing up healthy children.

Social bonding is a biological process that ensures our connection with each other. As we experience relationships, our brain chemistry is activated through the release of hormones, leading to increased social bonding and a sense of well being and contentment. We experience increased levels of the neuropeptides, oxytocin and prolactin and of the endogenous opioids, the endorphins, leading to increased social bonding and a sense of well-being and contentment.

Whilst understanding the biology is less important, we describe this to illustrate that relationships are at the heart of who we are as human beings. We are designed to relate to each other socially and in this way feel good within ourselves. This is the foundation for love and emotional health. A parent experiences this social bonding as closely connected with what Panksepp calls the 'CARE' brain system. This is an operating system in the brain which organizes the emotional tendency in the parent to take care of and nurture the child. The child in turn experiences social bonding as a feeling of attachment security. When a child experiences a secure attachment, he is able to derive safety and comfort from a caregiver. At the heart of our humanity is our need for physical closeness, for touch, for intimacy. It is no surprise therefore, as Jaak Panksepp points out, that societies that encourage these within relationships are the least aggressive in the world.

## Theories of attachment and intersubjectivity

Love is an essential ingredient in raising our children. The gift of love is a gift to the child of security, connection and developing capacity for relationships. As we will explore in later chapters, PACE is a parenting attitude that directly provides the child with these essential experiences. Two psychological theories underlie the use of PACE and inform us about the importance of love. These are attachment theory and intersubjectivity. We will introduce these here and return to them throughout the book.

### Attachment theory

A little boy born in London in the early 1900s was raised by a paid nanny – not an unusual circumstance in wealthy families during that time period. Those fortunate to have a nanny who could give them the experience of love and security grew up emotionally healthy. This little boy had such an experience, but he sadly lost this attachment figure when she left the family home during his fourth year. He later told his own son that he was 'sufficiently hurt to feel the pain of childhood separation – but was not so traumatized that he could not face working with it on a daily basis.'[22] This early childhood experience led to a lifetime of study as John Bowlby grew up and followed a career as a child psychiatrist, with a particular interest in the impact of maternal separation on children. Sir Richard Bowlby recalls that:

> My father spent his career unravelling the complexities of the mother/infant attachment bond in the hope that the knowledge would influence the way society supported parents in caring for their children. He said: 'If we value our children, we must cherish their parents.'[23]

Sir Richard Bowlby relates how his father was uncertain as to what to call his theory describing the parent–child bond.[24] Initially, he thought that he might call it a 'Theory of Love' but he feared that it would not be accepted as sufficiently scientific if he did so. Love was not recognized as central to mental health at that time.

And so attachment theory was born, a legacy so helpful to us when exploring how to parent children who have had early experience of separation, loss or disrupted parenting. In 1953, John Bowlby entitled his book *Child Care and the Growth of Love*,[25] establishing love as central to attachment theory. In this book he equates the love and pleasure of a mother as spiritual nourishment for the child.

We would like to add a word for fathers. Mothers were very much under the microscope during the development of attachment theory, and much that was written focused on the mother–child relationship. This was in common with the culture of the time; child care was very much seen as the mother's job, whilst fathers occupied a role as wage earner. In modern times, we understand the importance of both parents to a child. Attachment theory has developed into a theory about parenting, biological or not, mothers or fathers. Children need parents to help them feel secure so that they can safely expand out into the world.

What attachment theory does so successfully is identify the importance for the child of a warm, intimate and continuous relationship with parents within which both find satisfaction and enjoyment. As Bowlby says, 'In no other relationship do human beings place themselves so unreservedly and so continuously at the disposal of others.'[26] In providing these intense and intimate relationships parents also gain:

> A child needs to feel he is an object of pleasure and pride to his mother, a mother needs to feel an expansion of her own personality in the personality of her child: each needs to feel closely identified with the other.[27]

The idea of a continuous relationship has caused much political debate and controversy over the years, both as mothers are encouraged into the work place or back into the home, depending upon meeting the needs of society as defined by the politicians of the time. Continuous, however, does not mean that a parent has to be ever-present for the child. The child experiences the parent as continuously present even when apart. The child is held in mind by the parent and can carry the parent in his heart wherever he is.

Children are born, attachment theory suggests, predisposed to seek security from their primary caregivers. These attachment figures keep them safe from harm and facilitate their journey into the world. An attachment bond is formed which allows the child to seek security and comfort from the caregiver and ensures that the caregiver offers nurturance to the child. Note that in terms of ensuring safety and security this is not a reciprocal relationship. Parents are a secure base, keeping the child safe, not the other way around. The child moves outward to explore and learn in the world, coming back to touch base again as needed.

Children therefore have a range of attachment behaviours that signal to the parents that they need comfort – for example, a child might cry, cling or follow the parent. The child is letting the parent know that at this moment he needs attention and nurture. Similarly, the child has a range of exploratory behaviours that signal that he is ready to investigate the world around him. These behaviours are characterized by moving away from the parent and taking an interest in events and objects in the world. The sensitive caregiver is able to read these signals and support the child on a moment-to-moment basis. A secure attachment forms between them. Beginning early in life, children use this experience to understand how relationships work. An internal working model – a template or memory of the relationship – is formed; this will be a guide for the children both in the present and with future relationships. Children learn what to expect from other people as a result of this early experience.

---

Jamie and his mum have gone to visit friends. They are invited in and Jamie, a naturally confident and sociable child, runs in to find the toys. Jack, a more timid child, stays closer to his mum as he ponders these newcomers to his home. Mum hugs him reassuringly and allows him to gravitate to Jamie in his own time. Soon both boys are playing happily together and the parents enjoy a cup of tea. There is a ring at the doorbell. Both boys pause in their play and look to their mums. Jack's mum moves to the door and Jack quickly follows her. She lifts him up and they greet the local vicar together. Jamie moves a little closer to his mum and watches carefully. The vicar greets the two boys. Jamie tentatively moves forward, but keeps a hand on his mum's knee just in case. Jack stays firmly by his mum. Jamie's mum gets her purse for the vicar's collection. Jamie draws back from the play to see what his mum is doing. He readily takes the money from her and takes it to the vicar. The vicar departs and soon both boys are engrossed in their play again.

---

In this simple scene we can see the gentle movement of attachment and exploration, supported by each mother. In their own and different ways, the boys signal to the parents their level of security at each moment. The parents respond, the children feel safe, and play proceeds at its own pace. The sensitive attunement each mother displays towards her own son displays her ease at interpreting the level of anxiety or confidence being experienced moment by moment. The mothers provide reassurance when needed and facilitate play at other times. The boys are developing secure attachments, and this in turn enables them to develop trust in others and self-reliance in themselves. They will grow up able to approach the world with confidence, knowing that they can seek help when needed.

But what happens when secure attachments do not develop? An attachment figure less able to understand or respond to the signals the child is giving is described as insensitive. The child lacking a sense of security organizes his behaviour in different ways. The child works harder in order to feel safe.

For example, a parent might find it difficult to respond when her child signals a need for comfort. She might experience this as overwhelming and she gives the subtle, or sometimes not so subtle, message that she will withdraw at these times, rejecting or ignoring the child's need. The child adjusts to this behaviour by minimizing his attachment behaviours: 'If I don't display my need of you, then maybe you will stay available to me.' In attachment theory, this is described as an avoidant attachment.

Another parent may be inconsistent in her response to the child, sometimes being available, sometimes being irritated by the child. Faced with such unpredictability, the child responds by forcing predictability. He becomes attention needing, ensuring the parent's continuing attention by not being fully reassured or soothed by her. This is described as an ambivalent resistant attachment.

The child faced with frightening behaviour in a parent has a much more difficult time feeling safe. Fear triggers the innate need for comfort. The child turns to the parent instinctively, but it is the parent who is the source of fear. A young child disorganizes in the face of this unresolvable threat. He quite literally does not know what to do, his behaviour reflecting this hopelessness.

With her colleagues, the eminent Professor of Psychology in California Mary Main, explored how, when the haven of safety is also source of threat, a child is unable to organize his behaviour to feel safe.[28] With increased maturity, this child will learn ways of managing this level of fear. He is likely to become highly controlling, developing a range of behaviours in order to give him some fragile sense of safety. Thus a child might be coercive, aggressively demanding attention only to reject this attention once given; if the parent becomes angry, the child switches to more submissive, coy behaviours, only to move back to angry when the parent begins to respond. The child is the puppet master, pulling on the parent's strings. Other children are more self-reliant in their behaviour, trying to manage on their own rather than appearing to need the parent. These children can even be caregiving, taking care of the parent rather than being taken care of.

A small proportion of children are unlucky enough to have had no experience of an early attachment relationship, either because of severe neglect or impoverished institutionalized care. These children do not develop selective attachments, as there is no one available to allow this process. These children can be disinhibited, indiscriminately friendly, but unable to engage in mutually satisfying relationships, or they can be inhibited, withdrawing from social contact rather than approaching others.

If you are parenting a child with an attachment difficulty, he will not be able to elicit care and comfort from you in a straightforward way. Attachment is a relationship dance: the child signals and the parent responds. When a child experiences insecurity in his attachment relationships, he leads the relationship dance in a way that meets his expectations of his parent. He may act as if he does not need nurture at times of distress, or he may seek comfort and nurture when stress is low. He signals a need not related to current circumstance, but in line with his expectations of how you will respond. Helping a child to learn to feel secure with you means responding to what he hides as well as to what he signals. In this way he can begin to respond to your availability rather than to his expectations. Mary Dozier, a professor of Psychology at the University of Delaware in Newark, USA, has described this parenting as being both sensitive and gently challenging to these hidden and expressed needs.[29]

Children with severe attachment difficulties are the most afraid of being parented. They will display a range of challenging behaviours that help them to feel a sense of control over you. They may lie or steal, urinate in unusual places, refuse to eat or hurt your favourite pet, all behaviours that help to reduce their feelings of fear and helplessness. They are highly reluctant to give up the fragile but hard-earned sense of security that these behaviours represent. It will take all your patience and a highly predictable environment to lead such a child to a state where he can relax his control and dare to trust that you will not hurt him.

Understanding the attachment experience of your child and how this translates into his current relationship can help you to respond in ways that build his sense of trust and security. As you gently lead him into different ways of relating to you, he will be able to experience a more secure attachment relationship, providing a solid foundation for his increasingly ambitious exploration of his world.

## Intersubjectivity

In the last section we considered that an important part of the love a parent gives to a child is the safety and security that this offers. This is only part of the story. The gift of love is security, but it is also much more. When we love someone, we are touched by them. They influence us in a multitude of ways, and we seek to share this influence with them. In return, we touch them; in being influenced, we also influence. Love is a mutual relationship. In loving a child, a parent is opening herself up to this mutual influence, and in the process both can grow stronger. This is intersubjectivity, a contingent and responsive relationship, which allows each partner to discover what is unique and special about the other and share this understanding together. How we see ourselves – our very sense of self – is an outcome of these intersubjective relationships, starting in the love between parent and child.

---

Consider a baby playing with his parent. They are each engaged in a mutual game of peep-bo. Suddenly, the parent stills; her face is neutral and she stares into mid-space. The baby looks confused as he attempts to re-establish contact with the parent, and within a minute he is visibly distressed. Arms and legs waving, he cries and fusses until the parent returns to him. Quickly, the parent re-establishes her relationship with the infant. The baby settles and can play once more.

---

This is a description of the 'still face experiment'. It provides a vivid and poignant example of how important a reciprocal relationship is for a very young infant. The relationship needs to be immediate, and present, with each response contingent on the action of the other. This synchronicity brings the relationship alive. Within contingent relationships both partners share the emotional experience. If the experience is one of play, the parent and child will gain a sense of joy and fun. The emotional state of each will be magnified as they jointly engage in the experience. If the child is experiencing distress, the parent will match this emotional experience without getting distressed herself. This will help the child to regulate his distress; he will be soothed by the experience. In this way the child develops an ability to regulate his own emotional states. The experience of emotional regulation within a relationship will lead to a growing ability to manage emotional experience, and thus to grow and develop through this experience. In addition, the experience of shared attention and complementary intention within a relationship will lead to a growing ability to attend and to cooperate. The child is learning to be a social being, able to relate to and enjoy being with other people.

Without this synchronicity the child does not experience connection, and lack of connection is a dangerous state. Safety for a dependent child, self-awareness for a maturing adolescent and a feeling of wholeness for a mature adult are only found in connection with another. Intersubjectivity is at the heart of relationships. In the still face experiment, brief as it is, the relationship is no longer live and contingent; the infant knows that something important is missing. An infant is born for connection. When connection fails because the parent has become unresponsive, the infant is quickly unsettled by the experience.

Colwyn Trevarthen, Emeritus Professor of Child Psychology and Psychobiology at the University of Edinburgh, Scotland has extensively studied this contingent relationship between parent and child.[30] He has observed how babies need reciprocal relationships; the subjective experience of the parent becomes the subjective experience of the child. He termed this *primary intersubjectivity*, an absorbed relationship within which each becomes totally focused on the other. Young children form their identity within such absorbed relationships. The parent experiences the child as delightful; the child knows he is delightful. The parent experiences the child as hateful; the child knows he is hateful. The child organizes his developing sense of self around the parent's experience of him.

---

Imagine a young child playing with his father. He becomes excited and accidentally upsets the cup of coffee the father placed on the table. The father is angry and chides the child for his clumsiness. He tells him that he is naughty. The child accepts this intersubjective meaning of the event, and deep in the core of his developing sense of self, he takes home a lesson that he is a naughty, clumsy child.

Let us give the story a happier ending. The father reflects on this incident and knows he has been overly harsh. He has had a stressful day and did not want to clear up spilt coffee. He takes his son in his arms. He tells him it is all right; he should not have left the coffee there. He reassures him that he is not naughty. Deep inside the child, his core is rewritten. He may do naughty things but he is not naughty. He is loved enough for his father to repair the relationship. Things can go wrong but he will always be loved. He is loveable.

---

Primary intersubjectivity develops to include secondary intersubjectivity. Now the child can learn about the wider world of people, events and objects through his experience of the parent's experience of these. He discovers the meaning of these to his parent and learns about the world for himself. His ability to think begins in these shared experiences. The world, self and others all come to make sense to the child, and this too impacts on his developing sense of self.

When the friendly vicar entered the home where Jamie and Jack were playing, they had no previous experience of him. Each child looked to his own mother to know how to respond to this unsought interruption to their play. The parents were relaxed and so the children relaxed. Jamie, ever the more sociable of the two, even approached and interacted with him, but both could play in his presence. If the parents had been anxious or uncomfortable, the boys would have remained wary, seeking closeness to their parents to protect them from this unknown threat. The experience of the stranger will have a different meaning depending upon the meaning given to it by the parents. Parent and child have found intersubjective meaning in the experience.

---

A mother and son are walking in the woods. The mother, distracted by a chance meeting with a friend, does not notice her son wander away. Suddenly aware of his absence, she scans around for him. She is gripped by a feeling of panic when she can't see him. She turns a corner and there he is. He stands quite still, his own panic clearly visible. He sees her and cries. The mother bends down and holds her small son, absorbing his fear, worry and relief as they are reunited. His sobs lessen as he experiences the safety of his mother's embrace. Calm again, he looks around. A ladybird has landed on a leaf quite close to him. He is transfixed. Mum looks to see the source of this interest. Smiling, she places the ladybird gently on his hand, and both share the joy of the small creature walking across his finger. The ladybird stills, its wings outstretched, and then it is gone. Mother and son take each other's hand as they resume their walk.

---

This small scene describes the gift of love a parent gives her child. She will keep him safe and offer security, and from this secure base they can truly explore the world together. Whether in fear or joy, they share intersubjective experience, and in the sharing the child comes to know himself and the world a little better.

Imagine the experience when the moments of intersubjectivity do not come.

---

A mother and son are walking in the woods. The mother, distracted by a chance meeting with a friend, does not notice her son wander away. Suddenly aware of his absence, she scans around for him. She feels cross that he has got lost, and calls out angrily. She turns a corner and there he is, a mixture of fear and defiance on his face. She calls to him to get back here right now. He turns away as if to run. Shouting at him, she grabs him roughly by the hand. They resume their walk. The ladybird flies away unnoticed.

---

## The importance of connection

The capacity for relationship, with its reciprocal connection and influence, develops with the love of a parent. The child learns to know, to understand and to relate to self and to others. Born to be a social being, the love of a parent allows the child to fulfil this destiny.

The emotional life of the child therefore comes alive in the love of his parents. The child learns to feel, and to understand what he feels, in the arms of loving caregivers. Love is a social bond that is instinctive for each of us. We are born knowing how to love. Love is, however, also deeply influenced by experience. The way we are loved as a child will influence how we love as an adult and as a parent. Love is a journey that begins at birth and accompanies us throughout life. It is a journey that can take some wrong turns at times. Stress, the parents' own early experience, illness, life events can all affect the way a parent loves a child.

Whether you are a biological parent or have come later to parenting your child through fostering, adoption or residential care, your own relationships and experience will influence the way you love the child for whom you are caring. Whatever has happened in the past, the journey continues now. The child may be deeply troubled by past relationship experience, but buried within the brain is the capacity to love and to be loved. The beauty of love is that it is two-way. Each influences the other. As you find new ways to love your child, you will be enriched by the connection that develops between you. As your child develops security and a deeper trust, you will both develop mental health and emotional well-being.

Today's journey begins in understanding. Understand your past, present and potential future. Know where you have come from, and with this insight seek strong, healthy relationships in the present. Fortified by relationship yourself, you will be able to offer the child the relationship experience he needs to heal and to develop.

## When connection fails

The centuries have seen many examples of failed connections between child and parent. Horrifyingly, this is sometimes in the name of science. Consider Harry Harlow, an American research psychologist at the University of Wisconsin–Madison, who was interested in the scientific study of the nature of love. His story is poignantly described by Harvard University psychologist and author Lauren Slater.[31]

Perhaps echoing his own childhood, growing up with a 'cold' mother, Harlow was interested in the impact on rhesus macaque monkeys when they were deprived of maternal contact. There are echoes of John Bowlby here: both appear to explore their own relationship history through the study they have chosen. Sadly, Harlow's studies were less compassionate. Anticipating the importance of food for survival, he provided the monkeys with a surrogate mother made of wire. This mother was the giver of sustenance. Alongside was a cloth surrogate mother, lacking the capacity to feed. The monkeys overwhelmingly preferred to cling to the cloth 'mothers', only leaving them for the minimum time needed to feed. Harlow had demonstrated the overriding importance of touch to infants. In ever-increasingly horrific experiments, Harlow demonstrated what happens to animals developmentally traumatized. Developmental trauma describes the experience of fear and terror from within the family, impacting on the development of the young mammal. The monkeys' experience of love and parenting was also an experience of terror and torment. Harlow's legacy was to reinforce our understanding of the importance of connection with a parent for infants to thrive, and the overwhelming need of a child to invest in any parent, however cruel, for survival. This was a legacy hard won by a group of defenceless creatures who demonstrated how emotionally damaging parenting without love is for developing mammals.

What is true for monkeys is also true for human young. Frederick II was Holy Roman Emperor in the thirteenth century. A proficient linguist, he wanted to find out what the 'natural' language of childhood is. He employed wet nurses and ordered them to raise a group of infants without talking, singing or cuddling them. The children were physically cared for but not nurtured. He hoped he would learn what the original language of humans is as the children developed without the influence of hearing language spoken to them. The experiment was a failure; all the infants died one after the other.[32] Language is a skill dependent upon being raised in linguistically rich environments; the experiment could never have succeeded. This did demonstrate, however, the absolute importance of nurture for survival. Without love, children will not thrive.

Over the centuries, events have conspired to prove this fact many times. From stories of so-called 'wolf children', longitudinal studies of children adopted from orphanages, to modern medicine's description of non-organic failure to thrive (faltering growth), we recognize that without adequate nurture children will not grow and thrive. It is heartbreaking to hear of a two-year-old child taken into foster care following experience of severe neglect. She was fed but not held or cuddled. She had the appearance of a malnourished child of three to four months – a clear demonstration that without love, even calorie-rich food cannot nourish the child.

Lewis and his colleagues[33] describe the fourfold increase in sudden infant death amongst babies of depressed mothers. Bruce Perry, a child psychiatrist and professor with Northwestern University in Chicago, has a particular interest in helping children traumatized during their early care. Writing with journalist Maia Szalavitz, he describes research showing that more than a third of children raised in an institution but without individual attention died before they were two years old.[34]

Through all these examples, we see the tragic results of a lack of connection on children's health, well-being and development.

Without love, children cannot connect, and this deprives them of safety and security. Without love, children are deprived of intersubjective experience, and they develop alone and lonely. Perry and Szalavitz have written:

> The most traumatic aspects of all disasters involve the shattering of human connections. And this is especially true for children. Being harmed by the people who are supposed to love you, being abandoned by them, being robbed of the one-on-one relationships that allow you to feel safe and valued and to become humane – these are profoundly destructive experiences. Because humans are inescapably social beings, the worst catastrophes that can befall us inevitably involve relational loss. As a result, recovery from trauma and neglect is also all about relationships – rebuilding trust, regaining confidence, returning to a sense of security and reconnecting to love.[35]

Tragically, children can learn to survive without safety, security or connection, but this is at a cost. The children take control, and in doing so they learn to fear other ways of being. They avoid intersubjective experience. They do not want to connect because they fear that this will only confirm what they already know: they are not loveable and they will never be loved by you.

The challenge for the parent is to help these children open up to love and safety in relationships; to help them revise their view of themselves and of others. Healing comes from being part of a social world. Only with a sense of belonging and love will a child start to heal. Opening up to being loved means loving in return; it is an intersubjective experience. Embracing this experience means trusting enough to give up control. This will not come easily to a child whose faith and trust has hurt him so much. Your commitment to this child means loving despite his inability to love you back, offering security and intersubjective experience through countless rejections, touching him with your hand and your heart, even though his touch in return is harsh, painful, rejecting and unforgiving. This is what therapeutic parenting is. It requires faith that one day this child will open up to you and accept all the love and caring you have to offer.

As you offer kindness to the child, be kind to yourself. Find supportive and helpful relationships to join you on this journey. Accept that parenting a child who resists intersubjective experience will inevitably lead you to withdraw from this experience at times. As you parent with PACE, you will be more deeply aware of your child's and your own struggles. As you understand and accept these struggles, you will be able to admire the child's courage and tenacity. With playfulness, acceptance, curiosity and empathy, you will be able to find your own courage and tenacity. Eventually, this will open up security and intersubjective experience for both of you. As Margot Sunderland reminds us: 'Taking time to understand your child's painful feelings will deepen the emotional bond between you.'[36]

Even a few minutes a day of concentrated time for each other can help an emotionally vulnerable child to experience a parent as liking him. This may be puzzling, confusing and difficult to accept at first. The child might try to spoil this time, to demonstrate that he is not worthy of being loved. You will need all the stubborn persistence you can find. Over time you will undermine the child's solid belief that he is hated. He will be confused, and in confusion he will entertain different possibilities: 'Maybe you do like me; maybe I am likeable.' A tentative connection is formed. This in turn will strengthen the child for coping with the more difficult aspects of being parented. Previously, discipline has been evidence to the child of your meanness, your hatred of him. Now he will question these motives. Instead, he may come to understand that love has two hands: it is kind and nurturing, but it is also boundaries, guidelines to live by. Being held in two hands brings safety and comfort.

## Conclusion

This chapter has explored the multifaceted emotion that we call love. This emotional bond, with its biological underpinning, is at the centre of a child's security and development. A parent's love provides commitment for, but also joy in, her relationship with the child. This commitment brings security and connection for the child.

Parenting a child who has not had this experience early in life can be challenging. Parenting with PACE provides a foundation for bringing these things afresh to the child. With playfulness, acceptance, curiosity and empathy you will develop connections with your child that will last you both a lifetime.

## STORY

## A Mummy Finds Out How to Look After Her Baby

Once upon a time there was a mummy. She was a new mummy. She had never had a baby before. She wanted to look after her new baby really, really well, but she had a problem. She was not sure how to look after her new baby. When the baby cried, she was not sure what he needed. When he was content, she was not sure how to play with him.

Mummy was very worried about this. She tried to think back to when she was little. It was hard to remember when she was very small, but she knew her mummy had not looked after her very well.

Mummy decided she needed help. If she was going to be a good mummy, she needed someone to teach her. Very carefully, she wrapped her baby in a blanket and put him in his pram. She collected a few things she needed and set off to look for help.

The first person she met was another mummy. Surely another mummy would be able to help her? She showed the other mummy her baby and asked her, 'How can I be a good mummy?' This mummy taught her what babies need: how to feed them, change them and play with them. She gave the mummy some nappies so that she could keep her baby clean and dry.

Mummy carried on her journey, thinking about what she been told. Her baby woke up and cried. Carefully, she changed the baby's nappy. Still the baby cried. She tried to feed the baby but he didn't want the milk. She tried to play with the baby, but he still cried. Mummy felt like crying too. She still couldn't be a good mummy.

Next the mummy met a nurse. She told the nurse about her baby and how he would not stop crying although she had done everything she had been told. The nurse picked the baby up and cuddled him. The baby stopped crying. The nurse showed the mummy how to rock the baby and pat him on the back to help him feel more comfortable. Then she helped the mummy feed her baby. Finally, the baby fell asleep. Mummy thanked the nurse and carried on with her journey.

When the baby next woke, Mummy carefully changed his nappy and fed him. She rocked him and patted him on the back. Then she laid him in his pram, but he didn't go to sleep. He started to fret. Mummy didn't know what to do.

Mummy met a woodcarver. This man was a granddad. He told the mummy that when his grandchildren came to stay they liked to play with rattles that he had carved out of wood. He gave the mummy a rattle he had made. The mummy showed the rattle to the baby and he smiled.

Mummy walked on. She thought about all the things she had learnt about looking after babies: how to feed them and change them; how to pat them on the back so they felt more comfortable; how to play with them. Still she was worried. How would she know what her baby needed? When should she feed him or change him? When did he need rocking and when did he need playing with? Mummy had learnt how to look after her baby; she understood this in her head, but deep in her heart this mummy still struggled. The head learns by being taught; the heart learns by being loved. Mummy needed head and heart. She needed to be taught and to be loved.

Mummy felt tired and cold. She had walked a long way from home and she felt too weary for the journey back. Mummy did not know it but she had walked so far that she was near to the home of her fairy godmother. Her fairy godmother found her. She didn't say a word, just took her in her arms and cuddled her. She took her inside her house and sat her by the warm fire. Whilst Mummy was resting and getting warm again, the fairy godmother took care of the baby. She then made the mummy some warm buttered toast.

As the mummy ate the toast, she felt better. She started to ask her fairy godmother how to look after babies. The fairy godmother put her finger to her lips. 'No more questions,' she said. 'Let me take care of you and you will be able to look after your baby.'

Over the next few weeks, the mummy stayed with her fairy godmother. She enjoyed being taken care of. Her fairy godmother ran her baths and made her meals. Sometimes they played games. When she felt sad or worried, her fairy godmother gave her a cuddle and helped her to feel better. Gradually, the mummy began feeling more confident about taking care of her baby. She found that she knew when her baby needed feeding, changing, rocking or playing with. The mummy was puzzled. Her fairy godmother had not taught her about looking after her baby but she found she could do it. 'How do I know what to do?' she asked. The fairy godmother told her, 'Your head knew what to do, but you also need your heart to look after your baby. The answers in your heart have helped you to use the answers in your head.' Mummy looked puzzled. 'But how has my heart learnt?' she asked. The fairy godmother laughed. 'No more questions,' she said. 'Remember, just let me take care of you and you will be able to look after your baby.'

# PART I

# Play

# *2*

# The World of Play

Children need a range of play experiences to develop to their full potential. Throughout their childhood they experience the joy of play with parents, they engage in play with adults, they play alone and, of course, they play with other children. Some children play imaginatively, building and inhabiting worlds of their own design. Other children prefer something more structured – football in the yard, for example. In adulthood, although play may feature less, a playful attitude to life helps to deal with the typical stresses of taking on adult responsibility. Play allows us to express ourselves in a free and spontaneous way. As we enter a playful state, we are doing what we want with whom we want. In play we can truly be who we want to be.

Although there is debate about the role of play in child development, few would doubt the importance of play in children's lives. Play influences development in all areas.

Through play, children develop social abilities: they learn to share, to be sensitive to another's feelings, to understand rules, to cooperate. Alongside social interactions, the child is also developing a sense of identity. The child learns about herself in relation to others.

Cognitive development – the ability to think, understand and use knowledge – can be enhanced by play. Children develop increasing abilities to concentrate and attend; they learn to plan, to solve problems and to master language.

Play can also support emotional development. It provides opportunities to let off steam, to express anxieties, to reduce feelings of anger, fear and inadequacy, and to enhance feelings of control, success and pleasure.

Play is essential for all of us, but the right to play is seen as an integral part of being a child. The United Nations Convention on the Rights of the Child states that every child is entitled to rest and play and to have the chance to join in a wide range of activities.[1] This is a right that is compromised for children who have experienced early trauma, neglect, separation or loss. Bringing play back into these children's lives is a central part of helping them recover and fulfil their potential to be happy, healthy young people.

This chapter will explore the world of play, before we turn in the next chapter to playfulness within parenting.

## What is play?

The experience of being at play is one with which we are all familiar. We know what play is, we recognize it when we see it and we respond in playful ways when circumstances permit.

Defining play is more difficult. Are we describing behaviour – play as an action, or an emotional state – the feeling of being playful? Do we need to play to survive, or is it a developmental process, a way of developing skills and abilities? Of course, play is all of these and more. In play we can be intense, joyful, preoccupied or attentive. We may be alone in our play or actively interacting with others. Play can bring us into a state of joyful bliss or intense laughter. It might lead to a sense of accomplishment and satisfaction, but at times it can also lead to frustration and a sense of shortcoming.

Kim remembers watching a game of tennis – two top players competing for a place in the French Open semi-final. They were both 'playing' a game, and yet it did not look like 'play'. Intense concentration, determination, frustration and moments of satisfaction were played out between these two players as the first set proceeded. They were playing against each other, yet this did not look like a social situation. They rarely acknowledged each other, although each player was deeply aware of the other.

Were they playing or were they working as they attempted to win every point? It looked like hard work, with little sign of playfulness. Then suddenly one of the players gets into the 'zone', the state sportsmen and sportswomen describe when all effort reduces and the game takes on its own ease and pleasure. Suddenly, he can do no wrong; he places his racket and the ball flies back, unbeatable. Now we can witness a sense of play, which appears joyful and fun. The player looks comfortable, as he revels in his skill and athleticism. He truly is *playing* tennis. Of course it does not last; a few games later and the 'zone' has abandoned him. He is back to competing for every point. Play has become work once more.

So what has this observation of playing tennis revealed? That 'play' is difficult to pin down. It is not simply behaviour, an emotional state or a developmental process. Perhaps, ultimately, play is a state of being; maybe at its best it is a state of joy, fun and laughter. It is a time for relaxation, but also at times a state of intense focus and concentration. There may be goals, purposes or outcomes, but these are secondary to the experience.

Jerome Bruner is a research psychologist who worked at Oxford University in England. In his introduction to a book entitled *The Biology of Play* he suggests that 'whatever man can do seriously he can do playfully'.[2] It is not what we are doing but how we are doing it. He goes on to suggest that play is a feeling of tension and joy with a consciousness that it is different from ordinary life. In the tennis match, the work of winning a match, along with the career success, ranking and pay cheque that would accompany this, was, for a sublime period of the match, transformed into pure play.

This description has focused on adults, but perhaps observation of children will better define what play is. Let's take a look around a nursery environment. This is a lively, noisy environment. The children choose what to play with, until the structure of the day directs them to stop for a drink or to sit on the mat for a story. Whilst the latter are adult-directed activities, the majority of the play is child-directed. Adults are available to support when needed, to make suggestions, provide props or occasionally to resolve disputes.

---

Two boys are playing with model dinosaurs, mirroring each other as they play side by side. They do not interact, but their play appears companionable. Suddenly, their attention is distracted by a third boy, busy with his own activity. They turn as one to watch him. The bigger of the two boys suddenly snatches at something the third boy holds. He stands up, arms raised, and the boy freezes. He then gives a jump, smiles and moves away, his companion following him. Without words, these three boys have created a world of play within which they copy, observe, try out and eventually resolve potential conflict.

Whilst this mini-drama occurs, another group of boys and girls are making their own dramatic play. They have dressed up as doctors and nurses. A small girl is selected as the patient. She lies on the table, patiently awaiting her fate. The stage is set, the actors ready, but it is as if the children have forgotten their lines. They stand looking at each other, props in hand. One boy, more confident than the others, moves into action and starts busily examining the child patient. One of the girls, emboldened by her companion, also enters the drama, pretending to administer medicine as the boy turns away to check the 'chart'. The drama continues harmoniously as all three become absorbed in the world they are creating.

Just to the side of this action, a girl sits busy on a 'telephone', absorbed in listening to an apparent conversation and writing down the 'message' she is taking. Another child picks up the other phone and listens for a while. Puzzled, he looks at the receiver in his hand. He turns it around and listens again. He looks up and smiles self-consciously as he realizes there is no one on the other end; it is just pretend.

And so it continues as we make our way around the nursery. Children, solitary or in groups, engage in a range of play activities; some construct, some imitate and some imagine. They are aware of each other, and at times play cooperatively. They display varying levels of maturity and social awareness, but all are engaged in the world of play.

---

Play has been described variously as amusement, absorption and creativity. It can be seen as non-serious and non-goal-directed. Barbara Tizard, who was a research fellow at the Thomas Coram Research Unit in London, England, suggests that play is distinct from work and learning.[3] It can, however, be highly serious with a clear goal; imagine a child completing a jigsaw puzzle, for example. Children, and indeed adults, can be highly absorbed and creative whilst at play. Frustration in play can, however, lead to distractibility and lack of creativity. The more you think about play, the harder it is to define. We reach out to explore play and it slips through our fingers. Perhaps an understanding of the biology underlying play will help in the quest to define it.

## The biological drive to play

To understand play from a biological point of view, we can turn again to Jaak Panksepp, whom we met in Chapter 1. He has a scientific approach to understanding play which might help to define it. This is a 'bottom-up' approach, searching for meaning within the brain and exploring how biology underpins playfulness. It is a search that takes us not only to the biological foundations of play, but also to the impact play itself has on the unfolding of our biology. As Stuart Brown, American psychiatrist and founder of the National Institute for Play, succinctly puts it, we are 'built to play and built through play'.[4]

Panksepp[5] suggests that mammals are born with a range of abilities important for survival. These are instinctive; the animal does not need any experience to act. The actions they lead to, however, offer opportunities for learning, using higher cognitive brain areas. In other words, we act on our instincts but learn from our experience. He suggests four primitive brain systems which ensure survival. He calls these:

- *Seeking*: This leads to an intense interest in exploring the world, ensuring that we search for things that we need, crave or desire. This system motivates the child to interact with the world, stimulating development. Seeking is sustained by curiosity. We will meet this system again when we explore 'curiosity' in Chapter 6.

- *Fear*: In response to threat our *fear* system ensures that we freeze or flee, allowing escape to safety.

- *Rage*: Whereas *fear* provokes freeze or flee, *rage* provokes fight. When we experience frustration or anger, this system helps us to act, via a range of attacking behaviours.

- *Panic*: This system is aroused by fear of separation and leads to the experience of separation distress. It is the basis of our social attachment.

Alongside these primitive systems we also have a number of more sophisticated socioemotional systems which emerge at appropriate times during development. The one that is of interest to us in this chapter is the *play* system.

- *Play*: This is the earliest of the socioemotional systems. *Play* helps us to feel good, to experience joy and laughter. It is central in social interactions, ensuring social bonding.

Play is therefore an impulse, which needs no prior learning. Panksepp gives the example of a research project which revealed that rats denied social interaction early in their psychosocial development will play vigorously when given the opportunity. The instinct to play is a strong one. Only with extensive neglect in primates or humans will this instinctive drive reduce.

Play is an instinct but one which, in humans, is greatly modified by learning. Our prolonged childhoods and the sophistication of our brain development leads to an extended range of play behaviours. The higher brain areas unique to humans have their part here. These are the more broadly developed cognitive areas of the brain which provide the seat of learning. They are utilized in play, extending the learning experience and adding to the maturity of the developing child. As Panksepp puts it, the energy for play and its vitality, laughter and spontaneity come from the ancient, instinctive part of the brain, whilst the diversity of our play and of our learning comes from our higher brain function. The sum of who we are truly is more than the parts.

Humans are highly social animals; we thrive on social interactions. Our social engagement systems and the instinct to relate to others are well developed from birth. Infants seek out social contacts from within hours of birth, and the need for human companionship is a lifelong drive. This social bonding is enhanced by the playful side of our nature. Play and social engagement come together in laughter and fun.

The most primitive type of social play and the one most common amongst mammals is rough and tumble play, sometimes called roughhousing. Anyone who has seen puppies or other young animals at play will recognize this type of play. Almost like fighting, the animals roll around together, barking and biting at each other. Only the body language betrays the playful intent. Panksepp speculates that this type of play has multiple benefits for brain and body. The animal is learning physical skills, whilst being assimilated into the structure of the society it will grow up in.

Within rough and tumble play, the animals, or indeed young children, are learning about themselves and others. They learn their limits of aggression and also how to accept defeat gracefully. In the process, they are learning important rules about who to cooperate with and who to avoid. As Panksepp says: '...the brain's PLAY network may help stitch individuals into the social fabric that is the staging ground for their lives.'[6] In case this all sounds very serious, he also points out the large element of fun and laughter that goes alongside this play: 'Is it any wonder, then, that play is such fun – perhaps one of the major brain sources of joy?'

## Play and culture

Play is biologically based, but it is also a learnt behaviour. Human children demonstrate a large range of play behaviours extending well beyond the innate rough and tumble play that comes so naturally to them. Through learning, culture as well as biology influences how we play.

The examples of play considered so far reflect Kim's and Dan's own culture and experience. Whether on the tennis court or in a nursery, play has been considered from a Western cultural standpoint. Play, however, cannot be fully understood without considering the culture that gives it context. These cultural contexts have been studied by researcher Dina Feitelson, working at the University of Haifa in Israel. She points out that play will arise both out of physical conditions and the attitudes of the adults surrounding the children.[7] She cites the example of Kurdish Jews, whose culture actively encourages children to be seen and not heard. Typically, their two- and three-year-olds are quiet and passive. Upon immigration to Israel, these children became involved in the kindergartens, so central to Israeli culture. They are transformed into boisterous and active beings who enthusiastically entered into the play going on around them. It appeared to the Kurdish Jewish mothers that this strange new country was turning their children 'crazy'.

To understand play, therefore, we also have to understand the culture within which play is occurring. The social relationships, gender expectations and cultural traditions will shape not only social behaviours but also the play that children and adults engage in.

Even the most spontaneous of play has a large element of cultural influence to it. We give children pretend objects drawn from the world around them. Thus a model kitchen or the inside of a ship will encourage children to play within the cultural parameters of their experience. Even without the constraints of such toys, children will reflect their culture during play. Kim remembers a news report of a few years ago. A group of schoolchildren were pretending to inject themselves with heroin, a clear imitation of their home experience and the subculture they were living within. The school, as she remembers the report, was trying to ban this play, failing to understand that children will play what they observe and experience.

American researchers Nancy Curry and Sarah Arnaud observed children playing across a range of cultures in the 1980s.[8] Play was common across these cultures but types of play differed. This reflected the environments in which they lived and the roles the adults took. If they lived in a rural village this would be reflected in their play world, which would look very different to the play world of the child living within a mining community or in a city. Similarly, they enacted different adult occupations depending on their experience. The most involved play was with toys that were particularly relevant to the culture.

In play, and especially imaginary play, children become socialized into the culture within which they live. They develop a sense of self, both in terms of gender and role. Studies demonstrate the impact of Western culture, with girls acting out domestic themes whilst boys tend to act out themed fantasy (superheroes or space exploration, for example). When girls and boys play outside these stereotypes, others feel uncomfortable. Boys who like to play with 'girls' toys', for example, can be given a hard time. Girls who play more like boys are described as 'tomboys', a rather more accepted form of play! We mould our children for a world we anticipate they will grow up in.

Outside the arena of free play, we impose a further layer of culture on our children as we sanction certain activities. In the West, we enrol children in dance or judo classes, for example. Children join the local football club, Scout or Brownie pack. These activities provide culturally sanctioned playful experiences for the children. We appear to have come a long way from the biological roots of play, but perhaps not. Panksepp[9] points out that these activities would be 'emotionally hollow' without the ancient circuitry of playfulness. It is Panksepp's assertion that the lightness, joy and flow of play stem from the biological centres of the brain. Only with the *play* system can we generate the diversity of emotional behaviours upon which learning can operate. Play is biological, emotional and cultural.

## Play and child development

Alongside the biological and cultural influences previously discussed, play also meets a developmental need. Play promotes exploration and learning.

At its simplest, play is exploratory, investigating, finding out, extending knowledge – a response to curiosity. The infant or toddler repeats, practises and eventually masters behaviours that she has discovered through imitating others. Imagine teaching an infant to wave bye-bye or to clap hands. Brown describes play as beginning in movement.[10] For example, the infant plays with objects by picking them up and bringing them to her mouth.

The older child demonstrates a more functional approach to play as she manipulates objects. This play leads to improved understanding and the ability to solve problems. Exploratory and constructive play have an important role in helping the child understand the physical world.

Imitative and symbolic play allows children to explore beyond the physical world to the social world they inhabit. It is in this type of play that cultural influence is most clearly seen. The child imitates the world that she is observing, gradually extending this into more complex imaginative play.

Children are social beings. Play provides them with a window into the social world. As they play alone and then with others, they explore all that is social, and through this develop social competence themselves. From the parallel play of the young child – happy to be with but not yet interacting with her peers – through the conflicts and complexities of playing together – learning to share, to resolve difficulties and to think of others – to the cooperative and thoughtful play of true friends, children are learning about their own minds and the minds of others. They develop empathy and understanding, the root of trust and social success.

Imagination is at the root of being human. In imaginative play we are taken out of the here and now and freed from time and space. No wonder Brown suggests that imaginative play nourishes the spirit. He also points out the link between imaginative play and story making. As we nurture our children's imagination, we are increasing their capacity to create stories. Stories enrich our lives in many ways. They free us from the constraint of reality. Even as adults, we like to escape with a good book or film. For children, this story making is as easy as breathing. The children running around the playground apparently without purpose are actually part of a complex plot using a spaceship to move a civilization from a doomed planet to a new home. The little girl bent over her Puppy in My Pocket has just bred and shown the next Crufts champion, and her cousin quietly dancing in the other room has performed the whole of *Swan Lake* to rapturous applause. These children are honing abilities to create narrative, an important skill if we are to make sense of our life.

As humans, we don't just live life; we also make sense of it. We form coherent narratives to help us work through experiences. As we journey through life, we collect pieces of experience, which we need to integrate. In Brown's words: 'Stories are a way of putting disparate pieces of information into a unified context.'[11] Those who make coherent sense of their lives are free to move forward unhampered by the past. Those who can't are condemned to a cycle of endlessly repeating what has already gone.

> We continually make up imaginative story lines in our heads to keep the past, present and future in context. Since kids are embarking hourly on a new life adventure, they use their imaginative urges to keep a context for the emotional and cognitive symphony that is their developing being.[12]

Play and child development are therefore steady companions throughout childhood. Play in all its forms is an integral part of what makes the developing child fulfil the potential within her.

## Play within parenting

Playing with an infant or young child is a fundamental task of parenting. The quality of play that children experience with their early caregivers is important for their subsequent development. From birth, infants need to interact with their parents. Much of this interaction, when not taken up with feeding and care, will be playful. As Panksepp puts it: 'In most mammals, play emerges initially within the warm and supportive secure base of the home environment, where parental involvement is abundant.'[13] It is the parents who initially provide adequate stimulation, social interactions and the containment of anxieties that allow children to play and ultimately to develop.

An important part of parenting a young child is facilitating security of attachment; as child and parent bond, the parent offers and the child experiences security and understanding. This sense of safety offers a secure base from which the child will discover who she is, what she feels and how she can understand herself and the world around her. Two primary behavioural systems – the attachment system and the exploratory system – provide the innate drives that promote attachment to the parent and the ability to use this attachment as a secure base for wider exploration of self, other and the physical world.

Play is intimately involved in both attachment and exploration, although it is also distinct from both. Attachment will happen without play, but playfulness facilitates the attuned, responsive, contingent interactions that underpin the security that a child experiences with a sensitive parent. Similarly, exploration is not the same as play, but play can broaden and enhance exploration.

Attachment behaviours are innate behaviours that lead to feelings of increased security for the child. Knowing the availability and responsivity of the parent provides confidence within the child that she is safe and secure. The sensitive parent is attuned to his child, able to notice the moment-by-moment signals that the child is sending, leading to contingent responses and building a sense of availability for the child.

How is the parent able to attune to the child this way? This is where play comes in. From the moment a child is born, she is seeking a relationship to her parents. The young infant needs to experience an absorbed and attuned relationship within which she can discover this parent, and in doing so find out about herself. This absorption may initially be serious as the parent scrutinizes his young infant, but quickly it becomes playful. The parent coos and babbles to the child and is delighted when this elicits a response. Soon the parent and infant are taking turns, developing a playful conversation of noises, tongue thrusts and, as the infant matures, smiles. These early protoconversations become more sophisticated, as the infant's repertoire extends. Peek-a-boo and blowing bubbles become part of the playful interaction. As each discovers the other in play, as well as through care, the parent gets to know his unique and special child. He becomes aware of her moods and needs; he learns to read the signals she gives out and to respond in ways that continue to build security. This is emotional attunement at its best, a 'joyful union' which Brown[14] suggests is the most basic state of play, providing the foundation for more complex states of play which the child will develop throughout her life.

The child develops a sense of efficacy within the relationship. She discovers that she can make things happen; she can elicit a response that makes sense to her. As parent and child become emotionally in tune with each other, the infant experiences regulation of her emotion and connection with her mind. She is getting the experience she needs to grow into a self-regulating, self-thinking child. This early play experience provides a platform for both continuing security and care, but also for fun and laughter. Play builds the attunement essential for the parent–child relationship, a relationship which will eventually serve as the secure base for an ever-widening exploration of the world.

Imagine a father introducing his child to a nursery setting. The unfamiliarity of this environment will initially trigger the attachment system to activate. The child stays close to Dad, vigilant to the new surroundings, and to Dad's ability to keep her safe here. The attuned, sensitive parent allows the child this time to adjust to her new surroundings. The child starts to relax, and in relaxing she becomes more interested in this bright and exciting world she has just entered. The attachment system reduces in intensity and the exploratory system becomes active. Now the child looks around and with increasing confidence moves away from Dad to physically explore this strange new world. But watch carefully: this exploration is not yet playful. The child may wander around, not yet lingering anywhere for too long. She may pick up a toy and look at it. She may pause and watch the other children at play. She may even laugh at some antic observed in another child. Each captures her attention for a short while before she continues her inspection of all that the nursery has to offer. If she strays too far, she will search for Dad with her eyes, ensuring that he is supporting her still. A little further and she feels the need to return to him, to touch base before extending outward again to continue her exploration. Attachment and exploration are working beautifully together.

Only with further familiarity and a satiation of this initial exploration will the child begin to become playful in her surroundings. As her confidence grows, exploration will become more relaxed; now she will linger and start to play. She may spend time at the sand tray, investigating the feel of the sand between her fingers, exploring the way the toys can interact with the sand to build, to bury, to pour. Not yet completely relaxed, that may require a few more visits, but our child is now playing. And in playing her exploration is enriched; the drive to explore and the drive to play can now combine to provide a richer, more exuberant experience. What has begun in attachment security provided by the father has extended to include a wider exploration enriched by the playfulness that attachment security allows.

## How trauma and neglect impact on play

Children neglected and traumatized within their early parenting relationships miss out on the early play experience infants expect and need from their caregivers. Difficult early experience can have an important impact on the way that children play and on the subsequent influence this has on their development and capacity for relationships.

Play will only occur when physiological needs have been met. Play is inhibited, at least temporarily, if an animal is afraid or hungry.[15] Basic needs for safety, warmth, food and companionship must be met first. In fact, any event or situation that produces a negative emotional response will decrease the likelihood of playful behaviours. Play is inhibited by the negative emotion being experienced: 'When we are in peril, play will disappear.'[16] Brown goes on to suggest that the very absence of play further impacts on us, darkening our mood, reducing feelings of optimism and lessening the experience of pleasure.

Lilyan White, an animal researcher at Cambridge University in England, had a particular interest in the play of animals.[17] She notes the importance of novelty to trigger play. Novelty will lead us to explore and ultimately to play. Too much novelty, however, has the opposite effect. Novelty can also elicit a fear response, inhibiting play. We need a certain amount of safety and comfort before we can truly engage in play. Trauma gives novelty a dangerous feel. The child shuns novelty as she searches for sameness and predictability. Trauma can have a devastating impact on the child, affecting all areas of functioning. This is clearly seen in the play behaviours that children will engage in. Whether play is shut down or restricted to a repetitive re-experiencing of the event or events, play can be an early casualty of trauma.

Children who have experienced trauma in their lives may be hypervigilant to their surroundings. This reduces energy for play and leaves less concentration or attention for playful experience. The parent will need to provide safety and security in a predictable, consistent environment before the child will relax sufficiently to play in a more spontaneous, uninhibited way. Additionally, children may have strong negative feelings that are frightening and unpredictable. Reminders quickly trigger fear and they may experience difficult memories, all of which can interfere with play. Children may display inappropriate play behaviours that can be unsettling to others, including the parent. Sexualized behaviour, for example, might lead adults to withdraw from the child, reducing the amount of appropriate play experience that they are offering.

Not only traumatic experience but also absence of experience, as in neglect, reduces capacity to play. Studies with primates demonstrate the impact of social deprivation. Thus Panskepp[18] explores the work of researcher Chamove who studied young monkeys and chimps deprived of companions for several days. These animals quickly became despondent, demonstrating very little play initially when reunited again. No wonder Brown describes depression as the opposite of play.[19]

Children who experience neglect early in life demonstrate, like the chimps described above, a paucity of play behaviours.

---

Observe a family group of three now living in foster care. The eldest is a girl aged seven; she is accompanied by her three- and four-year-old brothers. They stand close to their foster parent, looking at the toys that have been put out for them. With some encouragement, they start to explore a little. The girl plays alone, building the Lego with a seriousness that belies the state of play. Her brothers are more obviously trying to maintain the attention of the foster parent. They alternate sitting on the parent's lap, each waiting for the moment when he can take up the prized place. The younger child has achieved this, so the older one picks up a tea cup. He is anxious to get back to the foster parent with the 'cup of tea'; in his haste he fails to notice that he has stood on the tray and upset the remaining cups. Finally, they both manage to sit on her lap whilst she reads them a story. Throughout this observation there is an evident lack of play. The children are quiet although persistent. This persistence is aimed at the foster parent, however, not the play things. The younger boys seek the foster parent's attention whilst the girl studiously manages without her. None of the children can relax into a world of imagination nor become absorbed in play.

---

Children who, when young, have experienced loss of significant carers, whether because of illness, death or abuse, will have more difficulty playing and using play to develop understanding and confidence.

For some children, as with the boys in the example above, their emotional need for physical contact and nurture will override their need to play. All their efforts are aimed at keeping the parent close, ensuring that the parent is available to them. This is a highly serious occupation which has an impact on the amount and quality of play that the children display. Even when playing, they will be keeping an eye and ear ready to abandon play in an instant if they feel their access to the parent is being curtailed. When they are playing with the parent, their focus will be on the parent, reducing the degree to which they can become absorbed in the play.

For other children, as with the girl above, they will feel safer when they are not connecting with the parent. These children have learnt to take care of themselves, not to display need of the parent. Whilst they might feel safer playing with the parents than trying to elicit care from them, the play will also reflect their need for self-reliance to some degree. They will become independent in play sooner, preferring to play alone. They thus miss out on interactions that might facilitate the development of play skills and impact positively on their development.

Still other children are so traumatized by their early experience that they have to stay in control at all costs. A need to be in control overrides all other desires. Play is lost to the large range of controlling behaviours that provide a fragile sense of security for the children.

Children who have experienced trauma and neglect early in life will need the stability and predictability of a safe home and parent before they can trust enough to discover the rich world of play.

## Helping the child who lacks early play experience

Children who experience inappropriate parenting from a very young age miss out on important playful interactions with a parent. These interactions begin from birth. They are very apparent during caregiving activities such as being fed, bathed and changed, as well as during those times when parents freely play with their awake and alert infant. Games of peek-a-boo, tongue poking and tickling offer delight to both child and parent. They also draw the child into relationships, laying the foundations for later social and emotional development.

When these early interactions are missing, play experience is limited. This will have an impact on later experience. The child might, for example, find it difficult to relate to other children. She may function at a younger emotional age than the children she is mixing with, finding it difficult to form friendships and to engage in cooperative play. This in turn will impact on other important developmental stages. She might struggle to develop social perspective-taking skills, the ability to understand the point of view of another. Psychologists describe children as acquiring a 'theory of mind', the ability to understand that others have thoughts, feelings, beliefs and desires, which might be different to your own. This understanding can be delayed or different for children who have had impoverished early relationship experience, leading to many difficulties interacting within the social world.

Developmentally, it is important for parents to be aware of the play needs of children who have encountered difficult early experience as a result of separation and loss, trauma, abuse or neglect. It will be important to consider what play skills the child has, and what she is lacking.

The child may be stuck at an earlier stage of development, needing the experiences of a much younger child before she can move on. Adoptive parents, for example, often describe their children's need to play at being an infant. Sometimes this may take the form of an animal – a puppy or kitten, for example. Kim heard of one child who wanted to play repetitively at hatching out of a dinosaur egg. At other times, the child might play at being a baby, even wanting to experience infantile needs being met – for example, being fed through a baby's bottle. When parents resist these play experiences, the child can become stuck with this need, continuing to play these experiences repetitively and insistently.

Play skills might be delayed. Children are progressing through the developmental stages of play, but more slowly than their peers. Expectations on them to act their age or to fit in with the other children can be very difficult. They may need more structure or supervision for their play. They might prefer younger activities or younger children to play with. They need more play with adults, or adult support in their play. Adjusting play to the emotional age of the child will be important, but can be missed, especially in a child who is cognitively brighter.

Children may demonstrate gaps in their play because of their early experience. They might, for example, have learnt to play rule-based games and be a dab hand at Monopoly, but be all at sea if given a doll's house or farm set to play with. Similarly, they may not have built up the level of concentration or attention of other children and need shorter episodes of play before changing activity.

The children might find it difficult to play with other children. They may lack the social skills or level of maturity that will allow them to cooperate and resolve conflicts. They may struggle to develop the intimacy of more reciprocal relationships, remaining isolated or moving on quickly from friend to friend. These children will need more support and supervision to help them interact successfully with their peers.

## Play as exploration of experience

An example was given earlier of children playing together and acting out a scenario about injecting drugs. This example revealed how themes in play can express something of the cultural experience to which children are being subjected. There may be another dimension to this play, as well as being an expression of what they have observed: the children may also be trying to make sense of their experience. When experience is distressing or even traumatic, play can be an important way to deal with this experience, reducing some of the impact upon them emotionally. When we observe children at play, we can also observe some of the tensions that they are experiencing in their emotional lives. Researchers and theorists have speculated that this type of play might help the children to experience some feelings of control over their fears and anxieties, perhaps even developing ways of coping with these.[20]

Play that reflects the anxieties and worries of children provides an important opportunity for adults to offer support. By observing the play, we obtain insight into the internal world of the child. This insight can help us to adjust our support to the children, further helping them to manage difficult experience. This is the basis of some therapies, called play therapies. In the world of play, the therapist can help the child understand and manage fears and anxieties, resolve difficult experience and find ways of experiencing being in control and coping.

Play can be therapeutic, whether at home or in a therapy setting. A parent can watch his child at play, gaining a new understanding of her experience and how she is making sense of the world. Playing with the child provides an opportunity to develop a relationship of trust. This relationship is an important support for the child as she explores her world and the experiences that she has encountered. In this way play can be used symbolically to express wishes and fears, fantasies, conflict and various perceptions of the world. The child can explore past and current experiences and can gain some awareness of and mastery over feelings. In the process, the child will be developing an improved sense of self-esteem and self-confidence and a different, more positive sense of identity.

A therapist has specialist skills to provide a safe place in which the child can explore her world and a therapeutic relationship to allow the child to express her feelings. Children do not always need this level of specialization, however. This type of therapy can also provide an uncomfortable and unmeant message that parents will not be able to manage the awful things that children are expressing in play. Parents can offer similar experiences for children, and with sensitive support can achieve something of what the specialist therapies aim for. In the process, the relationship between parent and child is strengthened. The parent develops greater understanding and this leads to more confident acceptance and empathy. The child will develop increased trust in the parent, strengthening feelings of security and safety. When the parent plays with the child, the child has opportunities to learn, develop and heal at a pace that she can cope with.

## A concluding example

When Kim first met Josie she was a withdrawn, passive 18-month-old child. She played little and appeared uninterested in the world around her. Traumatized by the physical abuse that she had received at the hands of her father, she was removed into foster care. Gradually, over the next few months, the foster carers helped Josie to experience a safe environment. They provided toys and activities and encouraged Josie to engage with these. Josie did learn to play

She explored the toys, she jumped on the trampoline, she even laughed at times. In all of this play she remained solitary, however, interacting little with her carers. Then one day she discovered play in all its richness. She came alive, laughing, as she explored her foster father's face. She looked deeply into his eyes and she giggled – a spontaneous, uninhibited giggle that came from deep within her. She reached out and touched her foster dad's face. Josie had finally discovered what she had needed from birth: a sensitive, attuned parent who could accompany her in her world of play. As each became absorbed with the other, the rest of the world faded into the background. Josie's biological need for play was being fulfilled, amplified by a relationship within which she felt safe and cherished.

This play experience will have positive developmental consequences: it will provide a cultural basis for Josie's development, and it will add another dimension to the parenting she is experiencing. At last, Josie is able to know that the world is not always a frightening place. She discovers instead a world where she is free to do what she wants and to receive responses to this from her caregivers. For Josie, the healing has finally begun. Play, within a caring relationship, is the key to freeing her from the trauma of her past.

# 3

# Playful Parenting

As we explore PACE within this book, you will see how each component is separate but also intertwined with the others. At times you will think explicitly about being playful, focusing on curiosity, demonstrating acceptance or providing empathy. At other times, and especially as you become more practised with it, PACE will become a whole, an attitude to parenting which encompasses all at once.

Each component has a special contribution, but only together will PACE work to its maximum. Curiosity is like the mind, contributing to thinking; empathy is like the heart, focused around feeling. Acceptance is the key that allows mind and heart to work together. Playfulness surrounds all three. In this analogy you might think about it as the air we breathe. The 'P' – the playful approach – brings 'ACE' alive. It is play that brings us the greatest sense of pleasure and joy, a fun connection to our child. As we put all of these together, we help the child to feel more secure within his attachment relationships, able to enter into and enjoy intersubjective relationships.

Play provides connection with children. After writing this chapter, Kim came across a book devoted to the topic of play in parenting. Coincidentally we chose the same title for this chapter as American Psychologist Lawrence Cohen chose for his book. He writes: 'Playful parenting is a way to enter a child's world, on the child's terms, in order to foster closeness, confidence and connection.'[1]

Within this chapter we explore how playfulness can become a central part of parenting. This increases connectedness between parent and child, leading to increased understanding and deepening of relationship. In turn, this helps parents experience more joy with their children, introducing the children to the pleasure and joy of relationships. Playful parenting can enhance the emotional development of the child.

## Playfulness in PACE-led parenting

Playfulness is an important part of parenting children who have experienced difficult past experiences. These children can be left with a strong sense of pessimism and fear that family life can never be different. When the parent provides a playful attitude, she is also conveying a sense of optimism that things can change, and that she experiences the child positively. The parent notices strengths within the child that she can respond to with play, humour and fun. Maybe this relationship will be unlike past experiences, and maybe there are parts of the child that can relate to this new relationship in a different way.

---

Katherine has had a difficult mealtime. This has resulted in her shouting at her mother and storming up to her bedroom without finishing her food. A short time later her mother brings up some clothes to put in her drawers. As she puts the clothes away, she casually talks with Katherine:

Mum: Bad day today?

Katherine: What do you care? (She lies on her bed and puts her face into her pillow)

Mum: It really feels like I don't care, uh? Is that because I asked you not to flick the food?

Katherine: You are always picking on me. It is never Justin's fault!

(Mum sits down and puts her hand on Katherine's back)

Mum: It feels like I pick on you sometimes, doesn't it? I sure am a fussy mum. How fussy do you think I am? Maybe this fussy?' (Holds hands about a foot apart)

Katherine: (Takes a quick look) No, much fussier!

Mum: This fussy? (Hands further apart)

(Katherine rolls over and takes hold of her mother's hands)

Katherine: No, at least this fussy. Now leave me alone. (Said without conviction)

Mum: I won't. You are far too precious to me!

Katherine: Not as precious as Justin! (Starts to turn away again)

Mum: (With mock crossness) No turning away now, young lady. (More seriously and with empathy) Katherine, you are so good at telling me how you feel. I guess I forget sometimes and need reminding that when I correct you about something, it brings all sorts of worries up for you. It is scary thinking that I might love Justin more than you, isn't it? *(Playful again)* I guess we need to play 'guess how much I love you?' again.

*(This Is a game that they have played together many times. Katherine guesses how much her mother loves her and Mum always comes back with more)*

Katherine: *(Adopting a patient voice)* You love me to the moon.

Mum: I love you to the moon and back.

Katherine: You love me to the bottom of the ocean.

Mum: I love you to the bottom of the ocean, through the earth and out the other side.

Soon Katherine is giggling as they come up with more outrageous ways to love her. Mum then hugs Katherine to her and whispers, 'You are getting better and better at knowing how much I love you, but I guess when I asked you to stop flicking the food, you just forgot.'

Katherine: I'm sorry I flicked the food. I fell out with Lucy today at school.

Mum: In that case, let me make you a sandwich and you can tell me about it whilst you eat.

Throughout this exchange Mum has maintained a playful but supportive attitude to Katherine. She hasn't challenged her fears. Katherine needs to build confidence that her mother does love her. This confidence has been unsettled by the upset at school, and Katherine is quick to spot what she perceives as favouritism at the meal table. Mum focuses on reminding Katherine of her love for her, helping her to experience herself as loveable and important. For the time being, Katherine needs to experience an exclusive relationship with her mum, within which she can experience some optimism that she is special and loveable. Encompassing other family relationships within this is something to work towards.

---

Once children start to gain some experiences of themselves as loveable in the relationship with their parents, they will be more open to enjoying positive experiences within these relationships. Parents can now build upon this to develop the experience of reciprocal enjoyment within the family. Until the child can believe in the love of a parent, he will remain prone to experiencing other family members as leaving him out. His belief is that he is not as good as, or is less loved than, other family members. The normal teasing and banter of family life will be a source of stress and worry. Once the child has experienced a playful and accepting relationship with a parent, family fun will be less threatening. The child is now open to becoming a reciprocal member of the family.

Relationship development can be difficult. The child may resist or actively work to spoil these developing relationships; the parent will inevitably have moments of stress or distraction which can impact on the child. Developing and repairing the relationship at times of rupture is the hard work of parenting. Engaging in playfulness and building in moments of reciprocal enjoyment can get the family through the harder work of building strong and continuous relationships.

## Playfulness in parent–infant relationships

The early play experiences between a parent and infant have often not happened in the lives of children with attachment difficulties. It is helpful to think about what has been missed.

---

Imagine a father and his baby son. The small infant lies on his back on a towel having just been lifted from his bath. He is kicking his feet and waving his arms vigorously. Equally vigorously, the father talks to him. He leans forward and kisses the infant's tummy. The infant laughs and dad laughs back. The infant looks away and the father leans back slightly. As the infant looks back, the father is ready to re-engage, leaning forward to kiss the tummy again. The infant gives a throaty giggle and blows bubbles with his mouth. Dad mirrors this action, blowing bubbles back. The infant becomes even more animated as he reaches out to his father's face. Suddenly he coughs and appears discomfited. Dad immediately soothes, commenting on the nasty cough, and the baby laughs again. Dad blows bubbles again and the infant mirrors the action. Laughing, he reaches out and explores Dad's face once more. Dad laughs as the tiny hands reach out and hold his nose. 'Come on then, let's get you ready,' he says as he reaches for the talcum powder; contented, the infant accepts being dressed.

---

As illustrated in this example, infants experience emotion from birth. This might, for example, be a feeling of calm contentment, angry distress or intense joy. These emotions are expressed through a particular state, which psychologists call 'an affective state'. Parents intuitively match their infant's affective state with a synchronized affective state of their own. This is the basis of regulation. The infant can experience emotion being regulated because of the parent's own matched but regulated state which has the same rhythm and intensity as their infant. Daniel Stern, an American psychiatrist specializing in infant development, describes this matching of affective states as 'attunement' and suggests that this attunement experience is fundamental for the development of relationship as well as the development of the infant.[2]

In infancy, a frequent state of attunement is experienced as playfulness. In addition, this playful relationship precedes a relationship that needs to provide discipline and boundaries on behaviour. The infant experiences his primary interactions as playful; only later will these interactions be expanded to include discipline and socialization experiences.

Parent–infant play is highly interactive and primarily focused on enjoyment of the relationship. The parent engages in rhythm, movement and laughter, which draws the child into a connection with her. This is aided by the exaggerated facial expressions, vocalizations and sing-song voice which come so naturally when you hold an infant in your arms. The child enjoys the repetition of these interactions, feeling safe in the sameness, and from this safety is able to enjoy moments of surprise when the parent does something unexpected. Think of a game of peek-a-boo, for example. These interactions generate energy between parent and child and this in turn brings the infant to life.

Playfulness between parent and child ideally starts in infancy. The child is born into a relationship that is joyful, attentive and absorbed with him and his uniqueness. Essential for healthy development, these early parent–child relationships provide the infant with two fundamental and essential experiences, as we saw in Chapter 1.

First, the experience of safety and security with another wiser and more mature caregiver; this is the experience of attachment security. The child is experiencing a hierarchical relationship. You keep me safe; I am kept safe by you. The child has no responsibility for keeping the adult safe.

Secondly, the experience of reciprocal influence with another person; this is a non-hierarchical relationship. Both are equal partners in influencing and being influenced by the other. This is the foundation of intersubjectivity.

With both these experiences the child will mature, able to enter into relationships from which he can derive security from another and within which he can experience reciprocity, the ability to influence others whilst being influenced by them.

Whilst a range of experiences offered by the parent underlie these experiences of safety and reciprocity, play can be seen at the heart of them. An attitude of playfulness brings joy into the relationship, providing a secure foundation and confidence which will survive the more difficult elements of relating. For example, the parent will feel more able to cope when her child is distressed, fearful or fretful. Similarly, the child will be more able to cope with times of relationship breaks, perhaps because the parent is distracted or stressed or because there has been a need for discipline and correction. A play-based relationship brings them both experiences of connection and pleasure that can make harder times easier to cope with.

The experience of playfulness – the joy and fascination of another within infancy – provides the child with his first experience of a positive and unconditional relationship: 'I love you for being you, not for what you do or how you respond. I will always love you no matter what. My love for you is not conditional on anything you say, do or experience.' Experience of such unconditional relationships builds confidence for the child that he is inherently good, worthwhile and loveable. This confidence helps him to deal with the range of relationships that he will encounter, including those that have a conditional element to them: 'I will approve of you if you do...' All of this begins in the playful encounters of infancy.

## Developing playfulness with older children

So what happens when children miss out on playful relationships early in life? This has an impact on their capacity for relationship, as well as on their own emerging development.

The child is older when he first experiences a playful relationship, the foundation of the infant–parent relationship. He has to manage relationships with parents who need to provide discipline and restrictions on his behaviour, without the initial freedom of just being together, free of the constraints that the need to discipline brings. Two developmental stages are being combined. The unconditional love and safety established in infancy is missing, reducing the child's ability to tolerate the more stressful acts of discipline that he needs for his own safety and socialization. For the child, this can lead to a belief that his behaviour is more important than he is. In fact, he may only see himself as his behaviour. The old adage of 'ignore the behaviour and not the child' rather loses its meaning when the child can only see himself through his behaviour.

The child may be mistrustful of playfulness observed in the parent. He may anticipate that the parent is trying to trick him; this is another way to get him to behave in a certain way; or even another expression of the parent's meanness to him. The challenge for the parent is to bring playfulness into the child's life so that he can experience the relationship differently, and learn to experience himself differently as a consequence.

In addition, the lack of good, early parent–child experience means that developmentally the child is less able to benefit from this experience now. The primary shared emotions of infancy such as joy and interest, excitement and happiness may have been missed. When these are experienced now, they will feel alien and even threatening. The child may find it difficult to regulate these states, or to use the adult to help with this regulation. He may quickly become over-excited, eventually spoiling the experience. Often what started as a good experience for the family is spoiled as the child cannot remain regulated with the emotion being generated. Alternatively, the child may withdraw from the experience, spoiling it for everyone in the process. The child may sabotage experiences before they can even happen.

## Playfulness as part of therapeutic parenting

Without good parent–infant experience based on moments of fun, laughter and play, the child misses the opportunity to discover the positive in self or other. These children will feel insecure within their attachment relationships, and will be unable to enter into or will actively resist intersubjective experience. The child does not know how to derive security from a parent, nor does he understand or value a reciprocal relationship.

Therapeutic parenting focuses on helping the child to develop a more secure attachment to the parent. It additionally offers the experience of intersubjective relationships, developing the child's capacity for reciprocal relationships. The child can experience being valued just for being himself, of being connected to another. Equally importantly he can experience influencing and being influenced by another.

As with the parent–infant relationship these relationships begin with play. The parent explores the strengths and uniqueness that is the child and enjoys and takes pleasure in these. This helps the relationship to be playful, enjoyable and deeply satisfying. The parent holds a positive and optimistic stance towards the child, within which she searches for and finds positive qualities – strengths that the child will build on. As the relationship between parent and child develops, the parent will experience a joyful fascination with the child. The child in turn will experience this as having a positive impact on the parent. Over time the child will come to enjoy this influence and want its continuing development.

---

Here is an example of a playful dialogue, witnessed by Kim, between a foster parent and her nine-year-old foster son, William, which illustrates this joyful fascination. We have been talking about how scary it is not to be able to trust your mummy to take care of you, and William has been able to talk about these fears. He looks at his foster parent and Kim wonders if he can see the love for him in his foster parent's eyes:

Parent: There it is. Can you see it?

William: Yes, there is one bit just there.

Parent: Are you looking lots. Really concentrate because if you really look guess what you will see? *(William stares intently into his foster parent's eyes)* There it is.

William: *(With excitement)* Yes, you love me! *(They have a big hug)*

Parent: I will love you whatever happens, for ever and ever and ever. I will love that big smile. I will love those deep brown eyes. I will love that mischievous laugh. I will love all of you. I will love you until you are a grumpy old man *(William laughs)* or even when I am a grumpy old lady.

William: *(With excitement)* You are!

Parent: Do you think so? Then you will have to love me lots as well. Because I love you no matter what.

William: That's why you are my mummy!

Parent: Well, that's the way I want it to be. That's what I want more than anything…

Parent and William: …in the whole, wide world. *(They hug together)*

---

In this extract, the playfulness between mother and foster son has allowed the child to get an experience of his impact on another person. The mother has reacted to him as a unique individual with his own characteristics. This has provided them both with a rich connection which has increased the pleasure and joy in their relationship.

This can sound very daunting, even hopeless, if you are currently experiencing your relationship with a child as negative and spiralling downwards. How can you begin to be playful when the days are full of so much conflict? We do not want to underestimate how difficult this is and how discouraged you may be feeling. We would encourage you, however, to search for moments of playfulness within you. As you will see further on in this book, we will also be introducing you to the attitude of acceptance, curiosity and empathy. These will also assist in the process of bringing a lighter and more playful element to your parenting. As you understand your child more deeply, accept the reasons for his behaviours more intensely and are able to empathize with the struggles he is engaged in, you will also be noticing the uniqueness and the strengths that are your child. You will become less irritated with the defences that your child uses to keep his own particular demons at bay, precisely because you understand these demons more fully.

In understanding your child, you will judge him less and as a consequence be able to be more playful with him. As you take on a playful presence within the relationship, you will also be conveying a sense of optimism. The child does have strengths and things can be different, better. The playfulness within the relationship brings a lightness that communicates hope, even at the darkest time. Conflicts and problems are difficult but within this relationship they can be managed.

Small moments of playfulness will bring small moments of optimism. These in turn will feed on themselves, eventually leading to more sustained moments of reciprocal enjoyment within the relationship, and within the family as a whole. In turn, these times of fun and humour, of enjoyment in the relationship will sustain each of you through the harder times that will inevitably also be there. The times when you smile together, look deeply at each other and even laugh in delightful companionship will cement the relationship, giving each a reason for being part of the family. Reciprocal laughter provides the foundation for safety and acceptance and reduces any sense of shame and fear that the child might be experiencing.

The child will experience these playful moments as unconditional acceptance of himself and will learn to provide unconditional acceptance back. Commitment within the family will be increased as the relationships are experienced as special and unique. The child may still be struggling with affection. Intimacy may still be a little way off, but playfulness can give the child experiences of a kind of closeness that will help both of you get through the harder times.

Over time, playfulness will become an accepted part of family life for the child. This moves beyond the episodic playfulness of laughter, jokes and humour, to a playfulness that is about a way of life. The relationships that develop are open and light, with less emphasis on agenda and what must or should happen and more on flexibility and responsiveness. The relationships become open to each other as both child and parents become open to the experience of each other. In a previous book, Dan explores this type of playfulness as relationship:

> Their primary intent is simply to be together, nothing else matters. Any conflicts, responsibilities, and frustrations are set aside. These playful times are truly moments of deepening, broadening and healing for the ongoing relationship. They are moments when each becomes absorbed by the other. When such moments occur they are not likely to be forgotten and whatever conflicts occur in the future are experienced within a context that holds onto the relationship that exists under the conflict.[3]

From this description it can be seen how much the playful and light qualities to relationships are important for the building of security; the child experiences being loved unconditionally, just for who he is. This builds hope that he is loveable and that the loving, supportive relationships he is learning to enjoy will continue. In return, the parent experiences hope that he can parent this child, developing a relationship that is bigger than the mistakes each of them might make and providing a sense that problems are not insurmountable. Striving for a playful element to the relationship is therefore part of building a secure base for the child, increasing security of attachment and opening the child up to reciprocal relationships both now and in the future.

As playfulness becomes an accepted part of family life, which the child can engage in, it can also become an important source of learning for the child. Humour can, for example, help the child to view events from different perspectives, leading to the possibility that he is open to the experience of others. This in turn can enhance flexibility of responding.

Of course, relationships cannot only be about moments of togetherness and fun. Relationships are also about conflict, discipline and coping with separation. An important part of the parenting that is offered includes helping the child to cope with these tensions and to learn that he is loved and wanted despite the difficult times. The playfulness that the parent brings to the relationship and the encouragement and support that help the child enter into such playful states not only increase fun within the relationship but also provide an important level of security for the child. This security is a bit like a safety net, available to support the child when he is experiencing the stress of discipline or if he is coping with separation or increased anxiety for other reasons.

Children who have had difficult early experience and who have low self-esteem and a negative view of self can really struggle with playfulness from others. They are quick to view this play as being mean to them or trying to trick them in some way. As with a younger child, you may need to be very explicit about what you are doing. Let the child know that you are being playful because you love him and want to have fun with him, not to make fun of him.

For a similar reason, be careful of more personal jokes or sarcasm. Typically, the child will not experience this as playful. He will, sometimes rightly, interpret it as a criticism of himself. We all tend to use humour to help cope with irritating traits in another. It is a way of lightly saying 'I love you but I do feel irritated when you get bossy like that.' The child may not understand the subtlety of this. The parent is trying to communicate an irritation with a specific behaviour, but the child assumes that it is his whole self that is disapproved of. Families use playfulness and gentle teasing to address traits in each other that can be a source of conflict. By family members becoming jointly playful, the relationships become bigger than any source of conflict. It is easy, however, for children to see judgement and criticism of themselves instead. This leads them into the experience of shame, further distancing them from the relationships that they need in order to feel secure.

## Playfulness and its impact on the child

Children who have experienced neglectful or frightening parenting in the past, or who have had too many experiences of separation and loss of parents will become wary of closeness. Intimacy may be frightening to them or just very alien. Some children may fear getting close because of the very strangeness of the experience; some because they anticipate that pain will follow. Other children may resist closeness because they fear how much they like it and want it. If they embrace this experience and then lose it once more, they will feel hurt all over again. Having experienced loss in the past, they will be very sensitive to the likelihood of loss in the future. They often experience a deep sense of badness or worthlessness. They anticipate that when you understand this about them you will inevitably withdraw. They do not expect closeness to last.

For all these reasons, parents may experience difficulty getting close to their children and helping their children enjoy this feeling of closeness. Playfulness can be a helpful way of allowing some closeness that is not so scary for the child, because it is not so intimate. A child can enjoy a playful moment because it is just that, a moment. The child does not have to fear its loss because it is not the relationship, only an expression of the relationship. A playful experience has happened and cannot be taken away. It is enjoyed in the present. An intimate experience is the relationship, and therefore, in the child's fears, can be gone in a heartbeat, never to return. Playfulness is a way of helping the child to allow some closeness but in a way that is less scary. Playful is 'affection-light' and therefore easier to tolerate when affection feels alien or frightening.

Additionally, children who have experienced developmental trauma will have more difficulty than other children regulating their emotion. Feelings are experienced more intensely when children have these regulation difficulties: anger becomes rage, fear becomes terror, sadness becomes despair, and shame becomes intensified, getting bigger and bigger. Furthermore, the children can't regulate their positive emotions. When they experience excitement, joy or love, these also become difficult to manage and then they get transformed by anxiety.

Again, the child dysregulates as he tries to deal with these escalating emotional states. Playfulness can provide graded doses of positive emotion that the child can manage. Whether it is a brief moment of playfulness or a more extended experience, these playful times bring the child into connection with another. He can cope with this connection, and therefore he can use it to stay regulated with the positive emotion he is now experiencing. Through a playful relationship, the child develops increased capacity for emotional regulation.

The child then becomes more open to the positive and can build towards sharing a positive relationship within which he can experience the full range of closeness and intimacy. The child will experience playful moments with the hope that relationships can be different to those he has previously experienced.

Play also opens the door to improved reflective abilities. As the child laughs and giggles, he also becomes more reflective, more able to think about things, whether in the present or the past.

---

Kim was involved in a therapy session with a five-year-old girl and her adoptive father. The three of them were engaged in some simple relationship-based games – stacking hands, blowing bubbles and blowing each other over. The child suddenly worried that her father would not catch her if she fell. Typically, this child would not be able to talk about such fears; she would instead revert to being bossy and controlling as a way of helping herself to feel safe. On this occasion, however, she was able to talk about them and to remember how her birth father did not keep her safe at all. She was able to reflect, at least in a limited way, that having one experience of a scary daddy led to you being scared sometimes with your adoptive dad. The games, although simple and apparently unimportant, had created a relaxed setting in which the child could name her fears. It is also likely that the largely non-verbal games had impacted on her brain in such a way that the connections between verbal and non-verbal were increased. In activating non-verbal areas of the brain, the child's ability to think and reflect were also enhanced.

---

Playfulness is also a great way of protecting the child from feelings of shame. When the child is laughing, a different part of the brain is activated compared to when the child is experiencing shame.

When the child is experiencing shame, he will not be able to enter into playfulness. He will feel a sense of badness at his core, and this will lead to a withdrawal from play and from the relationship itself. He attempts to protect himself from the pain he anticipates as part of this relationship. Support and empathy for these feelings of shame and badness will allow them to reduce. The child will become able to re-enter the relationship, and this can become playful again.

Here is an example of how shame is likely to lead the child away from all interactions with his parent, especially those that involve playfulness and affection.

---

Mum: *(Animated voice)* Why, look at my handsome son! You're more lovely than a bar of chocolate and you know how much I love chocolate!

Son (age 8): No I'm not! I'm ugly! Everybody says that! You're my mum so you have to say that I'm handsome.

Mum: *(With a much quieter, gentle voice)* Oh, Jake, I'm sorry that I didn't notice that you seem to be having a hard time.

Son: The kids laughed at me and called me Freckle-face! I hate these freckles, I hate them!

Mum: Oh, that must have hurt, Jake. That would be so hard to hear.

Son: They are ugly, Mum. They look dumb, all over my face. The other kids don't have them or not so many anyway.

Mum: That's probably true, son. You do have a lot. I didn't think that you disliked them though. I thought you were sort of proud of them. Like they made you feel special in a way.

Son: The other kids don't think so. They think that they're silly and stupid.

Mum: And it's hard to hear them say those things, even if they don't mean them.

Son: Why would they say that if they don't mean it?

Mum: I don't know, son. Maybe because they know how well you usually do with friends, and school, and sports. Maybe they were looking for something to find that wasn't so great about you and all that they could come up with was to tease you about your freckles.

Son: Why can't they just like me the way I am?

Mum: Maybe they do, son. Maybe they just feel a bit jealous sometimes that you seem to do well at just about everything, at least most of the time.

Son: So maybe they don't think my freckles are ugly?

Mum: Maybe not, son. The kids I knew when I was your age didn't think a kid's freckles were ugly. We liked who the kid was and it didn't matter if he had freckles or not.

Son: You think that's true now?

Mum: I do, son.

Son: I usually like them. Last week I tried to count them.

Mum: How many did you count?

Son: I got up to 87 and then Billy came over.

Mum: And you know what? I think Billy would like you the same if you had eight or 800.

Son: I do too, Mum.

Mum: So there you and your freckles are!

Son: And I really am more lovely than a bar of chocolate?

Mum: Son, you're more lovely than a mountain of chocolate that went to the moon.

Son: And I won't make you fat either.

Mum: You better be careful what you talk about there, son.

Son: I'll love you if you weigh eight pounds or 800, Mum!

---

In this conversation you can see how the boy's worry about his friend's teasing has led him to feel that maybe he is ugly. As his mum refers to him as handsome, it triggers his deeper worries about whether he is actually ugly and he enters a state of shame. He cannot enter into the playful interaction that Mum is providing. Mum is sensitive to this and moves from playfulness to curiosity and empathy. As her son experiences his mum understanding and accepting his worry, he can reconsider this worry and his sense of shame reduces. Now he is ready to be playful.

Conversely, when a child is enjoying a playful relationship, he is much less likely to enter into a state of shame and despair. Moments of rupture will be easier to cope with. The child will be more open to believing that he is loveable and to believing in the relationship that is on offer.

Play, therefore, can have an important developmental impact upon children. This results in improved capacity for regulation and reflection. In addition, cognitive abilities within the child can be enhanced through play. The child may come to the playful experiences with a reduced capacity for attention and concentration. As an infant, the ability to concentrate and attend expands because of the support offered by the parent and her own ability to concentrate and attend. Without this early experience, the child may need shorter, briefer, playful episodes within an attentive relationship. From this start, the child's abilities to concentrate and attend, both within the relationship and then outside of it, will gradually increase.

Overall, then, by bringing a playful part into your relationship with your child you will also be promoting his recovery from his past experience of trauma, neglect, separation and loss. The child will experience a relationship with a parent that is different from his past relationships. He will experience moments of being happy, of enjoying the relationship. He will also experience his parents as being able to help him regulate this experience. This will hold out hope that relationships can be different, and indeed that maybe he can be different with the support of these relationships.

## Maintaining playfulness

The experience of parenting a child without positive early parent–infant experiences can place a disadvantage on the relationship. The early acceptance and openness to each other at a time when the infant is less autonomous can provide a secure foundation for the later development of autonomy. The child remains open to the guidance of the parent. This experience can be missed for a number of reasons. For example, the parent and child may not have known each other during the child's early years. Alternatively, the parent may have had periods when she was unavailable to the child, perhaps because of her own stress, post-natal depression or other pressures she was coping with. This places an inevitable strain on the relationship. The parent is now parenting a child with complex difficulties, a reluctance to enter into a relationship and with a conflictual or withdrawn attitude. This can pose a significant challenge to enjoying acceptance and openness in the relationship. The foundation of playfulness is missing.

When the shared interests and joint history that children have with their parents is missing, the parent has to create playfulness out of current experience, but without this rich historical experience to feed it. Similarly, when both parent and child have had a difficult start to their relationship, the positive foundation to this relationship is missing. Play is now coloured with all the other aspects of the relationship, including distrust and suspicion, sensitivity to discipline and the lack of a close, reciprocal relationship which both parent and child can believe in. All of this can place a relationship under severe stress, which can lead to fundamental difficulties for the parent.

Dan has recently completed a book with a colleague that describes the five neuropsychological systems in the brain that are crucial for effective parenting over time.[4] These systems involve wanting to be near your child, experiencing pleasure or joy in his company, being interested in him, seeing deep meaning in the interactions with him, and being ready to try to do what is best for him in all circumstances, regardless of how difficult the circumstances are for you, him or your relationship.

These systems involve many regions of the brain. When parenting is easy, the hormones oxytocin or prolactin from areas of the hippocampus and dopamine from the nucleus accumbens will increase your desire to be with your child and to enjoy his company. The hormones activate a desire to approach and remain close to a loved one. They generate the emotions of love and affection for the other.

When things are more difficult, the lower regions of the prefrontal cortex are more active, involving the insula and anterior cingulate. These are the reflective parts of the brain. If you experience negative feelings towards your child – for example, fear or anger – it is these parts of the brain that help you to manage these difficult emotions. Your thoughts and awareness of the 'big picture' of parenting help you to inhibit any detrimental reactions to your child that might stem from your negative feelings. You will cope with feeling angry or afraid without this impacting negatively on the relationship you have with the child. These same parts of your brain also help you to experience empathy for your child. You will take a greater interest in him and will also be able to experience how important you are in his life.

Biologically, the joy of parenting can become switched off when the relationship is experiencing difficulties. This can lead to a state of 'blocked care', as the systems in the brain become compromised. The parent goes through the motions of parenting the child but cannot experience the pleasure of this parenting.

Blocks to enjoyment can arise for a number of reasons. The parent may have longstanding difficulties that get in the way of her parenting. Difficult parenting experience in her own childhood or severe relationship difficulties in the past might result in early bonding difficulties for the parent. The experience of compromised past relationships colour the potential for this relationship, leading to difficulties from the start.

Alternatively, the parent may be struggling with acute stress stemming from a more current crisis or difficult period in her life. Again, this can interfere with early bonding or can create problems parenting in the present. The parenting becomes a chore on top of the current stresses, with diminished joy or pleasure in the relationship. If a parent has experienced the joy and meaning of parenting in the past, both as a parent and as a child being parented, then she is more likely to re-establish her readiness and ability to care for her child when the current stresses are diminished or when she receives care herself from a partner, friend or therapist.

Finally, the difficulties in parenting might stem from characteristics of this particular child. The blocked care becomes child-specific. For example, a child with trauma and attachment difficulties will not engage in reciprocal relationships very well, and this lack of reciprocity tends to undermine the activity of the five systems that are crucial for effective parenting. Similar difficulties can stem from parenting a child who has his own biological challenges that make it harder to parent him. Alternatively, there may be an aspect of this child that triggers for the parent memories of a past difficult relationship. In any of these eventualities, the parent is left struggling to develop a reciprocal relationship, impacting on her capacity to experience the child as rewarding and the parenting of the child as pleasurable.

---

A mother, for example, experienced a physically abusive relationship with her father. When her baby son is born prematurely, this mother has an intense sense that she has already failed as a parent. She picks up her fragile son and is overwhelmed by a sense of terror that her son can already see her failure and already hates her. She looks into his eyes and the eyes of her father look back at her. This mother and son do not bond well, resulting in attachment insecurity for the little boy. He grows up to be aggressive and controlling as a way of dealing with this lack of security. These behaviours only serve to confirm what the mother has always feared: that her son is like her father. She experiences no joy or pleasure parenting this child, only fear, discouragement and failure.

---

When a parent is struggling to experience any pleasure or joy in the relationship with the child, playfulness can be a particular challenge. The play, humour and fun of a relationship are the first to disappear when stress increases. In this case, it will be essential for the parent to have her own support relationships within which she can be taken care of.

An opportunity to experience some fun and joy in such supportive relationships can begin the process of rediscovering or creating such experiences in the relationship with the child.

Respite from the daily parenting grind, opportunities to focus on non-child related activities and the experience of competence from other activities can all help to emotionally charge the parent again.

Respite can also provide opportunities for reflection. A first step in increasing empathy for the child can arise from gaining an understanding of the child and the difficulties that the child presents. As the parent understands more deeply, she will accept what her child is bringing in a way that can lead to increased support and love for that child. As she experiences these feelings, she will be in a better position to reintroduce fun and playfulness into the relationship.

In some cases, parents may find it helpful to find a therapeutic relationship within which they can explore their current difficulties without fear of judgement or criticism. Opportunities to reflect on past difficulties and their impact on current difficulties can help the parent to separate past from present. The parent will start to notice what is unique about her child rather than only viewing the child through the lens of past experience. Recognizing what is unique in the strengths and characteristics of a child can start the process of developing a relationship that is unique and not just a replay of what has occurred in the past. This in turn can help the parent to experience the joy and pleasure of parenting this child.

Gaining support for ourselves can seem like a very low priority in a list of needs, demands and requirements that our life dictates for us. When we lose capacity for joy and pleasure, however, prioritizing our needs is a must. Looking after ourselves allows us to bring all that we are to our relationship with our child. By prioritizing our own needs for support, recreation and relaxation, we are also prioritizing our child's need for a positive, playful relationship from us.

## In conclusion

In this chapter we have explored the playful element of PACE. Playfulness is at the heart of the relationship parents have with their infants. This can build a foundation for the ongoing development of that relationship. When this early experience is missed, the parent is challenged to introduce playfulness within the relationship at a later developmental stage. This brings a range of difficulties, combined as it is with the other parenting tasks of keeping the older child safe and providing appropriate boundaries and discipline.

Therapeutic parenting requires an element of playfulness for its success, but this attitude of playfulness can be difficult with a rejecting or hostile child. In addition, the parent brings her own history of stress, relationship difficulty and distrust of her own sense of pleasure and fun. Supportive relationships, playful opportunities outside of the parenting relationship and deeper understanding of the child can all help to bring fun and pleasure back into parenting.

We can be at our most connected when we play with our children. The joy of play can bring pleasure to a parenting task which is often grinding and thankless. Small moments of play can, over time, truly develop into a deep, enriching and playful relationship between child and parent.

## STORY

### The Naive Buccaneer

### By Gregory J. Delve[5]

The Ocean was a great, green field. Wind buffeted its surface, causing its emerald waves to writhe. The captain, four feet in height and an experienced seafarer, stood tall upon the sturdy gate, smiling a proud smile that only a boy who thinks himself the best and most strapping young man who ever sailed the seas could get away with. And get away with it he did, for it was the opinion of this naive buccaneer that he *was* the best and most strapping young man who ever sailed the seas.

This buccaneer also had a very specific aim in mind. He wanted a ship, for, as everybody knows, captains require a ship. Any old ship would not do, for he wanted a particular ship. It lay on the edge of the field – a great, thick trunk, with upturned roots at the prow and branches sticking out of its deck. And so, without further ado, he was down from the gate and ploughing through the waves. He found a sword on the way, long and brown, with a twig attached to it.

He crawled through the perilous waves until he was at the prow of the ship. Grasping an upturned root, he began to climb. He hauled himself on to the ship and gave a triumphant bellow. He dashed forwards and pounced upon his foes, who, though invisible, fled before his might. He grabbed the mast to steady himself, stabbing left and right until he was satisfied that all had either fallen overboard or surrendered to him.

'Who here challenges my right to captain this vessel?' he cried. 'Who amongst you has the courage to take me on?'

'I do!' It was his treacherous elder sister. She must have followed him.

'Black-hearted Jessica! You challenge me?'

'Only for what is rightfully mine.'

The siblings shared a self-confidence that had led them both to want to be captains. Black-hearted Jessica stood before her brother, arms folded, her outfit of T-shirt and jeans neatly topped with an authentic-looking tricorn.

'Well, you can't have it. I saw it first.'

'You didn't.'

He struck, but she nimbly dodged and grabbed his wrist. She prized open his hand and tossed the weapon overboard.

'No! What do we do now when the kraken arrives?'

'Kraken?'

'You take the wheel; I'll keep an eye out for it.'

Not entirely sure if he was bluffing, she ran to the other end of the ship, and began steering.

'We're on course for land!'

'Good! It's right on our tail, so hurry!'

Her eyes widened as she realized that she was only moments away from being consumed by a terrible sea monster. She spun the wheel and pulled on some ropes.

'I'm getting your sword! Take the wheel!'

Then she jumped into the water. Thrashing in the great waves, she grabbed the sword before hauling herself back on to the deck.

The captain took it back from her in an instant. 'I'll defend us whilst you get us to shore!' And with that he began swinging and stabbing at monstrous tentacles.

'We've run aground! We'll have to swim the rest of the way!'

They ran to the side of the deck, where they came face to face with the terrible jaws of the kraken. 'This way!'

They ran to the prow of the ship, and they climbed down together, jumping the last few feet and landing in a spectacular heap in the sea. Without a backwards glance, they ran hand in hand until they reached the gate, and clambered on to the shore, where it was safe.

'We made it home!' he said delightedly, for the shore was none other than his own back garden. Then, with a gleam in her eye, Black-hearted Jessica took his sword and ran him through. His eyes widening with shock, he gave a delighted cry of 'Oh!' and collapsed on the lawn, clutching the sword under his arm.

'And that,' said Jessica solemnly, 'was the end of the best and most strapping young man who ever sailed the seven seas.'

He opened his eyes, and Jessica helped him to his feet. 'Come on. Mum sent me out to bring you in for dinner. I'll race you back!' And with the cold wind in their hair, brother and sister raced away, their adventure left for another day.

Jessica burst into the dining room, followed closely by her brother.

'That's not fair! You're so much faster than me!'

'That's because she has longer legs than you,' laughed Mum. 'Yet it seems they didn't help either of you to arrive on time for dinner.' Gazing fondly at them, their mother rose from the table and fetched their plates from the kitchen.

'Mama, I saved Jessica from a kraken today!'

'Did you now?' His mother smiled, steering him into his seat. 'Why don't you tell me about it during your meal?'

'You did not save me. I had everything under control,' Jessica said, taking her place opposite him at the table.

'You didn't. You nearly got eaten. And then you killed me!'

Their mother raised an eyebrow. 'Did you, Jessica?

'Well, what did you expect?' Jessica grinned. 'After all, I am his big sister.'

# PART II

# Acceptance

# 4

# Acceptance of the Inner World of the Other

We are now moving on to consider acceptance. This is perhaps the hardest of the four parts of PACE to describe and to understand. We all know what it is to play, to experience empathy and to be curious. Generally, we can see the value in these, even if we struggle to do them at times.

When we think about acceptance, however, it can raise more questions than answers. What are we accepting? If we accept, are we being too lenient or tolerant of misbehaviour? How will a child learn if we 'merely' accept? What do we mean by acceptance?

In this chapter we focus on what acceptance is, and why it is so important in the parenting of children. The central message is that accepting the inner life of children, alongside unconditional love, is at the heart of the parents' relationship with their children. This does not lead to tolerance of misbehaviour and it does not stop parents teaching them. It does mean that teaching and discipline will rest on the strong foundation of deep and meaningful relationships, relationships that provide an important sense of security for the children.

Lionel Shriver is author of the award winning novel *We Need to Talk About Kevin*,[1] an exploration of the relationship between a mother and son. Can a relationship be built around the horror of the son's killing of seven students and two staff at his high school? It is also a study of culpability: do the sins of the child rest with the sins of the parent? Faced with such an abhorrent act, can the mother find a way to love her son unconditionally? It could be argued that this story is also a story of acceptance. Can the mother accept the experiences that she and her son have had, experiences that led to an act with such appalling consequences? As the book unfolds, the question is asked again and again: How can a mother find acceptance in the face of such a challenge caused by Kevin's behaviour?

Fortunately, it is rare to have our acceptance threatened to such a degree, but there are challenging behaviours that can threaten to compromise acceptance. These range from acts of aggression, deceit or rejection of others to the equally difficult harm that young people can inflict on themselves. Parents want to influence their children. They want their children to be happy; they want family life to be easier. Such influence begins with acceptance. A parent considers the thoughts, feelings, wishes, intentions, values, perceptions, memories and judgements of his child and incorporates this understanding of the child's inner experience into his interactions with her.

In this chapter and the next, we will explore how you can respond to the inner life of your child. We will be suggesting that your most powerful influence in your child's life comes not from evaluation but from simply accepting your child's inner life. It is through understanding and acceptance of our children and their innermost experience that we build relationships. This relationship development can result in behaviour change but, importantly, this is in the context of increased security. When we stop evaluating behaviour as right or wrong, acceptable or unacceptable, and truly understand the inner experience that led to the behaviour, acceptance becomes an important part of a solution. This includes discipline and boundaries, but only alongside relationship development, security building and a deeper and richer emotional development for the young person.

## What is acceptance?

Acceptance is most easily seen and described in the relationship between a parent and infant.

---

A few years ago, Dan was watching his daughter engaging with his granddaughter. It was time for a diaper change and Mum was cheerfully doing so. She was engaged in animated and giggling dialogue with her daughter as she went about the task of giving her a dry diaper. Just as she was finishing, her daughter urinated into this diaper. Mum first responded with surprise, then a loud giggle, then a dramatic discovery that this diaper was now wet, as she proceeded to find a new one. All the while, her daughter joined her with these evolving emotions from surprise to laughter to quietly anticipating another diaper change. The

entire sequence was accepted by the mother, and hence by the daughter.
There was no evaluation of the behaviour involved.

---

While it is easy to accept the behaviour of a young child, beyond infancy this changes. As a social species, we evaluate one another's behaviours with regard to whether or not these are in accord with our group's values. This is true whether the group is the family or the much larger community, be it cultural, religious or national. These behavioural evaluations lead to our responses, designed to encourage or discourage these actions. Such responses might involve rewards, praise, trophies, privileges and celebrations.

On the other hand, they may involve unwanted consequences or criticisms, loss of privileges or rewards, or removal from the group through loss of membership or prison. Families and larger groups therefore develop a network of rules, formal rewards and punishments, as well as group mores and laws to facilitate appropriate behaviours. There may be differences with regard to the nature of the rules, how rigid or flexible they are, along with the nature and extent of the behavioural responses to the individual's actions, but rule making is a consequence of living in social groups.

It is easy, therefore, to assume that the primary way we influence another's behaviour is by setting clear behavioural expectations and then providing positive and negative consequences for expressed behaviours. This position is based on the belief that if we reward or provide a positive consequence for a behaviour it will increase, whereas if we don't reward or provide a negative consequence for a behaviour, it will decrease. By providing a 'correction' for a behaviour, we expect to influence its course.

While tempting because of its simplicity, such a focus on behaviour alone often fails to create the degree of influence expected. The impetus for this view of behaviour change comes from psychological research, often involving the behaviours of pigeons and rats. Such 'reinforcers' are not as effective for humans because our motivations are more complex. We are motivated at least as much by long-term goals, complex thoughts, feelings and wishes. We are also able to focus on the motives of others. These are as influential as the immediate 'reinforcers' that we encounter.

We are also motivated by reciprocal relationships. We have more of an impact on another when they are also having an impact on us.

The human brain is designed to function within relationships. The type of relationships that our brains desire are the ones where we have a reciprocal impact on each other. If your child does not have any influence on you, you will have less influence on your child. We influence each other through complex interactions much more than by simple behavioural responses to specific actions.

This more complex view of mutual influence rests on our ability to understand the inner life of each other. Most of us would quickly agree that knowing a child's inner life with respect to a given behaviour and situation is likely to assist us in deciding how to intervene. There is likely to be more disagreement regarding what to do with this knowledge.

One option would be to evaluate and attempt to change this inner life of thoughts and feelings. Thus, if your child says that she wants something, you might try to convince her that she should not want it. If your child says that she does not like someone, you might try to convince her to like that person.

A second option – and the one that is strongly recommended in this book – is for you simply to accept your child's thoughts, feelings or wishes with regard to the situation, without trying to change them. In this option you may set a limit or provide a consequence for her immediate behaviour, but without evaluating the underlying reasons for the behaviour. Only the behaviour is evaluated; her inner life is met with acceptance.

Acceptance therefore means becoming aware of and understanding the other's thoughts, feelings, wishes, beliefs – that is, her inner life – without trying to change it. You simply experience what her experience is and understand it as it is, not as you might want it to be. There are no strings attached with acceptance. You are open to her inner life. You deepen your experience of her experience, rather than focus on trying to influence it.

One of the clearest examples of pure acceptance is in the practice of mindfulness. Mindfulness, long-existing within spiritual traditions and more recently in psychotherapeutic interventions, stresses the value of acceptance of the person's inner life as well as the overall present reality, whatever it is. Within a mindful state, the person is open to becoming aware of and accepting whatever she is experiencing in the present moment. Her attention may gently focus on her breathing, noticing it, becoming more deeply aware of its rhythms and regularities, its continuous presence in one's body. In mindfulness there is a letting-go of any effort to control whatever one is aware of. Without the mental effort to change or control the object of our awareness, we become more fully aware of its qualities and meanings.

---

Dan discovered the value of mindfulness, though he did not know what it was called, out of necessity when he was a child. He often had to see a dentist because he had not put much energy into caring for his teeth. He had many cavities, which required drilling and filling. His particular dentist did not believe in providing a local anaesthetic for such procedures, and Dan experienced how painful this could be. During one such procedure he noticed that if he simply became aware of the sensations caused by the drill, the pain seemed less. His open awareness led to acceptance of the sensation in the present moment, and the pain, for the most part, faded to a small sense of discomfort. He also began noticing that the various drills and locations actually produced many interesting types of sensation, some of which were not uncomfortable at all. He was amazed that by remaining open to and accepting of the sensations, they actually changed and became something that he did not try to avoid. When he mentioned this to his older brother, who thought he was a bit unusual anyway, he did not receive an accepting response!

---

American psychiatrist Dan Siegel, who is Co-Director of the Mindful Awareness Research Center, summarizes our understanding of mindfulness by describing it as 'being aware, on purpose and nonjudgmentally, of what is happening as it is happening in the present moment'.[2] Tara Brach, psychologist in Washington, DC, defines mindfulness as 'the quality of awareness that recognizes exactly what is happening in our moment-to-moment experience'.[3] American neurologist James Austin tries to capture the one-of-a-kind nature of mindful awareness when he speaks of 'being mindfully attuned to the fresh individuality of each present moment as it evolves into the next one, and then the next one'.[4]

Although these specialists in mindfulness mostly focus on the individual's experiences when alone, the same principles apply when in relationship with another. When we fully accept the other, we become aware of features of her that we otherwise don't notice. We become highly sensitive to her experience, which, when we do not judge, evaluate, control or try to change it, emerges much more fully than it otherwise would.

## Acceptance and behaviour

---

A number of years ago, Dan was asked to treat a 12-year-old adopted boy who had touched his ten-year-old adopted sister in a sexual manner. His sister was receiving treatment with another therapist. His parents were very angry with him for his behaviour but also deeply worried about the implications for his future. They now supervised him closely but he refused to talk with them about why he had acted that way.

Dan suggested that their presence might help this boy to communicate his experience of himself and his behaviour towards his sister, but only if they were first able to accept his wish to engage in that behaviour. They initially found it hard to do, fearing that by accepting his wish, they would be seen as approving of his behaviour.

When the boy's parents were able to understand the value of just accepting his wish, Dan began joint sessions with the three of them. In the third such session, the boy told Dan and his parents that he had seen an uncle sexually assault his biological sister when he was six years old. He said, in tears, that he wanted to be sure that his adopted sister's first sexual experience was not terrifying, as it had been for his biological sister.

In the sessions that followed, he was able to explore his own terror over what he had seen and his subsequent memories of it. His parents were able to experience empathic acceptance of his inner life and understand how it led to his behaviour towards his sister. They could do this whilst being clear that his behaviour was not safe for him or his sister. They would ensure that he did not engage in that behaviour again. Acceptance of his experience and limits on his behaviour helped the boy to feel loved, cherished and safe.

---

Humans tend to thrive within families and larger groups when they experience themselves as being accepted – without condition – for who they are. Your unconditional acceptance of your child generates a foundation of safety and worth that will increase her motivation to follow your family's customs and achieve its goals. Acceptance is likely to increase her readiness to communicate, to explore and learn about the interpersonal world. Acceptance is also likely to strengthen her relationship with you, to resolve conflicts and to increase her motivation to engage in behaviours that are valued by the family (though possibly less so by her!).

How can you practise acceptance while at the same time evaluating and responding to behaviour? The answer lies in where acceptance and evaluation are directed. We believe that acceptance – radical acceptance – will have a profound influence on your child's behaviour, and her overall sense of herself when it is directed to all aspects of her inner life: her thoughts, feelings, wishes, intentions, memories, perceptions, values and judgements. When her inner life is fully accepted, not only are behavioural conflicts easier to resolve, but such conflicts are also less like to occur in the first place. Paradoxically, when you focus only on behavioural goals and consequences, then conflicts and 'behavioural problems' often increase and your influence over them decreases. When you focus more on accepting the inner life of your child – including differences between her inner life and yours – behavioural conflicts and 'problems' tend to decrease.

There is a long history in religious and cultural traditions of accepting the person while judging behaviour as unacceptable – 'love the sinner and hate the sin'. Through the acceptance of what is, whether a physical or psychological reality, you are in the best position to determine what, if anything might be done to modify it. 'There is nothing to fear but fear itself' is a belief that has definite merit. When a person is frightened by a thing or event, she is better able to address it if she first allows herself to be aware of her fear, observe and understand it, within the context of acceptance. If fear leads to panic and a perceived 'need' to make the fear stop, the person is less likely to understand either the fear or how to deal with it.

This contrasts with other religious traditions where the thoughts, feelings and wishes of the person are not always accepted. 'Impure thoughts' are likely to warrant the need for confession among many Catholics. Coveting the wife or goods of one's neighbour is against two of the Ten Commandments. What underlies these prohibitions is the belief that by thinking about an activity or wanting something to occur, the person is more likely to engage in the activity and make it occur.

Imagine if we were to tell you not to think about an elephant. Most likely you were not thinking about an elephant before this. You may not have thought about an elephant for the past month or two. Now that we have said not to think about an elephant, we have put the thought in your mind. Telling you not to keep that thought is likely to increase your thinking about elephants. Imagine, however, that you accept the presence of an elephant in your mind, maybe wonder about it or remember past experiences with elephants. Your mind will soon drift to other content that is more interesting; you will stop thinking about the elephant without trying to do so.

In psychological circles too, there is a belief that when we obsess about doing something, we are more likely eventually to act upon our desires. Even though this may be true, the question is what to do about the obsessions. It is likely that by first accepting that they exist and then reflecting upon them, they will more easily reduce, compared to trying to control the obsessions by not thinking about them.

Most individuals equate their thoughts, feelings and wishes as aspects of themselves. When someone evaluates these qualities, the person often feels judged and criticized as a person. She is likely to become resistant to others' attempts to change her. Telling your child that she should not want another child's bike, that she should not think about playing football during maths classes and she should not feel anger towards her teacher is not likely to be effective in changing her thoughts, feelings or wishes.

Imagine telling your partner that – although you love her – you would like her to change her personality Your partner is not likely to oblige! If, however, you tell your partner that one of her behaviours is difficult for you – maybe she reads during your evening meal together – she may well understand and change her behaviour. What happens if you add to your request your assumption about why she engages in that behaviour – perhaps that she is self-centred? She is likely to become defensive rather than change her behaviour.

Such evaluations of the inner life of another tend not be met with gratitude and behavioural change. An individual is more likely to become motivated to change her behaviour when she is certain that the other accepts her for who she is. When we are able to separate the behaviour from the person himself and only evaluate the behaviour, the other is more likely to be motivated to change this behaviour.

Acceptance of your child, therefore, is likely to be the most effective starting point in influencing her behaviour. She is more likely to both trust your motives for addressing her behaviour while remaining confident that you value her as a person. If she knows that she is liked and valued as a person, unconditionally, she is less likely to take any criticism of her behaviour 'personally'. She is then less likely to become defensive in response to the behavioural criticism. Her 'self' remains safe under your gaze when she experiences your acceptance.

## Acceptance and the brain

The work of the American neuropsychologist Stephen Porges has much to offer in our understanding of the importance of acceptance. Dr Porges developed a well-respected model of an important aspect of the brain's functioning: the polyvagal theory.[5]

This theory suggests that there are interwoven systems in the brain that function to facilitate our ability to become engaged with others: the social engagement system. The first responsibility of this system is determining, in a split second, whether or not we are safe with another person. This is a preconscious awareness emerging from deep centres in the brain. If we sense that we are not safe, we engage in either mobilization defences (fight or flight) or immobilization defences (freezing, playing dead, dissociation). When we sense that we are safe, a neural system activates involving the ventral vagal nerve complex. The vagal nerve complex is an aspect of the autonomic nervous system that regulates heart rate, breathing, digestion and other bodily responses. The older dorsal vagal nerve complex mobilizes the body for fight or flight or immobilizes the body in states of hiding or freezing. The newer ventral vagal nerve complex is known as the social engagement system in that it facilitates an open and engaged awareness of others within safe relationships. The vagal nerve complex is only present in higher mammals. It enables us to engage reciprocally with others in an open, receptive state of awareness. This system primes us to relate to others using non-verbal communication involving facial expressions, voice modulations and rhythms, gestures, postures and touch. We develop these skills when we feel safe. Infants become quite good at them if conditions are right. When we do not feel safe, however, we are more focused on self-protection, limiting our open engagement with the other person.

We are presenting Porges' work because of his conviction that the social engagement system, and the open, reciprocal, engaged state of awareness that emerges when we are safe, is activated when we sense that we are accepted by the other person. In contrast, the defensive systems – either of mobilization or immobilization – are activated when we sense that we are being evaluated by the other person. Porges is speaking of all evaluations, both negative and positive. This is important because evaluations are at the core of behavioural management programmes, which use consequences, rewards and punishments.

Whilst behavioural evaluations are a necessary part of caregiving, they will be most effective if embedded in acceptance of your child. With acceptance, the social engagement system is activated. When your child experiences an evaluation, she begins to move into the defensive system. That tendency can be held in check or minimized if she knows within her core sense of self that she is unconditionally accepted, even if her behaviour is being evaluated.

Regardless of whether or not the behavioural issue is resolved, and no matter how long it takes, acceptance remains constant. This suggests that it is the social engagement system and its underpinnings in acceptance that enhance a parent's ability to influence his child much more than consequences do.

We find it fascinating that the older vagal nerve quiets the breathing, lowers the heart rate and becomes motionless in order to protect the self (playing possum). In this state we decrease our contact with and awareness of what is outside of our body. Compare this to a toddler being scolded by his parent: she tends to freeze, hide, become motionless and avoid eye contact. The newer vagal nerve quiets the breathing, lowers the heart rate and primes the body to be receptive to the other person, becoming more open and fully engaged. In this state we increase our contact with and awareness of what is outside of our body. When a toddler is enjoying being with his parent, she tends to be fully engaged in the present moment. Her eyes focus on the parent, whilst being attuned with all of her parent's expressions.

## Shame and guilt

An exploration of the emotions of shame and guilt provides excellent examples of the value in accepting the person and evaluating only her behaviour. Shame is an emotion that pertains to the self, arising from the sense that 'I am bad' or 'I am unloveable.' When the self is experienced in this way, the resulting shame is very stressful and painful. Because of this, many people try to avoid feelings of shame by either denying the feelings themselves or denying the behaviours that activated such shameful feelings. The former response is reflected in children saying 'I don't care! It doesn't bother me!' when confronted with a behaviour and its consequence. The latter is reflected in children saying 'I didn't do it!' Shame therefore tends to elicit lying (I didn't do it), making excuses (it was an accident), blaming the other person (she took my game), or minimizing the consequence of the behaviour (she's not hurt badly, she's exaggerating how much it hurts!). Shame is such a painful emotion that an individual confronted with her behaviour will avoid thinking about it. Her response is often one of rage: 'Don't talk about it! I don't want to think about it! You're bringing it up because you want to make me mad!' We explore these reactions as a 'shield against shame' in Chapter 7.

Shame, therefore, is a self-centred emotion. It functions to protect the self from perceived attacks from others. In shame we hide and avoid eye contact with the other, leading to isolation. It interferes with efforts to resolve a conflict and to repair a relationship. Shame is thus likely to decrease attachment behaviours, such as coming to the parent for support in response to a problem.

The pain of shame tends to create the habit of avoiding difficulties and problems. It creates the desire to 'deal with it tomorrow' rather than face it today. The risk that a discussion will create shame is often the reason that such a discussion does not occur. The shame of a 'bad habit' is likely to impede one's best efforts to change that habit. The shame of making a mistake is likely to be the reason why a person does not learn from her mistake.

In contrast to shame, guilt is an emotion that is associated with one's behaviour. In guilt, the person concludes: 'I did something wrong. I broke a rule. I hurt another person.' Unlike shame, where the person tries to deny the behaviour that triggered the sense of being bad, with guilt the person has the opposite tendency. She wants to repair the relationship caused by the behaviour. As a result, the person is motivated to acknowledge the behaviour, to apologize and possibly to engage in behaviour meant to restore the relationship. The person finds that in openly acknowledging the behaviour, the guilt begins to decrease. Guilt is an other-centred emotion. Guilt exists in response to the perception that one has hurt the other through one's behaviour. Guilt is associated with empathy, whereas shame is associated with reduced empathy for the other. To facilitate empathy and to encourage the development of a child's conscience, it is beneficial to reduce the child's shame, leaving room for the development of guilt.

Shame precedes guilt in the developing child. When you scold your toddler, it is normal that she experience shame. She will try to hide, become motionless and speechless. When you comfort and reconnect with the toddler, the experience of shame reduces. It is then possible to redirect or briefly mention the reason for the scolding. The toddler will be able to think about what she did and make sense of it. In this way your child begins to perceive the consequences of her actions, learns to experience empathy for the other and to experience guilt over the other's distress. Repairing the relationship through reconnection provides the child with the psychological reality that she is unconditionally accepted and loved even if a given behaviour is not. The child experiences the relationship as being more important than disapproval and conflict over her behaviour.

If a parent does not comfort and reconnect with his child, shame becomes too great. This child is not likely to begin to develop guilt over her behaviour. She remains in shame over her parent's criticism of her behaviour. She is convinced that her parent is dissatisfied with her as a person.

By communicating to your child 'I'm not angry with you, I'm angry at what you did', you are helping to elicit guilt and not shame, providing the foundation for the development of empathy. Sometimes, however, the results are not so positive. This might be because your anger at the behaviour is too pervasive or long-lasting. Alternatively, you may avoid repairing the relationship and reconnecting with your child. Sometimes parents use relationship withdrawal as a means of discipline, by not talking to the child or sending her away from them. This, too, is likely to elicit shame rather than guilt. Too much of this type of discipline is likely to compromise the development of empathy.

Researchers have demonstrated that continuing to experience the emotion of shame is associated with various psychological problems. According to Tangney and Dearing, these include 'depression, anxiety, eating disorder symptoms, subclinical sociopathy, and low self-esteem'.[6] The emotion of guilt, however, is not associated with any psychological problems. When a person is said to have 'too much guilt', the emotion experienced is more likely to be shame.

Since the locus of shame is the self and the locus of guilt is behaviour, it is understandable that a person would deny shame but can acknowledge and address behaviours associated with guilt. Behaviour is more readily changed than aspects of the self. If I feel a sense of badness about who I am, and this is not easily changed, then I am more likely to respond with denial or rage. This is a natural response when we experience attacks on our sense of self, our identity. We are not being accepted for who we are.

## Abuse and neglect

When a young child experiences abuse and/or neglect from her parents, her only possible conclusion is that she is bad, unloveable. Even later, although the older child may know that her parents' actions are not accepted by other adults outside the family, she is still likely to attribute this behaviour to defects in herself. Thus, abused and neglected children are almost certain to exist in a state of shame. This state is so pervasive and so painful that the child develops a variety of defences and symptoms to hide from it. Most commonly, she denies its existence or minimizes its impact on her.

The experience of abuse and/or neglect from parents also compromises the child's trust in other adults with whom she has a relationship (for example, foster parent, teacher, therapist). She may trust that the other adult will not abuse or neglect her, but she is unlikely to trust that the adult truly likes her or thinks that she is a good child. This leads to beliefs such as 'you will stop liking me when you truly get to know me' or 'you are pretending to like me, it is just your job'. The child may try hard to hide her 'evil core', anticipating that only then will others like her. This leads to a continuing sense of shame, which prevents the abused and neglected child from utilizing the more positive relationships to change her sense of herself. She cannot begin to experience herself as being good.

---

Dan briefly treated a four-year-old adopted boy, Ben, who had experienced profound neglect during the first year of his life. Ben then resided in a good foster home for two years until he was adopted. During the year that he had been living with his adoptive parents, he was very quiet and detached from them. He did what he was told, he played with them and in many respects he seemed to be developing well. More worryingly, however, was his lack of emotional expression and apparent indifference to receiving comfort or affection. Dan discovered that Ben had been more emotionally expressive and engaged with his foster parents than he was with his adoptive parents.

During the second joint session involving Ben and his adoptive parents, Dan was exploring – in a storytelling voice – Ben's early years. Ben listened quietly while he played with a few toys on the carpet. When Dan mentioned his foster parents, Ben became tense. Then Dan spoke of the day when the social worker told him that he would be going to live with a new family. Ben screamed, 'I was bad!' and covered his face.

Dan continued the story, now including Ben's belief that he was bad and that was why he had to leave his foster family. After accepting Ben's experience that he was bad, Dan was able to express empathy for Ben in having that experience. Ben cried strongly and when his adoptive mother picked him up and cuddled him, Ben cried in her arms.

If Dan had not accepted his experience but rather simply tried to explain to him that he moved because foster care is temporary, most likely Ben would have become quiet and withdrawn and would not have accepted comfort for his experience. Dan did later quietly speak of the temporary nature of foster care but only after first accepting and experiencing empathy for Ben's experience. He could then include that information in his evolving life story.

---

The attitude of acceptance is crucial to help the abused and neglected child begin the slow process of reorganizing her sense of self. Acceptance allows her to be open to the adult's experience of her. Through accepting the inner life of this child, the parent or teacher may gradually help her to know that any correction is restricted to her behaviour alone and not who she is. However, this process is slow and difficult. The child does not easily believe the adult who says, 'I'm not angry with you, I am angry at what you did.' The child, 'knowing' she is truly bad, will more readily believe that the adult does not like her and is soon going to send her away.

Thus the abused and neglected child often perceives rejection rather than acceptance from the adults around her. Often she reacts with anger or withdraws into isolation. She tries to pretend that the adult is not important to her. She may ensure that the parent is truly not important to her by dissociating from any developing feeling of closeness or trust. This is not pretence; this child is convinced that she is not loveable. A life that involves being an actual member of a family, cherished for who she is, never to be abandoned, is not accessible to her. She is not like regular children; she is an outcast, unwanted, unloved and lacking in value to anyone.

Whilst many children take acceptance from their parents and other adults for granted, this is not true of children who have experienced abuse or neglect. These are the children who are most in need of acceptance. While it is easy to acknowledge this, offering this acceptance presents its own challenges. For example, the symptoms displayed by the child can be extreme and pervasive. The child's rejection of parent, teacher or therapist can be extreme. Even the most caring adult can lose sight of the child under such symptoms. Instead of demonstrating acceptance, the adult is left seeing and reacting to these symptoms.

Caring adults are not robots, but human beings who rely a great deal on being engaged in a reciprocal relationship with a child who, at least once in a while, demonstrates that the adult does matter. The adult can find energy to continue to care for this child when he believes that his efforts will make a difference. When there are no such signs, the best foster parent may begin to wear down, to reduce his commitment to the child and, eventually, to end the relationship. While the biological or adoptive parent may continue to provide for his child's physical needs, he may also begin to disengage psychologically from the relationship with his child.

Such relationship breakdown is traumatic for the child. As a consequence, she is less likely to trust the acceptance and commitment of the next caring adult. It is also painful for the adult. He has a strong commitment to make a difference in the life of the child in his care. Faced with failure with his child, he is at risk of experiencing shame himself. Such experience of shame can lead even the most caring adult to blame the child for the failure. Unintentionally, the adult may convey this blame through non-verbal communication that the child is 'unworkable' or a 'lost cause'. When the adult gives up on her, the child is likely to experience further confirmation that her deep sense of self, her own pervasive shame, is warranted.

If a parent is to continue to accept his child, even while addressing intense, continuous misbehaviours, he will need ongoing support to be able to care for this child day after day, month after month. Helping this adult to perceive what is positive about the child – to like the child under the behaviour – may make the difference between success and failure in this relationship. It may take only one such relationship – one relationship in which the child begins to truly experience unconditional acceptance – to enable the child to reduce her sense of shame. She can then discover who she is under the symptoms and who she was prior to the abuse. She can begin to learn how to develop a life based on the sense of self that this relationship nurtures.

---

An adoptive parent told Dan about the improved functioning of her adoptive adolescent son over the prior six months:

Dan: So how have things been lately with your son?

Adoptive Mum: So much better. It is such a relief.

Dan: That's great! Any idea what might have influenced his progress?

Mum: I changed. I was thinking about him and me one day, just thinking. And I realized that he is my son and that I would accept him as he was. And I would do that even if he never changed. I'd still push him to change his behaviours, but I'd continue to accept him even if he did not.

Dan: That was it?

Mum: That was it. And you know what? I didn't tell him what I was thinking, but within a few days I started to see a change in him! Somehow he seemed to know.

Dan: That you would always accept him?

Mum: Yes, even if he never changed. And he began to change!

---

## Acceptance and intersubjectivity

The nature of intersubjectivity and its crucial role in your child's developing sense of self, perceptions of others, and understanding of the world was described in Chapter 1.

Acceptance of your child – of her inner life – is central in ensuring that your child will become fully engaged in the process of learning through intersubjective experiences.

Intersubjective experiences are those in which the subjective experience of one member of the pair influences the subjective experience of the other. Intersubjectivity means being open, perceptive, engaged and accepting of the experience of the other. If you do not accept your child's experience, your child is likely to hide her experience from you. You are then unlikely to be able to assist her in making sense of, deepening and organizing the experience she has of herself, another person or an event. When a child is not confident that her parent will accept her inner life, she begins to hide her thoughts, feelings, wishes, memories and intentions from him. This leaves her trying to make sense of what is happening in her life and, more importantly, who she is, without help. She is left to try to manage difficult situations on her own.

When your child is alone with her inner life, she is less likely to develop the habit of reflecting on it, wondering about it or understanding it. She does not know what she thinks, what she feels or what she wants. She might remember an event, but she is less likely to remember her experience of that event. She does not develop words for her inner life and she is not able to communicate what she is experiencing to others. A vicious circle develops in which she is more isolated from both others and her own inner life. She lives in uncertainty about much that occurs in her day-to-day living. She is uncertain about who she is; her sense of self is often disjointed, incoherent and filled with gaps.

When your child's inner life is accepted by you, she is more likely to take an interest in it, to begin to understand it and to communicate it. In communicating her experience of herself or an event, she becomes open to your response to her experience. This is what intersubjectivity is all about. The parent notices the child's experience, without evaluating it; experience is not right or wrong, it just is. The parent then shares his own experience of the child with her. In this way the parent influences how the child organizes her experience. This is characterized by openness, acceptance, curiosity and empathy. The child becomes open to the way her parents experience her and the world. This is the core of the parents' influence on the child's development.

---

Imagine that a boy, Bob, has doubts about whether or not he was being fair to his friend when he turned down a request to go to a game. Notice the difference in the following two vignettes.

The first conveys a mother who substitutes her thinking for her son's:

Mum: *(Spoken with the voice of a rational judge)* So you told him 'no'. What's the problem?

Bob: Yesterday I told him that I'd probably go and then I decided that I didn't want to.

Mum might respond in a range of ways, each representing her desire to think for her son:

1. Well, you didn't promise and now you decided, so forget about it. It's his issue if he is bothered by it.

2. It's a waste of time just going to the game anyway. You made the right choice.

3. If you led him to believe that you were going, even if you didn't promise, then you should go. Don't disappoint him.

4. He's your good friend. You should go even if you don't feel like it. He'd do it for you.

Bob: Thanks, Mum. I'll figure something out.

When Bob expressed distress and uncertainty to his mum, she tried to fix the problem and decide for her son. She assumed that if she knew the factors involved, with her experience and distance she could know what was best for Bob. That assumption is likely to be invalid in many situations. The reasons for Bob's uncertainty will be due to many social and emotional factors that cannot be quantified. If Bob follows her advice, he may realize too late that what he did was not the best choice for him. Even more difficult for Bob's development would be a developing reliance on his mother's decisions for him. This would interfere with his growing awareness of his inner life and his ability to choose between competing thoughts, feelings, values and desires. Alternatively, he may give up all reliance on his mother's help when he has to make difficult decisions. Again, this would restrict his development. In avoiding her efforts to decide for him, he now has to make all his decisions alone.

Contrast this brief interaction between Bob and his mum with the following one. Here the mother remains intersubjectively present while accepting her son's doubts and struggles over his decision.

Mum: *(Spoken with the voice of an accepting parent)* So you told him 'no'. What's the problem?

Bob: Yesterday I told him that I'd probably go. Then I decided that I didn't want to.

Mum: I see. He thought that you would probably go and now he's disappointed.

Bob: Yeah, he really wants to go, and it wouldn't bother me that much if I went.

Mum: Seems like you're trying to balance your concern for your good friend's strong feelings with your own feelings that are not so big.

Bob: Yeah, Mum. I know that he'll be OK about it if I say 'no'. I just wonder if maybe I should go since it is so important to him that we go together.

Mum: And he'd not be OK going with one of his other friends?

Bob: He would. But I think he just has a lot more fun with me. We get along real well.

Mum: I get your struggle, honey. That balance between what you want and what your best friend wants. Having a good friend makes these choices difficult. However, knowing that he is your good friend will give you confidence that you'll still be good friends no matter what you decide; especially as you're working so hard to make the decision. He is important to you, and you are to him, and you both know it.

Bob: So you're not going to tell me what to do, are you?

Mum: And get in the middle of your friendship? No way!

Here, Bob shares his doubts with his mum and they both explore their experience of these alongside his thoughts, feelings and intentions. After such non-judgemental exploration, he is in a much better position to decide what to do. Bob's mum is not evaluating her son's behaviour, but simply sharing her experience of his experience of his uncertainty. Bob will be in a better position to make many such decisions in the years ahead than if his mother decided for him.

---

## In conclusion

When you think of loving your child, this is likely to include thoughts of unconditionally accepting her, 'for better or worse'.

Within your commitment to your child, you know that you will 'stand by her' no matter what. You may totally disagree with or even reject her behaviour, but you will remain with her regardless of the consequences of her behaviour. Acceptance becomes a bit tricky when you are engaged in discipline. Yet that is when acceptance is needed the most. Your steady acceptance while disciplining her gives her safety and confidence. Her behaviour is not going to destroy your relationship with her and your love of her person. As you accept and show confidence in her ability to understand and organize her inner life, she will develop this inner life more fully in ways that are likely to evoke pride within both of you. She will develop her unique path, whilst maintaining closeness to you throughout her adulthood.

Dan's granddaughter, age three, recently told her mother a number of times over a period of two weeks that she did not love her. Her mother completely accepted this statement about her daughter's inner life. She responded in varying ways with playfulness, curiosity or empathy. Her daughter quickly lost interest in exploring both that concept of not loving her mother as well as how her mother might respond to it. She discovered something very important, namely that she was safe to tell her mother whatever she thought, felt or wanted. The next week, when she did something that caused her mother to correct her, she stated, 'I'm not sorry.' She lost interest in this expression even faster.

For Dan's granddaughter, acceptance is a lived reality that gives her the freedom to explore her inner life within the safety of her mother's love.

# 5

# Parenting with Unconditional Acceptance

In the previous chapter we discussed the value of acceptance in human relationships, and the parent–child relationship in particular. Now we want to focus on the realities of bringing acceptance alive in day-to-day parenting. Describing acceptance is harder than it might seem. Acceptance is like the air we breathe. We tend to take it for granted, although both parent and child would be aware of its absence quickly if it were not there. When we try to write about acceptance, we find that we are writing about playfulness, curiosity or empathy. These qualities move quickly into the foreground, while acceptance moves quietly to the background. Yet without acceptance the other three qualities of PACE would have much less impact on your child and your relationship with him.

Acceptance refers to an attitude of open engagement with your child. You are aware of how he is with you and how you are with him. You allow your simple awareness to dominate your experience. You are not trying to change him; you are simply aware of how you are together. Without this experience of acceptance it is more likely that your child will become defensive. He might experience your communications as an evaluation of himself, and will seek to protect himself. He might become angry, hostile or self-blaming. All of these take away from the relationship.

In being open to your child's experience, you are allowing this to have an impact on you, to influence you. His experience then has meaning for you. From this position of acceptance you will have an impact on your child. Understanding his experience will affect how you communicate this to him. This in turn affects how he experiences you. Acceptance brings intersubjectivity to life.

This chapter will also address the difficulties of experiencing and communicating acceptance. Like the other features of PACE, providing acceptance is easier said than done, especially if you did not experience this very much yourself as a child. Acceptance is hard when your child's behaviour is challenging. It is hard when you are tired and have ten other responsibilities facing you. We hope that you accept yourself when you have difficulty experiencing acceptance for your child. With self-acceptance, it is easier to once again experience acceptance for your child.

## The storytelling nature of acceptance

You might recall, in the last chapter, we described acceptance and the social engagement system in the brain. When this is activated, the relationship comes alive, as each is deeply involved with the other. This system is activated by a sense of acceptance, communicated by voice modulations and rhythms, facial expressions, gestures, posture and touch. The way you talk with your child will also have an impact.

Imagine you are telling a story. If you adopt a monotone or a lecturing style of telling a story, you are unlikely to engage your audience. They will become distracted and disinterested. So it is when talking with your child. To help the listener to become absorbed in a story, free from distractions, you adopt a certain style of talking. This is highly engaging, bringing the story to life. This is the same style of talking which will engage your child. A storytelling quality to your voice helps him to become absorbed with you. He can then experience your acceptance of him and his experience. Sometimes this engagement is animated and sometimes it is quiet. Sometimes you initiate the interactions and sometimes you are responsive to your child's initiatives. Throughout this reciprocal activity you remain open and engaged. The intention you convey is one of simply accepting him, being aware of him, and understanding his inner life.

Acceptance is conveyed most clearly by your non-verbal communications. Your eyes and facial expressions are both receptive to and fully engaged with your child. Your vocal expressions contain modulations and rhythms. As you picture this, notice how much more it resembles the act of telling a story than giving a stern lecture. Your movements and gestures are spontaneously expressing your full interest in your child and your enjoyment of the present moment with him.

Equally important is the joint rhythm between your non-verbal communications and his. You are matching his affective expressions. Sometimes you will take the lead and notice if he matches your lead;

more often you will start with what he is experiencing. If he is quiet and sad, you are quiet as well, showing your acceptance of his emotional state. If he is agitated, you are animated and regulated, helping him not to become dysregulated. By matching his affective expressions, you convey your full acceptance of his present experience. In these moments of full engagement, your child senses your acceptance and becomes engaged with you.

As you become more accepting of your child and his experience, you will naturally feel more empathy for him. This empathy is conveyed alongside acceptance in the same way. We will explore this further in Chapter 9.

## Bringing acceptance into parenting

In this section we will explore ways of demonstrating acceptance to your child. We will address the important issue of how to remain accepting of his inner life even when you need to place limits or expectations on his behaviour.

### Accept your child's inner life; evaluate only his behaviour

We have stressed in the previous chapter the value of accepting your child's inner life even though you need to place expectations or limits on his behaviour. When you accept his thoughts, feelings, wishes, perceptions, intentions, memories and judgements, he is much more likely to accept your boundaries on his behaviours. If you honestly communicate to him that it is fine if he disagrees with you, thinks that you are unfair or wants what you don't want, then he is more likely to meet your behavioural expectations. If you suggest that your differences of thought, feeling and wishes indicate that he is wrong and you are right, he is more likely to resist your expectations.

---

Let's imagine a dialogue between Jane and 12-year-old Bryana, her daughter. Actually we will imagine the dialogue twice. The first time Jane conveys an attitude of evaluation and judgement. We will then replay the conversation, but this time Jane will express acceptance for Bryana's experience. To set the scene, Bryana has asked to spend the weekend at her friend Jenny's house. Jane is agreeable to Bryana spending most of Saturday with Jenny but not the whole weekend.

Bryana: That's so unfair! You never let me have any fun!

Jane: You're the one who is unfair! You are so wrong about that!

*Note how Jane immediately responds by telling her daughter that her experience is wrong.*

Bryana: You don't! You always say that I have to stay home, get my work done and hang out with the family!

Jane: Well, you are a member of this family, you know.

Bryana: Yeah, if it's what you want, then it's for the family. If it's what I want, I'm being selfish.

Jane: You better watch what you're saying.

*Bryana thinks that her mother views her wishes as selfish. If that is her experience, it suggests that she has doubts about her mother's perception of her. It would be wise to understand these doubts, rather than being angry with her for expressing them.*

Bryana: But it's true! You always seem to think when I want to do something for myself that I am being selfish, that I don't want to do my share at home!

Jane: You're only 12, Bryana. You're not ready yet to be independent and come and go as you want.

Bryana: I don't ask to. I just want to spend one weekend with Jenny. This is the first time I've asked to do that in a couple of months.

Jane: And I said 'no', so you should just accept it and quit feeling sorry for yourself and thinking that I'm a horrible mother.

*Again, Jane is not accepting her daughter's thoughts and feelings. Rather, she judges them as simply 'feeling sorry for yourself'. She also says that she is wrong for criticising her mother's actions.*

Bryana: I'm not feeling sorry for myself! You're so mean to say that!

Jane: You have no right to say I'm mean. I'm being very reasonable. You're the one who is being mean about this.

*Jane judges that her thoughts are reasonable and her daughter's thoughts are unreasonable. She goes further and says that her daughter has no right to express her inner life if it disagrees with Jane.*

Bryana: Of course, it's always my fault.

Jane: You're the one who got all upset over a reasonable denial of your request.

Bryana: I wish that you'd just listen sometimes and not always try to run my life! If I don't agree with you, I'm some kind of ungrateful daughter.

Jane: It does seem a bit ungrateful to me that I do so much for you and I let you do so much that you want to do. You are just never satisfied. You think I'm mean when I'm probably one of the best mothers in the neighbourhood!

Bryana: Yeah, you should get a medal!

Jane: No more of your sarcasm! You need to start facing the fact that you are the unreasonable one here, not me. This is your issue, not mine.

Bryana: Like I said before, you always think that it's my fault and that you're never wrong.

Jane: You don't really believe that. I admit it when I make a mistake. You're just saying that to try to make me feel guilty so that I'll give in to you. It's not going to happen.

*Jane continues to criticize her daughter's thoughts and feelings. As a result, the conflict is escalating. It is much more now than an argument about how to spend the weekend. It is about their relationship as well as the rules of communication and openness. Jane is communicating that her daughter is not permitted to hold or express negative evaluations about her mother's behaviour, while Jane is permitted to hold negative assumptions about her daughter's motives and behaviour.*

Bryana: Now you know what my motives are better than I do. I'm trying to make you feel guilty. And if I say that you're wrong, I'll be wrong again, and unreasonable!

Jane: This conversation is a waste of time. You don't want to listen to me at all. You'll argue for ever because you want your own way and you're not going to get it.

Bryana: You never listen! Know-it-all!

Jane: You've crossed another line, Bryana. Now you're not going to her house on Saturday either.

*The escalation has now led to consequences that further create stress on their relationship. This could have been avoided if Jane had accepted her daughter's thoughts, feelings and wishes, while remaining firm on her decision about the weekend.*

Bryana: Great! You're meaner than every other mother I know. All my friends feel sorry for me that I got stuck with you.

Jane: Go to your room. I don't want to talk with you.

Bryana: Being alone in my room is a lot better than being with you.

Jane: And stay there until I call you for supper!

Bryana: Don't bother; I'm not hungry.

Jane: That's fine with me.

*During this dialogue Jane evaluated and criticized her daughter's experience – her thoughts, feelings, wishes and beliefs. She appears intent on convincing Bryana of the weaknesses of that experience, and then telling her what she should think, feel, say or want. Jane's goal appears to be to force Bryana to change her experience. This is much deeper than not spending the weekend with her friend. As a result, the dialogue leads to increasing defensiveness on the part of both mother and daughter, along with emotional distance, anger and escalating consequences.*

*

Now for the replay. Notice how different this dialogue goes when Jane offers Bryana acceptance.

Bryana: That's so unfair! You never let me have any fun!

Jane: It seems to you now that I never let you have fun?

Bryana: Well, maybe sometimes, but why can't I stay overnight?

*Here Jane accepts her daughter's thought that Jane never lets her have fun. In doing so, her daughter is able to reflect on what she said and qualify it.*

Jane: The whole family has been so busy lately. I thought this weekend would be a good time to have some family time.

Bryana: Could we do that on Sunday night?

Jane: Well, I was thinking more like Saturday night and then an early start Sunday to go for a walk up by the lake.

Bryana: But I really want to see Jenny!

Jane: I understand that, honey. You can spend most of Saturday with her.

Bryana: We'll just start having fun and then I'll have to leave!

Jane: It's hard, Bryana, to juggle the things that we all like to do separately with what I think we need to do as a family. I'm sorry that it makes you unhappy that I want us to focus more on family time this weekend.

Bryana: I'm not being selfish!

*Jane tries to express understanding and empathy for her daughter's distress, but Bryana experiences her words as criticism. Notice next that Jane does not say that her daughter's experience is wrong. Rather she apologizes for speaking in a way that leads her daughter to think she is being accused of selfishness.*

Jane: I know. I'm sorry it sounded like I thought you were being selfish. I meant that it is hard for all of us to give up some things that we want to do. Not just you. And I get it that you'd rather be with Jenny this weekend. I'm sorry if it seems that I'm asking you to give up more than the rest of us.

Bryana: Well, it does seem that way. Like I'm the one who has to make the sacrifices for the good of the family. I don't see you or Dad or Julie giving up much.

Jane: So it does seem to you that I'm asking more of you than the rest of us. If it seems that way to you, I can understand why you'd be angry about it.

*Jane conveys understanding of her daughter's thoughts and then makes it clear that her anger makes sense too; her daughter thinks that she is being asked to do more than the other members of the family. If she thinks this, then she would feel angry. Jane is not defensive. She accepts her daughter's inner life.*

Bryana: Well, you don't want to go away on your own this weekend. I'm giving up Jenny; it doesn't seem like anyone else is giving up much.

Jane: You're right about that, Bryana. I don't think the rest of us had any big plans.

Bryana: Then why am I the one that has to give up the most?

Jane: You are giving up the most this time, so it is harder for you. Other times it has been harder for someone else, and it will be that way in the future, too. But this time it is harder for you. I can understand your disappointment, and how it seems unfair. I can see why you might be angry with me.

*Jane acknowledges that her daughter is giving up more this time, while expressing her thought that at other times the others give up more. She does not argue about this, just expresses her perception, being confident that her daughter will see it the same way too, but only after her distress in the moment is accepted.*

Bryana: It does seem that way, Mum.

Jane: I can see why it might, honey. Anything I can do to help?

Bryana: Let me spend the weekend with Jenny.

Jane: I can't, honey. Anything else?

Bryana: Just don't expect me to be all happy and cheerful up at the lake.

Jane: That's a deal.

*This is not the time to tell Bryana that she is not entitled to be unhappy and 'ruin it for the rest of the family'. Accepting her thought that she might be unhappy is probably the best way that Jane can increase the likelihood that Bryana will enjoy the family walk.*

\*

In the second dialogue you will notice that Jane's intent was to accept and understand her child's experience – as expressed by her thoughts, feelings and wishes – and to wonder about it, using curiosity. This helped Bryana to reflect on it as well. Jane then focused simply on trying to experience Bryana's experience with compassion, demonstrating empathy. When Bryana experienced her mother's accepting presence and communications, she was much more able to accept her mother's decision that Bryana could not spend the weekend with her friend.

You might be tempted to think that such disagreements are unlikely to end so easily as in the second dialogue. We can only encourage you to focus on accepting your child's thoughts, feelings and wishes, connected to your conflicts. You may be surprised at the lack of escalation that follows as your child accepts your decision more quickly.

---

## Loving your child's uniqueness means that you accept that he is not the same as you

You might recall in our discussion of mindfulness in the last chapter our quotation from James Austin when he speaks of 'being mindfully attuned to the fresh individuality of each present moment as it evolves into the next one, and then the next one'.[1] When you are mindfully aware of your child, accepting fully how he is experiencing his developing life, you will discover what is unique about him. You will experience the one-of-a-kind special qualities that comprise who he is.

You want your child to develop according to his temperament, interests and abilities. You want him to develop his potential, shown in his spirit and his dreams. To truly realize this, you will need to accept his inner life, even when aspects of his inner life differ from your own. You need to understand that his thoughts, feelings and wishes are not necessarily wrong in order for your thoughts, feelings and wishes to be right. You may both be right, from within the differing perspectives of your experiences, ideas, perspectives, wishes, thoughts and feelings.

You will need to trust in your child's developing abilities to know what is in his best interests. This means that you will have to accept that at times he may make mistakes and learn from them. This may be better for his development than making his decisions for him, preventing all possible mistakes, or trying to rescue him if he does make a mistake.

If you raise him well, he will develop his own autonomous abilities to know what is best in a given situation.

This means that you will need to reduce your desire to be in control of his life. If you try to exert pervasive control over him, he is in danger of becoming dependent on your decisions, not developing the skills needed to think for himself. Alternatively, he might resist your efforts to control him, engaging in behaviours just to assert his independence from you, even if, at times, he does not really want to do what he is doing. Have confidence in him and you will support him to become the person he dreams of becoming.

---

We will again use our imagination twice. This time we will describe a conversation between Jon and his 15-year-old daughter, Rachel. She has decided not to participate in the school drama club. In the first instance, Jon attempts to convince his daughter that she is making a mistake. He doubts her decisions and wants to change her mind. In the second instance, he accepts her thinking and accompanying decisions, even though he sees the situation differently.

Jon: I don't understand why you're not going to be in the club this year when you enjoyed it so much last year.

*In this statement Jon is using a tone of voice that implies there is something wrong with her decision.*

Rachel: It's not the drama, Dad, it's the clique of kids who want to dominate it. They make your life miserable if you don't agree with them. I don't need that.

Jon: But you will run into people like that your whole life, Rachel. You can't set aside what's important to you just because you'll come into contact with some people you don't like.

*Jon immediately tries to use reason to talk Rachel out of her decision. If he had accepted her experience and then replied with curiosity and empathy, she might have reflected differently about her decision. However, it would still be her decision.*

Rachel: I hear you, Dad, and I've given it a lot of thought. I have some great friends doing other stuff and I want to hang out with them more. The kids in the drama club this year are just mean and I don't want to have to bother with them.

Jon: But the advisor will be there. You can let her know if you have a problem and she'll keep them under control. You just like drama so much and I don't want you to miss it.

Rachel: No, Dad, I've decided. I've thought of all that and I just don't want to do it.

Jon: I hope you know what you're doing. I hope you don't regret it when it gets close to the date of the play.

*Jon's final comment is said with a tone of voice that implies he does not accept her decision but is just resigned to it. In this way, he is conveying his belief that her decision is wrong.*

*

Jon's response to his daughter's decision would most likely undermine her confidence in her own ability to know what is best for her. This might lead to a lack of confidence within Rachel that leads her to rely too much on him or others to make decisions for her. On the other hand, she might be less likely to get his thoughts in the future when she is struggling with making a decision. Children need to have parents available to guide them, to give them the benefit of the parent's life experiences, but not to decide for them.

Now we can see how it would be different if Jon accepts Rachel's decision to know what is best for herself.

Jon: I don't understand why you're not going to be in the club this year when you enjoyed it so much last year.

*While the words are the same as in the first example, the tone is more relaxed. He is conveying a sense of non-judgemental curiosity. This reduces the sense that he is asking questions in order to decide if his daughter's choice is right or wrong. He is interested in her decision rather than wanting to make a decision for her.*

Rachel: It's not the drama, Dad, it's the clique of kids who want to dominate it. They make your life miserable if you don't agree with them. I don't need that.

Jon: Oh, that's too bad. So you still like drama, you just don't want to have to do it under those circumstances. Those kids sound pretty awful.

Rachel: They really are, Dad. They're just mean to anyone that they don't like. I've already seen them in operation. They really said some cruel things to one of the other kids.

Jon: So they make life miserable for everyone. Have the teaching advisors done anything?

Rachel: They don't see much. These kids kiss up to them so they can get the best parts. But when they're not around, they make fun of the kids who are trying out for those parts.

Jon: I'm really sorry, Rachel. I know that drama has meant a lot to you. My guess is you've really been struggling with your decision. Not an easy one to make.

Rachel: No it wasn't, Dad. But once I made it, I felt so much relief. I have more time now to be with my good friends. I feel good about what I'm doing.

Jon: Since you do, honey, so do I. My bet is you'll end up having a good school year in spite of those kids.

Rachel: Thanks, Dad. I think I will.

In the second dialogue, Jon raises similar issues. This time, however, his tone conveys acceptance, while still being available to help his daughter with her difficult decision. He reflects with her about her ambivalence, wanting to understand it, but with no intention to change her mind.

---

## Acceptance helps develop, organize and strengthen the child's inner life

Your child's behaviour, how he acts from day to day in living his life emerges naturally from the way his inner life is developed, strengthened and organized. There is research that shows that children who have experienced a very difficult life, characterized by abuse, neglect and loss, often have great difficulty being aware of and expressing what they think, feel or want.[2] Their memory is often incomplete and they have difficulty developing plans, goals or meaningful interests. Their inner experience has not been valued or even seen by the adults in their lives. As a result, their behaviour is often impulsive, unpredictable and disorganized. They have difficulty working towards goals and regulating their emotional states.

In contrast are children who have what is called a coherent, autobiographical narrative. Such a child has a life that is organized around a meaningful story, a way of making sense of his own experience. He is aware of what he thinks, feels and wants. He is able to make sense of what has happened and is happening, as well as what he does, in a way that fits the pattern of his sense of himself, his sense of his family and the larger social world.

When you accept your child's inner life, you are making it safe for him to explore it, to discover what he thinks or feels without doubting whether he should have these thoughts or feelings.

If he does not experience your acceptance, he will be less likely to accept his inner life himself. This means he will be less likely to make sense of, organize and modify what he finds there if it does not fit other aspects of what is important to him. If he does not accept his inner life, he is likely to ignore it or be ashamed of it. He may act on it in ways that are just not congruent with his larger interests, desires and values. His behaviour will appear more disorganized and chaotic as a result.

---

Imagine that you have a five-year-old son, Ryan, who comes running into the living room screaming that he hates his big brother, Anthony. If you want to understand and convey acceptance of Ryan's inner experience leading to his strong statement, you will need to resist the following temptations:

- to ask Ryan what happened in order to correct it
- to tell Ryan that he should not hate his brother
- to tell Ryan not to let his brother bother him
- to tell Ryan not to play with his brother for a while and then things will be better.

None of those actions is likely to help Ryan to become more aware of the intense and complex feelings and thoughts that he is having about his brother. If you would like to use the current moment to assist him in the important developmental task of identifying, organizing and expressing his inner life, you need to focus on acceptance of his experience. This will help Ryan accept it as well. He will become more fully aware of it and start to make more sense of himself, his brother and their relationship. In this case, you might have chosen the following responses to his screams of hatred towards his brother:

> (*Matching the intensity of Ryan's voice*) You are so angry with Anthony now! Something must have just happened with Anthony, and you don't like it!

Such comments are likely to be followed with some wondering, using curiosity to explore what Ryan has experienced.

*(With a voice tone conveying a desire to understand rather than evaluate)* What's this about? You two were laughing a lot before, and now you're so angry! What's up?

As Ryan tells you what happened from his point of view, you can again accept his experience, conveying empathy for this experience.

Ah! It seemed that he was making fun of you! If he was, no wonder you'd be angry with him. No wonder.

Now you can deepen Ryan's understanding of his own experience of his brother and their relationship further. You might, for example, wonder how he makes sense of what happened in light of their ongoing relationship. This will help Ryan become more deeply aware of what he is experiencing.

*(Said with a curious, almost surprised tone of voice)* It seemed like he was making fun of you. I wonder why he would do that. You two often have such a great time together!

Ryan is likely to respond to this with an expression of ambivalence about his brother. This might lead to your accepting this ambivalence, while conveying as well your sense that relationships with brothers are often complicated.

Having a brother can be hard at times! And confusing! Sometimes you love him so much and other times you're so angry with him. Sometimes he drives you crazy and sometimes he makes you feel great. Brothers!

In this example, Ryan's experience of his relationship with his brother is being deepened. In the process, he will become more deeply aware of his inner life and will be learning how to make sense of this experience in the light of current events in his world. Instead of managing Ryan's relationship with his brother, or telling him how he should feel about this, you are doing something much more helpful. You are helping Ryan to manage his own relationship with his brother. This will help him with many relationships in the future.

---

Accepting your child's inner life without reservation will help him to develop his own sense of autonomy, with organized plans, interests and values. He will become clearer about what he thinks and what he feels. Playfulness, curiosity and empathy certainly help his development of autonomy, but the foundation of it all is your acceptance of him. You might also support, even encourage, an open discussion about how you and he agree and differ about many things that you have in mind. Such discussions are not to determine who is right and who is wrong. Rather, they are to foster the ability to think, reason and be aware of what is in the minds of those having the discussion. If he is safe and confident in exploring and communicating his thoughts with you, he is likely to be similarly confident in discussions with his friends. Save your evaluations for his behaviour, which you do need to limit at times as he moves through his developmental challenges and opportunities. Envelop his inner life in your acceptance.

## Getting to know your child through acceptance, non-judgemental curiosity and safety

As you accept your child's inner life, not only will he be in the best position to develop and organize it, but he will also be much more likely to share his inner life with you. When your child has confidence that you will accept whatever he tells you about his thoughts and feelings, he will be more open and honest with you, even when he knows that you will not be able to accept his behaviour. If you evaluate his inner life, he will either keep it secret from you or tell you what he thinks you want him to say. As an adolescent, your child will become more secretive and less open with you, both in his thoughts and feelings and in his behaviour.

This does not mean that you have to agree with what he thinks, feels or wants. You may think differently about one of the school rules. You may feel differently about a neighbour who makes a lot of noise late at night. You may have different priorities about how to spend money set aside for a family holiday. The point to remember is that no one is right and no one is wrong when you differ about these matters.

If your young son thinks that you are very mean for not buying him a toy, accept his experience of you as mean. If you tell him that he is being disrespectful for sharing his thoughts about you, you will be conveying that you are not interested in his inner life. Of course, you may not be accepting about the way he tells you! His behaviour may be disrespectful but not his thoughts. Conveying empathy and acceptance of his experience of you as a mean parent will also create an opportunity to help him reflect on how he tells you this as well as how strongly he believes it.

Years later, your son says that he does not want to go to university. Rather than telling him that his plans to skip university are wrong, you accept that these are his wishes at this current time. Then you can wonder about them, helping you to more deeply understand them, rather than trying to change them. Your acceptance and open communication with him will help him to reflect on what he is thinking and feeling. He may even be able to reflect on your differing wishes, recognizing that you think differently from him, not that you are trying to tell him what to do. This will place him in the best position to decide what he wants to do based on his deeper knowledge of what you and he think and feel.

Simple acceptance and support of his feelings as a young child, struggling with not getting a toy he desires, have laid the foundation for him to be able to handle the much more complex thoughts, feelings, wishes and desires of an adolescent. Importantly, he has also learnt that he can trust you to support him in making such complex decisions. He will also know that if he makes some decisions that prove unhelpful for him, you will be there to support him and to help him get back on track.

A lovely consequence of this acceptance is that it also brings you closer to your child. He will share, laugh and daydream more with you. He will try out his ideas and plans with you, knowing that he is safe to do so because you accept what he tells you about his inner thoughts, feelings, beliefs, wishes and desires. Emotional intimacy comes from being able to share whatever happens to be on your mind or in your heart in this moment.

As we illustrated in the example above, acceptance of a child's inner life does not mean that you have to conceal from him your thoughts about it. Acceptance is not the same as agreement. If you present your differing perspective, he is likely to listen and be influenced by you, especially if you are careful not to imply that you are right and he is wrong. You just have a different view. If you truly understand and accept his stated wish not to attend university, and then you present your perspective on the probable value for him if he chooses to attend, he is more likely to listen to your perspective, knowing that you are not devaluing his wishes.

At times you may not only disagree with your child's thoughts, but you may need to place limits on any behaviours that might result from his thoughts. Sometimes you need to make choices regarding your child's behaviour, when you believe that the behaviour is definitely not in his best interests. When your young child shouts at you that you were mean for not getting him a toy, you need to be clear that shouting is not an acceptable way of telling you about his inner life! Combining acceptance with limit setting can be challenging but it is important if a child is to learn that whilst his inner life is his own, adults will ensure that his behaviour is safe. If your four-year-old wants a second cookie, you can accept his wish for a cookie while being firm that he will not be having one.

If your teenager expresses his belief that he should be allowed to drink alcohol, you can accept that this is his belief. You will, however, also let him know that you have a different belief, and that you will act on this belief in order to keep him safe. You are clear that you do not want him to drink any alcohol even though he disagrees with that rule or law. You are placing your limit and expectation on his behaviour only. He is free to believe that he should be allowed to drink alcohol, while he is not free to act on his beliefs.

## Challenges to acceptance

In this section we explore some of the reasons why acceptance can be so difficult when you are a parent. Your hopes and fears can make it difficult to maintain an accepting attitude for the inner life of your child.

### Fears that unconditional acceptance will lead to selfish behaviour

You may have concerns that your child will become highly selfish if you demonstrate the acceptance we have been describing. Without appropriate socialization he will have little regard for others. Of course, socialization – helping a child to know what is acceptable or unacceptable within his family and culture – is certainly part of parenting, but this can be achieved while still maintaining an accepting attitude. We explored in the previous section how acceptance and behavioural limits can be combined.

It may be reassuring to know that you have his brain on your side. All the emerging research on the structure and functioning of the brain suggests that it is designed for cooperation, for experiencing empathy for others and for taking an interest in others.[3]

At birth, an infant's primary interest is in discovering who he is, who his parents are and the best ways to live in our social, cultural, emotional world. He wants to become like his parents and he imitates what they do. Even more importantly, he begins to experience their inner life, what they think and feel, their intentions, interests and values, as he models his inner life on theirs.

Your child's inner life will not be identical to yours, which, you are likely to admit, is a good thing. If you accept his inner life, you will be strengthening it in relation to yours, facilitating its development and organization. If you have empathy and an ability to share and cooperate with others, your child's inner experience will organize itself in a manner that also reflects these capacities. This will occur not through the rewards and punishments you give him, but mostly through the intersubjective relationship that you have with him.

Your child's brain is therefore likely to be working with you in guiding his development in pro-social ways. You can rest assured that your relationship with your child will be the primary way that you influence his development. Given these two realities, you can give up any need you experience to control your child's thoughts, feelings and wishes. For these same reasons, you can influence but need not control his personality development, interests and dreams. Simply provide basic behavioural expectations and limits, but especially be interested in who he is becoming. Let his mind and heart do the rest.

### You may experience a need for your child to surpass his peers

You may find yourself comparing your child to his peers on a regular basis. This might be due to your anxiety about his future. You want him to do well in life, and if his peers achieve more than he does, he will be at a disadvantage. While this may be true in certain areas, comparing him to them is not likely to increase his motivation or confidence to achieve. When you truly accept your child, you will let go of the goal that he surpass his peers. Judging his abilities and interests against others will only create in him a sense that he is not good enough for you. He may give up rather than face trying and failing. Or if he is good enough, he may believe that this is not because of who he is but rather it is because of what he is accomplishing. He may become anxious that he will not be able to maintain these accomplishments.

Discover instead what is unique about your child and his development and communicate complete acceptance of the person he is becoming. He will be much more likely to reach his potential than if you communicate that you are vigilantly comparing him to his peers and worrying about his future.

Another reason you may worry about your child's level of achievement compared to his peers may relate to fears that you will be judged poorly as a parent if he does not do well. His achievement becomes your achievement; his failure is your failure. Your competence as a parent is joined with his success. Such tendencies are understandable. You are a human being after all, not a robot. You have your own doubts and uncertainties, often related to your own past experience of success and failure and how you have been judged by others. Your past experience can all too easily become your child's future.

By strongly accepting your child, you will also reduce your own sense that your worth is dependent upon him achieving at a certain level. By strongly accepting him, you are likely to be able to accept yourself more fully. By accepting this aspect of your own inner life, you are likely to reduce its intensity. You will become more aware of the deep joy and satisfaction you receive from being his parent and giving him the opportunity to develop in ways that are important to him. You will have justifiable pride in your crucial role in his development, providing him with the unconditional acceptance that he needs to go forward in his life with confidence in himself.

Of course, this does not mean that you can't help your child achieve all he is capable of. Fears resting on your concerns for his future or your competence as a parent can lead to unnecessary anxiety. These are different to genuine concerns to get the best for him. You will want to give your child opportunities to fulfil his potential, to achieve his own goals and to develop his interests. If he has developmental delays or challenges, your responsibility is to be aware of them and provide him with an environment, and possibly specialized interventions, to foster these areas of his development. This will assist him in making progress to deal with these challenges.

However, you still need to accept these challenges as being part of who he is. This will enable him to accept them as well. This does not mean that he will not work to reduce them. Rather, it means that he is more likely to face them for what they are and deal with them to the best of his ability. If some areas of development will always be difficult, he is more likely to learn how to have a good life that takes them into account rather than deny them and leave himself vulnerable to disappointment and face repeated failures.

## In conclusion

Your greatest gifts to your child are unconditional acceptance and its close cousin, unconditional love. Others may guide him, be a mentor for him, support him and teach him, but he may never experience these gifts in his entire life if he does not receive them from his parents.

You may at times find yourself focusing almost exclusively on his behaviour, while taking for granted or not even seeing the unique child under the behaviour. This is easy to do; don't be hard on yourself. Simply be aware of it, accept yourself doing it, and you will return to the most basic quality of effective parenting – unconditional acceptance. Just as you accepted him from the moment that you became aware of him, either at birth or when he came to live with you, your ongoing acceptance of him will provide him with the 'wind beneath his wings' so that he can truly become the person he is destined to be.

---

### STORY

### Stripes and the Herd of Wild Horses

There are still wild places in the world, with mountains and green fields, where grass is high, almost touching the sky. The cool winds blow down from the north in the summer to make the running easier, and the warm winds blow up from the south in the winter to remove some of the bitterness from the cold. And, of course, in a land like this there is a magnificent herd of horses. Horses of strength and speed. Horses with long, golden manes. Horses so black that they are darker than a moonless night.

This is a tale of one of the horses of the herd. Not the strongest and not the fastest. But what does that matter to the herd? Each horse contributes to the good of them all. Each has a gift; each brings her own ability to see, to hear, to teach and to help. But this one horse – her name is Stripes – was not aware of having any gift for the herd. She was only aware of how different she was. And she hated this difference. She had come to hate herself. She hated her stripes. She looked like a zebra, though the herd did not know that since they had never seen a zebra. They just knew that she had stripes and none of the others did. In fact, none could recall any member of the herd ever having stripes before. Nor were there tales of horses in the past having stripes. Stripes knew this – she was the only one to ever, ever have been born covered with stripes. Not that her stripes had funny colours. No, they were light brown and dark brown, not pink or green. But still they were stripes, one after the next, covering her whole body.

Given that she hated herself, she was reluctant to join the others. She missed out as they jumped and bucked and called to the mountains, hearing their calls come back to them from the echoing heights. She did not even stay close as they grazed in the tall, rich grass. She did not want the others to look at her, so she often grazed alone at the edge of the thick brush, where the grass was not so good to eat. She didn't think that she deserved the good grass anyway. She didn't think that she deserved much of anything that the rest of the herd had. She thought that she was too different. She didn't talk to the others. Nor did she play with them. Nor teach the young ones. She didn't think that she had anything of worth to teach.

One day some others called to Stripes. Silver Streak, the wise one who guided the herd, wanted to talk with her! What had she done? Would she be sent away for being too different from the herd, of too little use? She approached Silver Streak who was standing on a knoll at the edge of the meadow. Silver Streak did not appear angry; rather, she spoke quietly and gently.

'Stripes, you are unhappy. You do not graze with us; you do not play in the meadows; you do not jump towards the sun. You are a member of the herd. These things that we do are for you to do as well.'

'Silver Streak, I am not like the others. I should leave. I have nothing to give.'

'Stripes, I am sorry that you think that about yourself. Now I understand why you stay away from us. Your thoughts about yourself must be truly painful. I would like you to stay at my side. I have hopes that you will discover what I see when I look at you, Stripes. My wish is that you will one day accept who you are and then discover the gift you bring to the herd. This I know from the wisdom of the ancient horses from the herds of the distant lands.'

'I will do as you ask, Silver Streak, though I fear that it cannot be so.'

'Stripes, I am glad that you agree to remain near me. I hope that you will come to trust me and my wisdom, and on that day we will discover the gift that you have for the herd.'

So Stripes and Silver Streak grazed closely together as the herd slowly made its way through the meadows, eating the grass always available to them in the next meadow and the next. Stripes developed a sense of peace and contentment at the side of Silver Streak. She enjoyed the companionship as well as the close grazing with the rest of the herd. She even learned to play a bit and to reach for the sky with her front hooves. She knew that Silver Streak valued her presence. She began to trust Silver Streak. Stripes felt as if she was a member of the herd. She began to accept herself. She came to accept her stripes, all of them from the darkest brown to the lightest.

One day, as the days and nights were turning cold, Silver Streak decided that this was the place where they would stay for the winter. There were dangers in continuing to graze when the winds turned very cold and the snows came. But there were dangers where they were as well. They could hear the mountain lions calling in the distance. Silver Streak searched for just the right spot for the herd, where they would be safe from the winds and from the lions and where there would be enough grass to last through the winter.

She found the place that she knew was right. She brought the herd close together and then she called Stripes forward.

'Do you trust me, Stripes?'

'Yes, Silver Streak.'

'Then I am trusting you with our safety. Go over to the edge of the meadow, where the brush is thick and where you can see over the far plains.'

Stripes did as she was told and the rest of the herd suddenly gasped all at once. Stripes had disappeared. Her stripes of shades of brown were the same shades as the brush overlooking the plain.

Silver Streak called Stripes back.

'Stripes, you will be our sentry, keeping us safe from any wandering mountain lions. They will not be able to see you in the brush because of your stripes. They would see any of the rest of us and then find a way to sneak up on us when we slept. You will see them and call to us and we will run to the far reaches of the meadows. Will you guard us, Stripes, as we sleep at night?'

Stripes shouted, 'Yes,' and the herd all shouted as one in gratitude. And Stripes became aware of who she was and her gift to the herd. And Silver Streak thanked her. And she thanked Silver Streak. And their winter was safe and they welcomed the spring as they began again their wandering through the high meadows.

**PART III**

# Curiosity

# 6

# Curiosity

## Finding a Different Perspective

> Pandora was trying to tame her curiosity, but at the end she could not hold herself anymore; she opened the box and all the illnesses and hardships that the gods had hidden in the box started coming out. Pandora was scared, because she saw all the evil spirits coming out and tried to close the box as fast as possible, closing Hope inside.[1]

There is a cultural distrust in curiosity; from this myth of Pandora through the story of Eve to the legendary curiosity that killed the cat, we are warned of the perils of being curious. It is an irony that in the myth of Pandora, Curiosity had to be contained and Hope was left inside. In this chapter we would like to provide a more positive view of curiosity. Rather than taming our curiosity, we should actively use it. Through curiosity comes improved understanding, creating, not trapping, hope.

Curiosity fuelled the scientific revolution of the 17th century, leading, in the West, to some of our greatest scientific advances. Barbara Benedict is an American Professor of English who has written a cultural history of curiosity. She suggests that it is discontent with our current knowledge or understanding that provokes curiosity. We want to pursue knowledge that is currently beyond what we know. When we are curious, we ask questions that challenge the status quo. 'Curiosity betrays the desire to know and therefore to be more than you are.'[2] This is a more hopeful view of curiosity, one that sees knowledge as progress.

Within child development, curiosity is the cornerstone of exploration, expanding a child's horizons, promoting development and advancing learning. The combination of curiosity and relationship is a potent mix that leads a child into a world not even dreamed of – a world of knowledge and understanding, but also a world where the inner feelings, desires and wishes of self and others make sense, a world of social success and emotional equilibrium.

In parenting, without curiosity the parent cannot know his child. True connection between parent and child is dependent on a curious parent who is prepared to look beyond what he can see and discover the inner world of the child. A parent who discovers the unique individual who is his child allows this child to impact on him, and in so doing allows this child to experience this impact and discover herself in the process.

Whether we are thinking about the child making her own unique developmental journey or the parent holding the child's hand during this journey, we need also to think about the power of narrative. Curiosity is story making. The stories we tell ourselves and others help us to understand and organize our experience. Human beings are natural storytellers. Throughout history, stories have been a way of making sense of our experience. Curiosity helps us to construct these narratives.

Therapists and colleagues Michael White from Australia and David Epston from New Zealand have explored how these narratives can be constructed and reconstructed within therapeutic interventions.[3] Within this and the next chapter, we will be most interested in the stories that develop between the child and parent, and the power of curiosity and narrative to lead to a different experience. This can fundamentally change the relationship between a parent and child. As parent and child construct and reconstruct stories of their experience together, perspectives can be dramatically changed and relationships healed.

This chapter will explore the importance of curiosity for children and for parents. Curiosity can truly change the way we see things, and this can make a crucial difference to the parent's ability to help the child feel secure.

---

Sarah's parents were not cruel, but they did have high expectations of her. Sarah's mother, Gillian, suffered from a long-standing depression, and her father, Bill, worked long hours to ensure sufficient income to pay the mortgage and the bills. On the authoritarian side of parenting, Bill expected Sarah, from quite a young age, to help her mother out, to be quiet when her mother was in bed with a headache, to carry out regular chores for her. Bill could be fun and playful with Sarah, but when he tired of this he would expect Sarah to stop making demands on him. This made him quite unpredictable at times.

Sarah tried hard to please her father, but she was only a child. She did not always read his moods; she sometimes stayed out with her friends when she should have been at home helping with the daily tasks, and at times she was noisy when she was expected to be quiet. Bill would quickly anger, and he told her that she was lazy and selfish. This is the story that Sarah grew up with. She understood herself through her father's eyes; she was the selfish, lazy child he described for her.

It was many years before Sarah would question this view of herself. A young adult, she was struggling to live alone, and bouts of depression and expectations of failure meant that relationships quickly ended. She was also struggling to come to terms with her sexuality and her father's disapproval of this. Sarah had little curiosity about this, just a bleak acceptance that this is the way things would be.

When Charlie came into her life, Sarah had few expectations, but Charlie was different. She gave Sarah an unconditional love that Sarah had not experienced before. Even more importantly, she awoke curiosity in her. Why did she not expect this relationship to last? Why did she see herself as selfish when Charlie saw a lovely, generous woman? What was lazy in such an industrious and dedicated person? As Sarah struggled to answer these questions, she realized that she was no longer the child that her father had described. She saw herself through new eyes, and in the seeing a new story emerged. Curiosity brings different perspectives, and this can truly change who we are and what we can do with our life. Sarah and Charlie remained together for many happy years.

## What is curiosity?

Pause in your reading and think about the things that you have been curious about today. The more you think, the more your list will grow. For example, Kim awoke to curiosity about why a certain song was in her mind. Whilst happy to enjoy a sunny walk in the hills, she wondered why the weather forecast had been wrong. She puzzled over the challenges a particular puppy was presenting whilst helping at the local puppy training class. She was curious about what food was in the fridge for lunch. She wrestled with this chapter and how to awaken curiosity in the reader. This list could be extended and extended.

We spend our lives wondering, thinking, reminiscing, puzzling, inventing, explaining and understanding. Without curiosity we could not do any of these things. Curiosity is part of who we are; it comes along with us as we journey through life. Todd Kashdan, an American psychologist who researches and writes about curiosity, suggests that it is being 'open and receptive to experiences that offer more than what is already known'.[4]

Curiosity is, then, as natural as breathing, and this is because we are born with an innate interest in novelty and a drive to explore and understand. Watch any infant or young child around you and you will see a wide-eyed wonder in the world. Panksepp, in his study of affective neuroscience, suggests that curiosity is an exploratory attitude that we all hold.[5] We are born with this need to know; it is a basic impulse which motivates all mammals to search, investigate and make sense of the world. Curiosity leads us to be actively engaged with the world we live in and to use this engagement to make meaning out of our experience.

Panksepp called this motivation to be curious the 'seeking system'. He describes this as an emotional system which, when activated, leads animals to be intensely interested in exploring the world and to become excited when desires are about to be met. Part of this seeking system therefore motivates us to find the resources that we need to stay alive – food, warmth and companionship, for example. Panksepp goes on to suggest: 'In humans this may be one of the main brain systems that generate and sustain curiosity, even for intellectual pursuits.'[6]

That is not all it does, however. Seeking is also connected to our need to understand our environment, to look for predictability; when things happen in a predictable way, we can relax, confident that B will follow A. Curiosity has helped us to find some predictability, and this in turn leads us to feel safe and thus open to new experience, to unpredictability. This balance between the predictable and unpredictable is what gives us our flexibility. Dan Siegel has helped to elucidate this.[7] Too little predictability and we experience chaos, too much predictability and we experience rigidity. Neither of these links to safety and the confidence to explore and move forward. The middle path between chaos and rigidity is flexibility. Flexibility stems out of sufficient predictability to provide feelings of safety, opening us up to curiosity and a need to know and to develop.

The final part of the seeking system represents our thirst for knowledge. We are curious, we have an interest in things, we seek for meaning.

Curiosity as part of this seeking system, Panksepp[8] suggests, is therefore a basic emotional state. When seeking is activated within our brains, it generates feelings of intense interest, engaged curiosity and eager anticipation. It is also very connected to our cognitive processes, the parts of our brain that are concerned with thinking and making sense of things. Curiosity adds to the content of our cognition, leading to cognitive changes, as it fuels our thinking and leads to the creation of ideas. Curiosity lies at the connection between our thinking and our feeling.

To understand the importance of curiosity within parenting, it will be helpful to explore curiosity in relation to other people. Taking an interest in another is an active process. In the story of Sarah and her father Bill earlier in this chapter, we saw what can happen when a parent has a non-curious, judgemental view of his child. Bill was not able to stop and consider Sarah's perspective. He judged her harshly, based on his assumptions that she was lazy and selfish. His judgement in turn led to Sarah's own judgements.

The nature of the intersubjective relationship between a parent and a child means that the child develops a sense of self via the parent's sense of her. Sarah's own understanding of herself was impacted upon by her father's judgements. The harsh nature of this judgement will have been painful for Sarah, leading to a need to defend herself. If it is painful to 'know yourself', you will stop seeking this knowledge. The father's judgement is made from a lack of curiosity – in effect 'stealing' Sarah's own curiosity. Neither sought for meaning in these judgements, and relationships were difficult as a consequence. If Bill had been able to stop and think about Sarah, he might have formed a different view. Of course, Sarah could behave in ways which might be seen as selfish and lazy at times – who of us doesn't? – but she could also be kind, generous and hardworking.

If Bill had taken an interest in his daughter, had opened his eyes to her, perhaps he could have seen these qualities also. Instead of judging harshly, he could have been open to Sarah in all her colours. He could have understood her, guiding her rather than imposing his will upon her. In not seeing, Bill had a less rich and rewarding relationship with his daughter, and Sarah had a less rich and more judgemental understanding of herself.

Curiosity is non-judgemental, a genuine wish to understand not prejudiced by our own assumptions or preferences. We are open to the other person, wanting to understand her, see the world from her perspective. We are interested in the experience of the other person. We want to discover how the other has made sense of her experience. Curiosity is motivated by a desire to understand rather than to change; following understanding, change might be welcome, but this is not the primary intent. Curiosity is therefore communicated without assumptions, judgements or solutions.

Earlier in this chapter we suggested that storytelling was an important way that we all make sense of events and experiences in our lives. We construct stories or narratives for ourselves and we communicate our experience through the communication of these stories. When we are curious about another, we are interested in these stories. Through our interest we join the other in the narrative, and by doing this we also have an impact on the narrative. We facilitate the other's deeper understanding of her own story. This might lead to more coherence in the narrative, as the other person more deeply understands her experience. Alternatively, it might lead to a different, fuller narrative, as we co-create the narrative with the other person. It is important to notice that curiosity is not taking over the creation of the story; we do not tell the other person what to think or feel. Rather, it is assisting the other person to more fully understand her experience, fostering her own curiosity so that her story becomes richer and fuller.

---

Let's stay with the story of Sarah and Charlie. We will eavesdrop on them as they curiously explore Sarah's experience.

Sarah: I know you will leave me, everybody always does.

Charlie: How can you know this, Sarah? How can you know what hasn't happened yet?

Sarah: Because that is what always happens. All my relationships end within three months. Why should this be any different?

Charlie: I am wondering about this. I believe when people are so certain about the future that somehow their past is involved. We might predict but we can't know what is in the future, but everyone has a past. Might this be the same for you? Do you expect us not to work out because of a past relationship that hasn't worked out?

Sarah: All my past relationships have been like that. They all end after just a few months. Why should this be any different?

Charlie: That sounds like circular reasoning to me. Past relationships have ended, therefore this one will. Why? Because they all do!

Sarah: When you put it like that, it doesn't make much sense, does it? But why am I so unsuccessful with other people?

Charlie: I don't know. What do you think? What do you think spoils things for you?

Sarah: Well, I don't know. I guess it's because I am so selfish. People don't like to stay with me because I am so thoughtless.

Charlie: Wow, Sarah, that really surprises me. Why do you see yourself as selfish?

Sarah: I have never thought about it before. It is something I have always known. I am selfish; my dad told me often enough. I grew up knowing this about myself.

Charlie: Oh, Sarah, I feel so sad for you. I know you had a difficult time with your dad, but how sad that he described you like that. I can't imagine what it is like growing up being criticized like that.

Sarah: It's just how it was. I just believed what he told me. I never questioned it before. I just assumed everyone could see this about me and therefore they left.

Charlie: Do you think there might be another reason why they left? It is kind of hard staying when you keep being told that it won't last. Do you think you might have pushed them away, perhaps? Maybe you couldn't believe in it, and you didn't allow the other person to believe either?

Sarah: I've never thought about it this way before. Goodness, could that really be it? I'm not sure what to think now. Have I created the situations because of my own view of myself?

Charlie: Well, I don't think it is because you are selfish. Look how you drop in on Mrs Baker every week. I couldn't put up with her endless moaning, but you keep on regardless.

Sarah: Oh, she is just a lonely old woman without any family of her own. I just don't like to think of her all on her own.

Charlie: Selfish, eh? Doesn't sound like it to me!

Sarah: Do you know, it is only just occurring to me that maybe I'm not always selfish. But if this isn't true, what else isn't? I'm not sure I am ready to have my whole world turned upside down.

Charlie: Maybe we can do it together. After all, isn't that what relationships are all about – discovering another person, and discovering more about yourself in the process? Maybe we will both see ourselves differently as we spend our lives together.

Sarah: Woa, slow down. I am just coming to terms with maybe it not ending. One step at a time, eh?

Charlie: See, now it is me being selfish. Of course let's take it slowly, but we do have a future, Sarah. I am sure of it.

Sarah: OK, perhaps. I'm just getting my head around selfishness being something we all do sometimes. It doesn't make me a selfish person. Do you know my whole view of myself has just shifted? My dad has a lot to answer for, but, you know, it was tough for him, with Mum ill and everything. I think he was just trying to hold everything together. I am going to have to think about this some more. I know that his judgement of me has had a huge impact on me, colouring how I see myself, and the relationships I have entered. It feels strange re-evaluating this now after all these years.

---

You will notice in the above example that this conversation is not simply about gathering information. It is about using curiosity to understand a situation. It is exploring beneath the surface of things to a deeper understanding of the inner life of the other. Curiosity therefore has to be more than questioning. Asking a list of questions, as in an interrogation, only stays on the surface of experience. One person asks, the other answers. Curiosity is much more of a collaborative venture. It is the joining of two or more people to share empathically their experience and discover together the deeper meaning of this experience.

When we show curiosity in another, we are acknowledging that we do not know. No matter how many times we may have encountered the same event, we still do not know how the individual in front of us experienced it. That person is unique and his experience of the event will also be unique. When we can suspend our own belief about the meaning of an event, we can be truly curious about the meaning for the other person.

Earlier we explored how Panksepp[9] understands the innate quality of curiosity as an affective state, an emotional system which motivates us to seek understanding. This suggests that curiosity is both rational and emotional. The rational implies thought, acquiring knowledge, using the cognitive processes in our brains. The emotional implies applying the rational with feelings, using the emotional processes in our brain. We understand (rationality) through our emotional states of interest, desire to know, fascination in the other's story and compassion about her experience. When we are both rational and emotional, we become deeply involved in story making with the other, facilitating reflection and conveying empathy for and respect of the other's experience.

## Curiosity and culture

Curiosity has a deep cultural as well as a developmental significance. Given that curiosity is such a central part of being human it is curious that we have such mixed feelings about it. We are told that 'curiosity kills the cat', implying that there is something deeply damaging in being curious, that what is hidden is indeed wisely hidden and we should not look for concealed knowledge.

Myths support this. Pandora opened the box; Eve ate the apple. Both gained in wisdom, but it is implied that this wisdom came at a cost. As Benedict explains, this was the view of curiosity that held sway in previous centuries.[10] For example, in the early 17th century curiosity was viewed as an impulse that was out of control, that it betrayed a desire to know more than is good for us. It was seen as the means by which humankind became trapped.

As we progress through history, we see an ambivalent view of curiosity, both as a force for good and for evil. Curiosity was equated with ambition during the Restoration period, as exemplified in the archetype of the scientist as ambitious new thinker. There were mixed views on whether such ambition was for good or ill. On the other hand, Samuel Johnson viewed curiosity much more positively as 'one of the permanent and certain characteristics of a vigorous mind'.[11]

This is the tension that remains with us to this day. Hidden knowledge can be seen as wisely hidden; consider Frankenstein's monster, an allegory for curiosity gone wrong.[12] On the other hand, curiosity opens up increased knowledge and understanding leading to development at the individual, societal and world level, as explored by Arthur C. Clarke in his story of curiosity, *2001: A Space Odyssey*.[13] Curiosity runs throughout the story, beginning with the apes, and the advantage conferred on the most curious of them, moving on to the discovery on the moon, which led to the final odyssey of Bowman as he explored worlds beyond any experienced before.

In this chapter we explore the more hopeful view of curiosity. As Benedict puts it, 'Curiosity is seeing your way out of your place. It is looking beyond.'[14] This is the view of curiosity that supports PACE. Only with curiosity can we move beyond our current relationship and move towards a relationship that offers the child greater security, and freedom from the trauma of the past. Only through curiosity will we find alternative stories, and help children to find alternative paths.

Here is a story to illustrate this point.

---

This is a story of the tree. Autumn in England is a lovely time of year. The colours as the leaves fall from the trees are beautiful, but, for Kim, watching autumn unfold is also a time of sadness.

As she watches the trees becoming bare of leaves, she anticipates dark days and long nights. She braces herself for cold and rain, and muddy walks with the dogs; seeing trees losing their leaves signals to her all that she doesn't like about winter.

Then one day she is listening to someone talking about the winter tree, and in an instant her perspective changes completely. He talks about the beauty of the tree that is revealed when the leaves are gone. Kim looks at trees with renewed curiosity, and she sees it. The beautiful shape of the trunk and branches, the light falling, revealing hues and tones unnoticed before.

Winter still contains long nights, mud and rain, but her enjoyment of winter walks has been transformed by this new story. The story of the tree has given Kim a new perspective, one that has in turn changed her responses.

The speaker was not trying to change views. His motive was to share his experience rather than to influence others, but as he told his story of the tree, Kim knew that she would never look at winter trees in quite the same way again. Through curiosity, our perspectives can be increased and our responses transformed.

---

## Curiosity within child development

Developmentally, curiosity drives the exploration that complements the need for attachment that a young child experiences. Within attachment theory John Bowlby coupled these two innate drives together, demonstrating how, as long as she feels safe and secure, a child will instinctively reach out to explore the world around her. Whereas distress and discomfort drive attachment, curiosity drives exploration.[15]

Whilst writing this chapter, Kim took her dogs out for a walk. With curiosity fresh on her mind, she watched them with renewed interest. From the way they sniffed the air as they jumped out of the car to the last look back as the walk ended, they curiously explored the world. Whilst a familiar, routine walk for Kim, to the dogs it was new and fresh. They looked, they smelled, they listened, they tasted, they touched. All their senses were absorbed in this discovery of the world around them. All mammals are born with this instinct to explore.

Human infants are no different. Innate curiosity awakens their interest in the world, and childhood is a voyage of discovery of self, other and the larger world around them. Unique amongst mammals, however, is the infant's dependency upon her parents. Curiosity, in humans especially, awakens within relationships. To understand the importance of curiosity within child development we have to be mindful of the importance of curiosity within relationships.

The infant is born into relationship. In a previous book, Dan comments that: 'Parents, from the moment that they are aware of their infant-still-in-the-womb, find themselves very curious about who their infant is.'[16] Children bathe in this curiosity as parent and child become absorbed with each other. Curiosity within relationship is soon joined by curiosity outside of it. The parent is on hand to facilitate the child's broadening curiosity as she learns about the physical world around her and, soon, the social world as well. Developmental progress, whether physical, cognitive, social or emotional, is enhanced by the relationship experienced with the parent. The world is translated through the eyes of the parents.

Throughout this journey of discovery, the child is learning about herself. This joint sharing of curiosity directly impacts on the sense of self that the child develops, and in turn this will impact on her continuing ability to enter into and benefit from relationships. As the parent discovers the uniqueness of his child, the child in turn discovers the impact she has on her parent. She learns to behave in ways that impact positively on her parent, and the parent in turn helps the child to discover who she is. A parent who delights in the cleverness of his child will have a child who believes she is clever. A parent who is absorbed by the actions of his child will have a child who is confident in her actions. A parent who can understand and support the distress of his child will have a child who can make sense of her inner experience.

Each impacts on the other in a curiosity-driven relationship that helps the child to understand, learn and make developmental progress. It will be clear from this discussion that the parent's sensitivity to his child will be an important precursor for healthy development.

Attachment theory, as explored in Chapter 1, explores the importance of sensitive parenting for secure attachment. A parent who is able to interpret the needs being expressed by the child and is prepared to step in and meet these needs will have a child who feels secure in the relationship. When the child has a need for comfort, she will confidently turn to the parent for this. When this need has been met, the child will confidently move outwards to explore and discover the world around her. The parent facilitates this exploration by continuing to be responsive to moment-by-moment needs. Children with this experience of secure attachment will be able to relax within their relationship with their parents, confident that the parents are available as needed. They can explore and learn in the world, and psychological development is enhanced.

Elizabeth Meins, a research psychologist from Durham University, England, has extended our understanding of sensitive parenting and its impact both on security of attachment and the development of the child.[17] She particularly points to the importance of 'mind-mindedness', the parents' ability to treat their children as individuals with their own mind. The parents understand what psychologists call 'theory of mind': that their children have their own minds, with their own thoughts, feelings, beliefs and desires. From infancy onwards, a parent responds to these inner qualities, helping the child to understand her own mind, to organize her experience and eventually to put into words what she is experiencing.

Mind-mindedness is an act of discovery. The parent is interested in his child's internal world, is genuinely striving to understand it. As he observes his child, talks to her, interacts with her, he is making guesses, tentative hypotheses about what the child might be experiencing. The tentativeness of this curiosity leaves him open to feedback, ready to abandon or adjust his guesses in light of the child's response to them. In this way the parent truly comes to understand the mind of his child, and can give this understanding back as a gift that will allow the child to come to know herself.

---

A parent is sitting playing with his child. As the child sets up her 'zoo', he chats to her:

> This looks like a big zoo. Where are the elephants going to go? Yes, that looks like a good enclosure for them. Ah, you have put the zookeeper in; what do you think he is going to do? Yes, I think he will feed the animals. They will be happy having lots of food to eat. Oh, you want some food, do you? What do you fancy? One of the zoo animal biscuits we bought when we did the shopping? Oh, I see, you want the cat biscuits. Do you think the lions are hungry? I wonder if Suki will mind if we give her biscuits to your animals. Maybe we should leave them for her. Do you think the lions would like these? Well, it will be bedtime soon; would you like to leave this here so you can play with it again tomorrow? You have enjoyed making a zoo today, haven't you?

Although you can only hear the parent's dialogue in this little scenario, it gives a clear sense of what the child is doing. Parent and child are playing together, the parent helping to expand his daughter's play as he follows her lead. Contrast this with a parent who already 'knows', without curiosity:

> This looks like a big zoo. Here, put the elephants here; they will need a big enclosure. No, the zookeeper won't go in there; put him here away from the lions. No, you can't have any food. You can't be hungry yet, you have only just had tea. No, don't get the cat biscuits out. That is naughty. Come on now, tidy all this mess up; it is bedtime. I don't think we will get the zoo out again if you can't play with it without getting upset.

This parent does not want to know what the internal world of his child is like. He already 'knows' without discovery. He instructs his child how to think and what to understand, and in the process he instils in her a dependency on others to tell her how to think. This child is not becoming self-aware, but is learning to understand herself only through the eyes of another – someone who has judged what her experience should be without trying to understand it.

---

With interested and open parenting, a child will successfully develop her own theory of mind, understanding not only her own mind but also the minds of others. The child, with the parent's help, is becoming a successful, thinking, feeling, social being, confident in her abilities and willing to continue to explore in the world. The curiosity of the parent – the willingness to understand the inner and outer worlds of the child – has in turn fostered the curiosity of the child. With curiosity, the child will continue to develop successfully as horizons broaden again and begin to encompass the wider world of school and expanding relationships.

## Curiosity within parenting

Curiosity therefore plays an important part in parenting children. Curiosity expresses interest in the child and her understanding of her own experience and of the experience of others. Curiosity also shows how much we love, respect and value our child. As in the first example of the parent and child playing with the zoo, we want to share her experience, help her to organize this experience and increase her understanding of her experience. Through our own curiosity we foster the curiosity of the child and thus enhance her development.

Children, especially young children, often do not know what they think and feel about an experience. The parent helps the child by leading her into a curious stance; together they can gain understanding. This process is called 'co-construction', a creative process in which they make sense of experience together. In this way, the child is learning not just to *be*, but also to *think*. She is gaining the habit of actively exploring her inner life, learning how she thinks or feels about experiences, finding words to put to her experience and therefore being in touch with her inner life.

As the child grows older, she will be more able to communicate this experience through words rather than behaviour.

## When curiosity shuts down

We have seen how instinctive curiosity is. A child is born curious, driven to explore the world around her. This curiosity is nurtured within relationships. As the child grows and matures, curiosity remains, expanded into a wider world of relationships. Children and young people experiment with who they are and consider who they want to be. Then, as adults, they are ready to take their curiosity into the world of work and parenthood.

Given the instinctive nature of curiosity, it is not surprising that children remain curious even through the most difficult circumstances. Given the social nature of curiosity, we would expect children to be most curious when with others. But what happens when difficult circumstances involve the relationships closest to the child?

When children find it difficult to feel safe or secure within their attachment relationships, their focus becomes much narrower. A lack of safety means that spontaneous and unrestricted exploration becomes much harder. As Todd Kashdan[18] suggests, when anxiety overwhelms the curiosity system, it is anxiety rather than novelty that determines what we think, what we do and how we feel. Anxiety becomes the driver, restricting our world and reducing our ability to learn and develop.

When anxiety is in control, we behave more and more in order to avoid the discomfort of anxiety. In the process, we do not learn to manage anxiety; because we have found high levels of anxiety intolerable, we learn to avoid smaller and smaller doses of anxiety. Our focus is on avoidance rather than exploration. We do not learn that we can survive anxiety or tolerate distress. This in turn means that personal growth is limited.

We will explore in the next chapter how the experience of shame also limits curiosity. Parents are vulnerable to feeling shame, especially when parenting is being challenged. A sense of failure, of getting it wrong, a feeling that you are not getting through to the child can all lead to a sense of shame, of not being good enough as a parent. This can be magnified in parents who already lack confidence in themselves, perhaps because of their own experience of being parented, or perhaps because of difficulties conceiving a child. This experience will also limit curiosity; the parent becomes angry, frustrated or despairing in his parenting role, further limiting the success he experiences, to the detriment of his relationship with the child.

The child who does not feel safe within relationships becomes narrowly focused on the relationship; she tries to organize her behaviour in order to increase her feelings of safety. This might be by becoming anxiously concerned with maintaining attention from the parent; exploration reduces as the child becomes focused on displaying her need of the parent, working hard not to let the parent out of sight and behaving in ways that keep the parent attending to her.

Whereas this child wears her anxiety very visibly, other children feel safer hiding it away. They work not to show how they are feeling and appear more interested in exploring than in seeking comfort or security. This exploration is, however, uncurious because the child's primary focus is on her safety.

She puts a lot of effort into hiding how she feels; energy for exploration is reduced. Whilst appearing to be focused away from the parent, the child is actually very attentive to his needs and moods. Apparent indifference or lack of need is actually the child's attempt to keep the parent close. There is little time for curiosity when so much attention is directed towards monitoring the parent's availability and suppressing negative feelings in order to ensure that this availability remains. In both these examples, therefore, the child's behaviour within the relationship is governed by the avoidance of discomfort. Curious exploration within the relationship shuts down.

This becomes an habitual state of being within relationships. As the child enters new, potentially healthier relationships, she continues to act based on a need to avoid discomfort. She never learns that this relationship might be a joyful opportunity to discover something different. The child cannot grow within the new relationships; she is too preoccupied in managing the anticipated discomfort learnt in the old relationships. The lack of exploration within the relationships means that the child cannot disconfirm the old beliefs that she still holds. Anxiety interferes with curiosity, as Todd Kashdan points out: 'By fearing anxiety, a person can't act on their curiosity. If overwhelming worry affects us early in life, then anxiety can disrupt a lot of opportunities during a critical developmental period.'[19]

We explored earlier Panksepp's[20] idea of a biological 'seeking system', motivating the child to be curious about the world. What happens to this system when a child is experiencing insecurity within her relationships with her parents? British Psychologist Glyn Hudson-Allez has explored this, suggesting that, in these situations, seeking is reduced and children become less playful and explorative. Learning about the world becomes secondary to safety.[21] Some children don't just feel insecure with parents or caregivers, but actually experience fear from these relationships. These are children who are traumatized within their most important relationships, because these are abusive, rejecting, neglectful or frightening in other ways. 'A frightened child will not play in a relaxed way, nor will she reach her potential through learning.'[22]

A frightened child is restricted in her experience of the world as it narrows to a tight focus on managing her own safety. Unable to rely on parents, the primary source of fear, the child attempts to find other ways to experience safety. A fragile security comes out of feeling in control of the relationship; the child may become aggressive or very compliant, self-reliant or coercively needy. These are desperate attempts to feel safe in an unsafe world. The emotional expression of this state is one of fear and anger; feelings of fun, playfulness and laughter disappear from the worlds of these children. There is little energy for the joyful exploration of the world.

Traumatized children process information very differently from calm children. Whilst most children thrive on some challenge in their lives – enjoying learning new skills and gaining mastery in their world – for the traumatized child, challenges are another source of fear or terror.

The experience of living in a state of fear has also impacted on the way their brains are working. The children are less able to use their higher, cognitive processes, the more complex parts of the brain involved in learning, problem solving and mastering skills. This means that the children respond to the world without thought, becoming reactive and instinctive in their responses. The trauma that they are living is killing the curiosity that they were born with. Instead of enjoying the novel, the challenge of learning, these children are scared by novelty; anything that is new, not yet known, is a potential threat. With the loss of exploration, curiosity shrivels and dies.

In the next chapter we will explore the parenting of children who have little curiosity, and consider how to bring curiosity into this parenting. This starts with maintaining your own curiosity. This can be difficult when parenting children who are insecure or traumatized. Feeling confident in your parenting can be difficult when children keep rejecting, clinging to or controlling you. This can gradually erode your confidence and increase feelings of anxiety, hopelessness or anger. Curiosity is easiest when you are experiencing confidence and joy in caring for your child. Curiosity is quickly lost when your own emotions lead to a sense of failure. You become focused on your sense of inadequacy, losing your more curious focus on the child. In this case, it is easy to become disconnected from your child, increasing anxiety for both of you.

It is even more difficult when caring for a traumatized child because you are at increased risk of becoming traumatized by her trauma. This is called secondary trauma. British social worker and experienced foster parent Kate Cairns points out how easy it is to experience a trauma reaction based on the trauma that the child is experiencing.[23] You do not need to experience the trauma directly; your sense of empathy with the child can lead to a reaction which is similar to the experience of trauma itself. Secondary trauma, just like primary trauma, is toxic to curiosity; when trauma enters, curiosity leaves, and you find yourself reacting without thought.

This risk of secondary trauma is greater if the parent has a history of unresolved attachment experience. This early experience of relationship trauma is triggered when the parent becomes supportive of and therefore exposed to his child's trauma. The parent is left dealing with two traumas, past and present, increasing the amount of stress he is experiencing and therefore multiplying the chance that he will be traumatized by this stress. We will return to managing these trauma reactions in the next chapter.

## In conclusion

Whilst views of curiosity have changed during the centuries in line with prevailing cultural beliefs, at its heart curiosity is rooted in our biology. We are curious, and curiosity will make us who we are.

Curiosity is a central part of a child's development and a central part of parenting. Curiosity is the fuel of children's exploration of themselves, others and the world around them. When we match our children's curiosity with our own curiosity, we understand and truly connect to them. This connection provides us with deeper acceptance and feelings of empathy for our children. This in turn leads to more responsive, sensitive support for the child in tune with her inner experience as well as her outer behaviour.

We started this chapter with the myth of Pandora, a warning against curiosity. Curiosity is, however, much more hopeful than this. Let's rewrite the story of Pandora based on a valuing of curiosity:

> Pandora had forgotten how to be curious. She spent her time reacting without thought, preoccupied with her own failings, and fearing her own inadequacy.

She feared opening the box, certain that it would only reveal more of her failures. Pandora was scared. She hid the box away.

A wise friend noticed Pandora and grew concerned. She was curious about why Pandora had so much fear. She discovered Pandora's story. She did not try to change her, but empathized with the difficulties she had faced. She explored Pandora's courage in carrying on despite her sense of failure.

Pandora looked up and saw a world she had forgotten about. One day she took down the box and, with her friend's help, she opened it. Curiosity was inside. Pandora embraced it and looked about her. The world expanded as she watched.

Pandora knew that she failed sometimes but she now also had hope that she could succeed.

# 7

# Staying Curious within Parenting

Curiosity is at the heart of PACE, and in this chapter we will explore the value of curiosity in maintaining the attitude of PACE.

Without curiosity, we are unlikely to find acceptance or to experience empathy. Curiosity helps us to find new perspectives, to more fully understand the child we are caring for. It is about understanding behaviour, but it also takes us beyond this to understand the motives, beliefs, fears and worries that drive the behaviour. We need to enter the heart and mind of the child, to fully understand the emotion that the child experiences and the thoughts that motivate the child. Only with this understanding can we find the deep acceptance that the child will experience as empathy for the whole of him.

---

Kate is struggling to get her 14-year-old daughter to school. Each morning she crawls deep into her bed and refuses to get up. Kate cajoles, nags and finally gets cross before a reluctant and grumpy Joanne gets up and dresses.

By the time she has dropped her at school, Kate feels as if they have both been through the mill. She is aware that her relationship with Joanne is very poor at the moment. This daily battle has pushed curiosity to the background; Kate has forgotten to wonder why Joanne is so reluctant to get up in the morning. In her frustration, she just attributes it to laziness and the awkwardness of early adolescence.

Curiosity and PACE might, however, lead to a very different, and perhaps surprising, outcome. She goes in extra early one morning to wake Joanne:

Kate: Joanne, time to get up now.

(Joanne *crawls further under the bedcovers*)

Kate: I am guessing you don't want to get up this morning, but I am wondering why this has got so hard for you. You always used to be up with the lark. What is the matter?

Joanne: Leave me alone, I just want to sleep.

Kate: I can see how much you want me to leave you alone, but it is important to me that you go to school. It used to be important to you too.

Joanne: *(In angry voice)* I just don't want to go. Right? Just leave me alone.

Kate: *(Matching the intensity of Joanne's anger, but without getting angry herself)* It is so important not to go, isn't it? You're really not enjoying school at the moment.

Joanne: *(A little calmer)* No, I hate it.

Kate: I get how much you hate it. Can you help me understand why? You used to love school when you were younger.

Joanne: Well, times change, don't they? Anyway, you wouldn't understand. I just don't want to go. Right?

Kate: Right, I've got it, and maybe I could understand a bit. Why not try me?

Joanne: You will only say I have to go. It's the law, as you keep reminding me. What is the point?

Kate: Yes, you are right, I do want you to go to school, but I don't want you to be unhappy. I am beginning to wonder if something is happening at school that is upsetting you.

Joanne: Just leave it, right. You wouldn't understand, and I don't want you to interfere. You will only make things worse.

Kate: You're worried that I could make it worse. Is that why you haven't talked to me? You think I would interfere. Like go into school and talk to someone. Is that what you are worried about?

Joanne: No, you mustn't go into school. I am getting up, OK. Just leave me alone!

Kate: Oh, Joanne, you're really worried I could make things worse. You don't want me to go into school. Is that why you aren't talking to me, because you think I would interfere and then things would be so much worse?

Joanne: Yes, I can't talk to you, OK. I will try and get up better in the mornings. Please don't talk to them.

Kate: OK, I see that's important to you, but I do want to know what has upset you so much. Do you think you could talk to me a bit? Maybe I could help without going into school?

Joanne: Will you promise not to tell anyone?

Kate: Oh, Joanne. I can't make that promise without knowing what is happening. I have to know you are safe, but I don't want to make things worse for you. Could we figure something out together?

Joanne: *(In tears)* I am so scared. If they know I have told you, they will kill me. It wasn't my fault, I didn't mean to do anything wrong.

Kate: *(Gently)* Was it very wrong? Let me help you, Joanne.

Joanne: It was the new boy, Mark, the one who started at the end of last term. I thought he liked me, but I'm not sure now. He asked me to give something to Justin. It was just a small packet. I didn't know what it was. Now I think it might have been drugs. He told me if I told anyone, the police would be after me. I know you will have to tell someone, but I didn't mean to do anything wrong. I'm sorry.

Kate: Now I understand. No wonder you have not wanted to go to school. You must have been so scared. We can sort this, though. Mark shouldn't have used you like that. I am glad you have told me. Let's have some breakfast and think about what we are going to do next. You are being so brave. I think we can sort this out and make sure Mark doesn't do this to anyone else.

Kate's curiosity has helped Joanne reveal a secret that has been causing her a lot of fear. Now Kate is not angry with her daughter any more. She understands how hard this has been, and she will help her sort it out.

---

The story of the winter tree in the last chapter is a metaphor for the story of our relationship with our children. If we want to transform this relationship, we will need to hold on to our curiosity, using this to search for alternative stories, stories that will transform our understanding of events, conversations and actions. We can then use this understanding to guide our thinking, leading to flexibility in our responses and strength in our relationships.

Curiosity is the key that helps us to expand our relationship with our children, helping them to build trust in us. We become a secure base from which they can grow, taking the steps that help them to explore a gradually broadening world. Curiosity can do that because it leads to increased understanding. We understand our child, the way he experiences the world and the behaviours he adopts to express this experience. With this understanding comes confidence: the confidence to respond, the confidence to help, the confidence to support our child. Without this understanding we are liable to become anxious, to experience failure, to feel defeated. Such experiences shut down curiosity and move us further away from a responsive relationship. Without curiosity we make rapid judgements, leading to non-reflective action.

---

Kim was on a family holiday when her son was 14 years old. Everyone was feeling relaxed and playful. They started to think about the future, exploring with Alex the things he might do. They teased him that one day he would be keeping them in their old age. Alex turned to them and very seriously told them that he did not think that he would grow up; he didn't see a future for himself.

This statement produced a strong response in Kim, a response that was full of anxiety and fear – a fear of losing him, a fear of failing him. She responded without thought, non-reflectively: 'Of course you will grow up, don't be so silly.' She judged Alex on the basis of his behaviour as reflected in the words he was using and her assumptions about this, rather than based on a genuine wish to understand what he was telling her.

He told her that he feared he would not grow up, and she judged this as a criticism of her parenting and responded defensively. Curiosity had failed her, and in so doing she failed to support her son with his own anxieties. It wasn't until they were back home that curiosity returned. Kim thought about this episode and started wondering about it; curiosity was back. She thought of her instant response, which centred around her fear of loss and failure. As she became preoccupied with her own meaning, based on her own fears, she lost sight of the meaning that might be present for her son.

What alternative stories might have helped her understand him more deeply? Alex could have been communicating his own fears and anxieties: 'You are asking me to imagine something that I find hard to imagine'; 'I don't want adult responsibility, let's stop this conversation now'; 'This is really scary for me, I have always feared growing up, taking the next step.' If curiosity had allowed her to imagine these alternative explanations she would have explored them with her son. Together they would have wondered about the fear he was communicating. Kim would have responded more sensitively, with more empathy. We can't always stay curious on the spot. Sometimes we need time for reflection, but the habit of curiosity will allow us to be prepared for the next time.

---

A failure of curiosity stops us seeking alternative stories, different explanations for what we are experiencing with our children. We are instead guided by our assumptions, believing we know and not pausing to discover. Without curiosity we are non-reflective; we react without thought and our reactions are generally more in tune with our own fears and anxieties than those of our children. A consequence of this might be that the child stops trying to communicate his experience. Feelings are left unregulated and often they emerge unpredictably, perhaps through challenging behaviour.

Curiosity starts with not knowing. When we do not know, we want to explore, to discover. This gives us a richness and depth to our theories. It is non-judgemental, so that we better understand the other and our responses to him. This leads to a deeper connection, a stronger relationship, within which the child feels more secure and more trusting of us.

Curiosity might be something that you do on behalf of the child, finding time to think about him, to wonder at his experience, to understand his behaviour. Alternatively, curiosity can be done with the child. You wonder together about the meaning of experiences. Both of these have their place in parenting.

Being curious with your child builds the relationship you have in many healthy ways. It increases the connection you have with the child as you come to understand him better. It helps the child to feel accepted and loved. It reduces the amount of nagging and lecturing you are doing; instead, the child feels that you 'get it' and becomes more co-operative in the process.

The child in turn is learning some important lessons from your curiosity. As you help him to understand and organize his experience, the child is developing important skills involving reflection, understanding his own inner world and being more open to exploring the inner worlds of others. This in turn will further build his regulation abilities.

As he comes to be more reflective, the child is also more in control of his own emotions. These are important skills that will help the child to manage away from you, to develop relationships and to experience success within these relationships. It will also increase his self-understanding. He will develop a coherent narrative of his experience, a sense of past, present and potential future within which he understands his experience and the journey he is taking through life. The child is building up his own stories, and these stories will be a guide for him as he moves out into the wider world.

Being curious with a child means wondering together. Parent and child figure out what is going on. In particular, they discover the hidden reasons why things happen. It might be figuring out why a child is behaving in a particular way. Alternatively, it might be figuring out why a child is feeling worried or fearful about something. Parent and child are story-making together, developing a narrative to explain something that is worrying or intriguing them.

This type of conversing with the child is non-confrontational; the parent is not interrogating, or trying to convey displeasure by asking direct questions. 'Have you taken my phone?' or 'Why have you come in so late?' are very different to 'I noticed you took my phone tonight; I'm wondering what that was about?' or 'I've been noticing that you have been staying out late a few times lately; I am concerned that something is bothering you?' In the former questions, the child will sense being in trouble. He is likely to get defensive, leading to disconnection between parent and child. In the latter, the parent is conveying a genuine interest in the child and discovering what is going on for him. This will reduce defensiveness and allow understanding and connection to develop between them.

When talking to a child in this way, it is important to be non-judgemental, to start with a 'not-knowing stance'. If you already think you know why a child is doing something, then you are not being curious; your assumptions shut down your curiosity. These preconceptions do not deepen understanding, but are shortcuts which divert from discovery. The parent does not want to work out why the child is behaving in a particular way; rather she wants to vent her own feelings or frustrations about the behaviour.

Notice the difference between saying to a child, 'You haven't done your homework again tonight. You really want to fail your exams, don't you!' and 'I notice you haven't done your homework tonight. What do you think that's about? I think maybe you are worried about failing your exams.' In the first example, conversation will stop and resentment will continue on both sides. The parent will continue to believe that the child is not trying, and the child will continue to feel that the parent is mean. In the second example, the parent may change her beliefs as the two of them explore this together. The child might say, for example, 'I am not worried about failing the exam, but I really don't get this topic. I tried asking Mr Smith, but he was busy. I just don't know what to do.' In this case the parent will modify her original guess as the two of them make sense of it together.

This type of non-judgemental wondering starts from the expectation that we may not understand now, but we can make meaning together. The parent does not know, nor does she expect the child to know. Meaning comes from the conversation between them. Of course, the behaviour is still there and presenting a problem, but joint understanding is more likely to lead to joint solutions; the child and parent together figure out what to do.

For this to be successful, it is important that the child does not experience his inner life being judged. Whatever sense is made of 'why', the parent accepts this. When feelings are understood without judgement, the child can cope with his behaviour being not acceptable, because it is separate from him. His thoughts, feelings and intentions are understood in a way that helps him to feel loved and valued. As we explored in Chapters 4 and 5, this deep acceptance will support him as he tries out different ways of behaving in the situation.

Sometimes a child will feel uncomfortable when his parent tries to figure out something with him. This might be very different from what he is used to or expects. He might think the parent is trying to trick him in some way. Alternatively, his feelings of shame and worthlessness might be so close to the surface that this is triggered by the simple questions the parent is asking, leading to more challenging behaviour. In these cases it can be helpful to show the curiosity more indirectly. The parent might wonder aloud, talk to a partner within hearing of the child or even talk to the family pet. With the focus less on the child, he might be able to tolerate the curiosity a little more, staying with it long enough to experience someone wanting to understand him.

---

Kim remembers being at a foster parent's house, whilst the foster daughter, Rebecca, was very distressed. It had been a difficult day, with Rebecca being explosive, oppositional and very difficult to soothe.

As Kim arrived, Rebecca had barricaded herself in the bathroom and was refusing to come out. The foster parent had tried talking directly to her, and it only seemed to worsen Rebecca's behaviour. Kim sat down near to the bathroom whilst she thought what to do. Seeing an opportunity, the family dog came up to her, eager for some attention.

Kim started talking to the dog whilst stroking him behind his ears.
She commented that Rebecca had been having a really tough day. She
wondered why it had been difficult. She asked the dog if he thought
that maybe she was worried about something, maybe about the family
contact that was coming up.

She commented that it must be very hard worrying about these
things; perhaps Rebecca was feeling very tired. This went on for some
time, much to the dog's pleasure. Gradually, Rebecca calmed and slowly
she came out. She still did not enter into conversation, but she did allow
the foster parent to cuddle and soothe her.

---

Thus far we have been considering curiosity in relation to the challenges
a child is presenting. Curiosity becomes part of the way we discipline,
helping a child to modify his behaviour so that it is more acceptable in
the family and wider community.

Curiosity in parenting is a lot broader than this, however. We are
also curious about the positives we see with our child. This is easy
with an infant and small child. Their ever-growing wonderment in the
world gives us a sense of our own wonderment in them. We delight in
and enjoy a child who is revealing the world afresh to us.

As the child grows older, it is easy to lose this sense of wonderment.
We become concerned about teaching right from wrong. We are
worried that the child will not be liked or will not be successful when
away from us. These concerns and preoccupations can stifle curiosity.
We take the positives for granted and become more focused on the
negatives. The need for discipline and correction can push curiosity
into the back seat.

It is important therefore to find time to enjoy the child's achievements,
to encourage his interests and to delight in his being in the world. As
we do this, we are also becoming more aware of our child's inner life
– what he is proud of, what he gets pleasure in, what he would like to
achieve. As we are curious about these thoughts, feelings, wishes and
desires, we are also helping the child become more aware of them in
turn. The child, with our support, is developing a greater awareness of
himself. He will take more notice of his successes, and his self-esteem
will strengthen and grow.

A small word of warning, though: be sure to stay truly open to your
child. It is very easy to allow our own hopes and desires to influence us,

to lose sight of what our child enjoys and create an expectation for him to be something we would like him to be. The child might feel obliged to meet these expectations, setting aside, or not even developing, his own thoughts, feelings and interests in order to meet those of his parents. Other children might take a different stance. They might rebel against the desires of the parents, growing further and further away from them in an effort to preserve their own sense of who they are.

Unfortunately, in the process, they become more governed by opposing their parent than in truly discovering themselves.

Being curious with your child can be hard work. You have to think on your feet, having some guesses at hand to wonder about and all the time monitoring your child's responses to what you are saying. Often this is not a 'natural' thing to do in parenting; it was not the way we were raised. We tend to parent our children in line with our own experience. For many of us, this means expecting the child to do as he is told and toe the line.

It is hard not to nag or lecture, especially when feeling worried about the child. We hope to talk him out of doing something or talk him into doing something else. The child feels judged. He digs his heels in and nothing changes.

If a parent wants to bring more curiosity into her parenting, it will be helpful to get into a habit of being curious about the child. Think and wonder about the child, and why he is behaving as he is. Building in opportunities to reflect can be a challenge in a busy life, but quiet times for reflection can save time later when you are not getting into endless arguments with the child.

It is also helpful to have people to reflect with. This might be a partner, a friend, another parent or a trusted professional. Time for reflection is an essential part of parenting with PACE. It is with reflection that curiosity is fully awakened and understanding deepened.

These times of reflection will give you a head start when talking to your child. You will have some ideas in mind that you can use to help you both figure it out. Importantly, though, the habit of curiosity will prevent you from getting too attached to your own ideas. You will have a genuine interest in understanding the child in front of you.

## Parenting children who have little curiosity

Children can lack curiosity for a range of reasons. We saw in the previous chapter how trauma can shut down curiosity; children stay hypervigilant to the potential fear in their environment, and this leaves little room for curious exploration.

Additionally, their brains are wired for danger. This means that the more emotional, reactive parts of the brain are in the driving seat ready to deal with any threat, whilst the more rational, reflective parts are inactive. The children react without thought, and opportunities for reflection are few. Maintaining a curious, wondering stance for these children can be challenging. Rather than enter into curiosity with you, the child is likely to respond with anger, rage or withdrawal as your curiosity becomes a further source of threat.

The challenge in parenting is to hold on to your own curiosity whilst you help the child to feel safe. Maintain responsive, available parenting, linked with lots of routine and structure. As you remain calm when your child is hyperaroused, the child's arousal level will gradually reduce. This in turn will lead the child to feel safer, and, as safety increases, the child will be able to experience less arousal and more times when he feels calm. The thinking part of the brain will switch back on as the emotional brain comes off high alert. Now the child can enter into curiosity with you.

Curiosity can also shut down for a child when he experiences parents who are not curious themselves. If parents do not wonder, if they experience little interest in their child's internal experience, then the child too will not wonder. Awakening curiosity in a child is an interpersonal experience. The child needs a relationship within which he can experience the other's curiosity. This will lead to joint curiosity, providing the child with the ability to be curious in his own right. When parents show little interest in their child, he is less likely to be interested in turn.

Another major block to curiosity in children is the perpetual state of shame that they experience, which becomes linked to a sense of badness. When early relationships have been poor, children often experience themselves as unloveable. The lack of attuned relationships, ineffective discipline and little repair when relationships disrupt can all leave children experiencing excessive levels of shame.

When children have experienced this kind of disintegrative shame over and over, the shame itself becomes part of who they are; it is built into their core sense of self. The children experience themselves as bad, and they anticipate that others will not want to help them. They will not want to enter into a curious relationship; they especially won't want to explore themselves in the others' eyes. Why be curious about how others see you when you anticipate that they will be looking at you without love, or even with hatred?

The child therefore will not wonder why he does things; he will just assume that he is bad or naughty, or flawed in some other way. Curiosity, which might reveal the badness within, will feel dangerous. Better not to look, not to have confirmed what you already believe to be true. The child is not curious, because curiosity feels like a voyage towards his shame. The child has an assumption that he is bad, and the shame of this means that he does not want to think or wonder about this.

Rather than open himself up to relationship, he puts up a shield. As we considered in Chapter 4, the shield against shame consists of behaviours that defend the child from having to see the reaction of others. He denies or minimizes his behaviour, he blames others when things go wrong, and, if all else fails, he rages against himself and others in his world.

Whilst these behaviours defend the child from the horrible feelings associated with a sense of shame, they interfere with curiosity. The child does not explore the relationship, so he never discovers the interest of others. He becomes cut off from feelings of being loved, valued and supported. Children who quickly experience shame they cannot regulate will find it difficult to trust and will be over-sensitive to signs that they are not good enough, that they are bad.

As with trauma, children experiencing shame also need parents who can hold on to their curiosity. The behaviours of the child can easily draw the parent into angry, frustrated responses. They fear the consequence for the child who constantly lies and appears not to take responsibility for his behaviour. They feel judged by other people, that the child's behaviour is a reflection of their parenting. All these reactions move the parent further from curiosity and into reactive parenting. If the adults respond to the behaviours that the child is displaying without understanding the feeling of shame underneath, this will only strengthen the shield. The relationship becomes more disconnected, perpetuating the shame and rage that the child experiences and keeping the shield firmly in place.

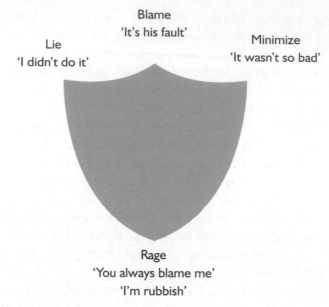

**Figure 7.1** The shield against shame

Curiosity can help the parent to look beyond the shame-fuelled behaviours, to the fear and distress that lies behind. When this is understood, the child will experience a greater sense of connection and will be more open to the relationship as a source of support and healing. He will risk lowering the shield and allow the parent to support him. With curiosity, acceptance and empathy, the child feels supported and at last his sense of shame can diminish. The shield weakens with the support that the adult gives him.

## Maintaining curiosity

If a parent provides a home without curiosity, then the relationship is less likely to grow.

Without understanding, we get caught up in a relationship that is unchanging: our child behaves and we react. Freud put this succinctly: 'A thing which has not been understood inevitably reappears; like an unlaid ghost, it cannot rest until the mystery has been solved and the spell broken.'[1] A parent cannot directly change a child's experience or the way it is communicated through language or behaviour. A parent can, however, change her own response to the child.

When Kim's response to the tree changed, the tree remained the same. Unlike the tree, a child enters a relationship with us; our experiences are intertwined. If a parent responds differently, over time she will notice the child change the way he behaves or communicates. A starting point for this is curiosity: the search for knowing what you do not know. Curiosity leads to a different understanding. You come to know the other's story more fully. With a different understanding comes a deeper acceptance of the child and his experience. The child experiences this increased understanding and acceptance through empathy and in turn feels more secure in your understanding.

One example of loss of curiosity is when we experience our child as evidence of our own sense of failure. We become driven by a narrative of failure that threatens to overwhelm us and we lose sight of our child's own story, the story that he is experiencing in front of us. This can be devastating for the child and the whole family.

---

Kim once knew a little boy, Jack, who had this impact on his adoptive family. Jack had been born to a mother who had quite severe mental health difficulties. She was preoccupied with her own needs and therefore could not meet the needs of her son.

There were fears that the child was being harmed in his mother's care and he was therefore removed into foster care. He settled into foster care relatively easily and presented no problems. At two years old, Jack is freed for adoption and he moves to his new home. Again, Jack settles easily and he gets on well with all family members. He appears to be a happy and sociable little boy.

For six months the parents enjoy their new son, constructing a story of success – the little boy that was meant to be with them. No one helps them to be curious about the impact of his previous experience. As they continue to offer Jack a close and loving relationship, Jack starts to change. He resists the relationships, especially with his mother. He becomes rejecting and self-reliant. He does not want to be fed, to be bathed, to be cared for. The most eloquent statement of this need for self-reliance is when Jack tries to change his own nappy.

His parents become frustrated, anxious, concerned. Their narrative of success is threatened as a new narrative about failure is emerging. It was going so well, now it isn't and so they must be failing in some way. The fear this creates shuts down curiosity as the family become trapped in a spiral of anxiety and worry. They cannot think beyond the fear that the adoption will fail, because the family are failing. Jack's fears increase as his parents react to their own fears and frustrations.

Kim's job is to help them get curiosity back, to consider alternative narratives related to the whole of Jack's experience. Perhaps 'mothers' remain a source of fear for him, linked to his early experience of a mother and his loss of past mothers. How long does it take for a little boy to experience the person taking care of him as a mother? What fears does this experience of being mothered evoke in him?

As the family enter into Jack's experience and begin to imagine what may underlie his fears, they are able to understand his need for control and self-reliance. They accept that for now it is too difficult for him to experience his need of this new mother, and they can empathize with his fear of close relationships. They continue to provide nurture for the needs that Jack does not express, but they are now attuned to the fears that this creates for him. Jack no longer experiences his parents as angry or frustrated but as continuing to be kind, caring and responsive. His fears start to reduce, and gradually he learns to trust in their availability and to dare to experience some dependence upon them. Jack has a successful adoption.

---

We hope this example illustrates how curiosity and the development of a deeper understanding of the other is supportive, accepting, empathic and ultimately strengthening of the relationship. The relationship can offer security and safety, and can support growth and exploration. Ultimately, it is a relationship that nurtures curiosity in the child. Freed from fears, he can explore the broadening world around him.

As Walt Disney so eloquently put it: 'We keep moving forward, opening up new doors, and doing new things, because we're curious… and curiosity keeps leading us down new paths.'[2]

## Parenting and socialization

Curiosity within an attitude of PACE is never more important than when we are trying to socialize our children. The importance of helping a child learn acceptable behaviour and reduce unacceptable behaviour is a powerful force in parenting, and one which can lead to the least reflective behaviours a parent can engage in.

When our children do something that we are proud of, when we are having fun or an enjoyable interaction, when we are guiding our child at his request, it is easy to stay reflective, to wonder about our child, to be curious about what he is doing and how he is experiencing. We remain non-judgemental as we look at the experience through our child's eyes, truly entering his experience with him.

At times of discipline, when we have a strong drive to stop our children behaving in a certain way, this sense of wonderment is quickly lost. We act instead on our own assumptions about the children's behaviours. They are doing it because they are naughty, selfish, deceitful.

We do not seek to understand the thoughts, feelings and intentions behind the behaviour. Instead, we judge the behaviour and in turn judge the child. As Dan has written in a previous book, we try to change the behaviour without understanding:

> It is within our parental socialization role that we often lose or diminish our curiosity. During discipline we often focus on our desire for certain behaviours, forgetting to wonder in response to the behaviours that are emerging. We lose sight of the fact that our child's behaviours, at least in part, are reflective of his efforts to develop a coherent narrative. Rather than join him in these efforts we often impose our own narrative on him.[3]

## Parenting and secondary trauma

Parenting children who are traumatized leaves a parent at increased risk of experiencing secondary trauma. Becoming traumatized by the child's trauma will lead to reduced curiosity and a more reactive response to the child. Sometimes the parent will become very active, frenetically trying to stave off the sense of panic being experienced. Other parents will become more withdrawn, not able to do the usual daily routines. Either way, the parent loses touch with her curiosity and becomes disconnected from the child, leaving him isolated and unsupported.

It is not always easy to notice this process happening to you. When a parent is experiencing parenting as traumatic, she tends to become more rigid and inflexible. Suddenly, the unimportant jobs must be completed, leaving no time to do other things. Thinking shuts down as she tries harder and harder to feel in control. More doing and less thinking means the parent becomes increasingly inefficient, and out of touch with herself, her child or others around her. This is when a parent needs good friends and family to support her. Others will notice what is happening more quickly than she will. Maintaining a good support network, time for yourself and time to relax are at their most important during times of increased stress, even though it is at these same times that you will feel you have least time for these things.

---

Margaret had been caring for Sam for three years, following two previous failed foster placements. He was now 12 years old, on the verge of exclusion from school and with a history of absconding. Following an early history of abuse and neglect, Sam was now rigidly controlling of everyone and everything.

He made a battle out of everything, arguing black is white, and night is day. On top of this, Sam stole compulsively and would lie without compunction. Margaret, who prided herself on her ability to turn around difficult boys, was losing heart. She did not feel that she had reached Sam at all, and he appeared not to trust her now any more than he did when he first arrived on her doorstep.

When Margaret's adult son, Gary, came home to visit, he was worried. Margaret looked tired and defeated. She was busily trying to sort out her paperwork, getting all her records up to date, but seemed to be going around in circles with it. She was fretting about finishing this and starting the evening meal. Gary suggested a takeaway and she snapped at him.

How would they eat healthily if she kept sending out for takeaways? She had implemented a complicated rewards and consequences strategy to try to bring Sam's stealing under control, but the consequences were piling up, and she could not see where to go with it. Gary tentatively suggested that she talk to her fostering social worker, but again this met with an angry retort – how did she have time for more meetings?

The next day Gary made one or two phone calls. He called his sister, Shelley, and the social worker. He arranged a respite weekend for Sam and recruited his sister to invite Margaret to her house for the same weekend. At first Margaret resisted, but Gary and Shelley united were too big a combination.

The weekend went well. They gave her time to rest and relax, and then sat down to talk to her. Quietly and calmly, they told Margaret what they were noticing and how concerned they were for her. Margaret was tearful; she agreed that caring for Sam was getting on top of her. The three of them drew up a plan. First on the list was to arrange a multi-agency meeting. Things were not working and she needed a new way forward with extra support. She promised Gary and Shelley that a priority would be to get some regular respite.

---

Margaret was lucky in having supportive children who were prepared to act on her behalf. This is not always easy, especially if you are used to being independent, and not comfortable in eliciting support from others. Needing support can feel like failure, not living up to others' expectations of you. This could not be further from the truth, however. Support is a lifeline, essential if you are caring for a traumatized child. Helping a child feel secure and surviving secondary trauma depends upon the relationships you have, almost as much as the skill you bring to your parenting.

Without support from trusted friends and relatives, a parent is unlikely even to recognize the trauma she is experiencing, never mind take steps to recover from it. Relationships can provide the sense of safety needed to gradually overcome the trauma. As curiosity returns, the parent will be able to take up the parenting challenge again.

## In conclusion

Curiosity increases understanding, acceptance and empathy. It leads to a more joyful and playful relationship, one in which the child experiences connection as the parent responds in tune with the child's inner experience.

Maintaining curiosity can be challenged by the sometimes bewildering and difficult behaviour that a child can display. This can trigger complex, non-reflective thoughts, feelings and behaviour in turn.

Holding on to reflection can maintain curiosity and provide a way of developing alternative stories, deepening understanding. You can't directly change the child's experience, but you can respond differently. This provides the child with a different experience, which can lead to different responses in turn. Curiosity is central to PACE, opening your eyes to new perspectives and new responses.

---

### STORY

### The Boy with All the Knowledge of the World in His Head

Once upon a time there was a boy. His name was David and he was very special. He was very special because he remembered everything he was ever told. This made him very clever. As time went by, he heard more and more,

16

and he stored more and more knowledge in his head. Soon he had all the knowledge of the world in his head.

Now David was a kind boy and he liked to help people. He liked to help his friends with their problems. Sometimes he helped them with their homework and sometimes he helped them with their hobbies. David enjoyed helping his friends. He enjoyed sorting out their problems and seeing how happy this made them.

David also liked to help his sister. This was a little trickier. Sometimes she let him help her, but other times she didn't like it. She wanted to be clever too, and she didn't like to think that David could do things that she couldn't do. She tried very hard to do things on her own and got very cross when David tried to help. Sometimes David got cross back because he wanted to help her and he was upset that she wouldn't let him.

David also liked to help his mum and dad. They were pleased when he helped them, but sometimes they wanted to help David in return. This was a problem. David knew he had all this knowledge in his head, but they didn't understand this. They thought that David needed help with all sorts of things that he didn't need help with. Sometimes David got cross with them. They would try to talk to him, but David found it very difficult to explain that he didn't need help because he had all the knowledge of the world in his head.

One day, David was at school when his friend Simon needed some help. He had a big problem and, knowing that David was very clever at sorting out problems, he brought it to David. Now, this problem was a very big one, and David went through all the knowledge in his head so that he could help his friend. He searched and searched for an answer, but despite all this knowledge he couldn't find one. This made David very anxious. This was difficult. He didn't like feeling anxious. Feeling anxious made him feel strange. He tried very hard not to feel anxious. So when Simon kept asking him for an answer, David could feel the anxiety building up. He did not like this at all and he got very angry with Simon. He shouted at him and Simon ran away.

Now David felt sad as well. Feeling sad was as bad as feeling anxious. If you feel sad, all the knowledge in your head can't help you. David worked very hard not to feel sad. He wanted Simon to come back, but he couldn't explain this to him. Instead, he turned his back and thought to himself that it was Simon's fault. Simon should not have a problem that all the knowledge of the world could not solve.

David was feeling very hot and bothered after school that day. He went home and was very cross with his mum. He would not have his snack and he would not play nicely with the other children. That night he had a judo lesson. Now, David liked his judo class. He liked to feel in control of all the moves and he was working hard for his next belt. Tonight, however, he did not feel like going. He was working very hard not to feel anxious or sad and he was feeling tired. David's mum was very clever. She could see that David was struggling with something big and she thought that going to his judo class might help. She encouraged him to go and even gave him a lift down to the hall.

David did feel better doing the judo moves. He focused very hard and he found that he wasn't feeling so cross and bothered. During the break, the judo teacher came up to talk to David. He had noticed how focused he was and he guessed that something was troubling him. David was feeling a bit more relaxed now and he found himself telling his teacher about the big problem that he could not solve and about his friend running away from him. He told him how cross he was when this made him sad and anxious. He thought that the teacher might laugh at him when he told him all this, but he didn't. He looked very thoughtful for a while and then he said that sometimes problems are bigger than all the knowledge of the world. Sometimes problems don't have easy answers, and you just need to be there for your friend.

David found tears in his eyes; he hurriedly fought them back so that they didn't show. How could he be there for his friend when he didn't have an answer? How could he be there when it made him feel anxious or sad? David's teacher helped him to see that although he was very clever, he wouldn't always have the answers. Sometimes he might need someone to help him. David thought about his mum and dad. They were sometimes sad, and Dad was very anxious when Uncle Bill was poorly. Maybe his mum and dad could help him when he felt sad and anxious. Then he would be able to help his friend.

That night David had a long talk with mum and dad. He told them about his friend. They told him how sad they were, thinking about him trying to deal with this all alone. They knew his life had been hard, and sometimes it felt as if parents were no help at all. David felt tears prickling the back of his eyes. For the first time in his whole life, he did not fight them but let them fall. Mum hugged him tight and even had a few tears herself. David suddenly felt safe and warm and cosy. He snuggled in tighter, enjoying the feeling that he did not have to solve problems all by himself. David discovered that tears were not all bad, and being comforted by your mum and dad was close to being the best feeling in the world. The boy with all the knowledge of the world in his head had learnt something brand new.

David discovered that there were more ways than one of being clever. He also learnt that having feelings was not weakness, and that feeling sad and anxious helped you notice when you needed some support from others. His mum and dad understood about some things even better than he did, and they could be there for him, to comfort and support him and even to help him when there were no answers. David was glad that he wasn't all alone, that he had his mum and dad and his judo teacher to help him.

The next day at school David found his friend. He told him he was sorry that he had been angry with him. He explained that he didn't have an answer to his problem but he would try and be there for him. He told him that he wasn't good at feeling sad or anxious but that he was working on it. David's friend gave him a big smile and said, 'It looks like we both have big problems; maybe we can help each other.' David smiled back. Even with all the knowledge of the world in his head, he still needed some help from other people. David was very clever, but sometimes that just wasn't enough.

# PART IV

# Empathy

# 8

# Empathy

## Connecting in the Emotional World

In this chapter we meet the last, but by no means the least, of the four components of PACE. This is empathy, the ability to feel with someone. Empathy is the glue that holds PACE together.

We begin our approach with empathy. Empathy for another motivates us to relate to that person. Without some degree of empathy we would not start to be playful, accepting or curious. Empathy and curiosity are partners; like identical twins, each expresses a different side of the same coin. Without curiosity, a genuine desire to know about, we would not seek to understand ourselves or others, but without empathy this curiosity will not open relationship up to us.

Empathy is also there at the endpoint. Without empathy playfulness, acceptance and curiosity would be in vain. Empathy connects us to the child through love and affection, a desire to protect, a motivation to help the child grow and, when needed, heal. Empathy communicates our playfulness, acceptance and curiosity. It is non-judgemental, allowing us to enter into the intersubjective relationship so important to the child's emotional growth and well-being. Resilience grows out of empathy. Playfulness, acceptance and curiosity would all be lost without empathy.

In this chapter we will explore the meaning and development of empathy and discover the power that is empathy and the devastating impact when empathy is lost.

## What is empathy?

Hermione looked at the pair of them with an almost pitying expression on her face.

'Don't you understand how Cho's feeling at the moment?' she asked.

'No,' said Harry and Ron together. Hermione sighed and laid down her quill.

'Well, obviously, she's feeling very sad, because she liked Cedric and now she likes Harry, and she can't work out who she likes best. Then she'll be feeling guilty, thinking it's an insult to Cedric's memory to be kissing Harry at all, and she'll be worrying about what everyone else might say about her if she starts going out with Harry. And she probably can't work out what her feelings towards Harry are, anyway, because he was the one who was with Cedric when Cedric died, so that's all very mixed up and painful. Oh, and she's afraid she's going to be thrown off the Ravenclaw Quidditch team because she's been flying so badly.'

A slightly stunned silence greeted the end of this speech, then Ron said, 'One person can't feel all that at once, they'd explode.'[1]

As the young people featured in the Harry Potter stories were finding out, humans are emotional beings, capable of a complex mixture of a large range of feelings. The ability to recognize and respond to these feelings is what empathy is all about.

Simon Baron-Cohen, professor of psychology and psychiatry in Cambridge, England, is an expert on understanding empathy and individuals who lack empathy for whatever reason. He identifies empathy as 'our ability to identify what someone else is thinking or feeling, and to respond to their thoughts and feelings with an appropriate emotion'.[2]

Empathy rests on the ability to sympathize, to feel for someone, to be emotionally moved by their experience; but empathy is more than this. Whereas sympathy is an innate response to the expression of emotion from another, empathy is an act of will, as we strive to get to know and understand the other. We actively build on our sympathy to move beyond 'feeling for' to also 'feeling with' the other person. Empathy is about shared emotion. We do more than observe; we enter into the emotional world of the other person. It is this ability to see what is hidden, to experience another's inner experience, that makes us a social species capable of mutually influencing each other.

As Hermione, Ron and Harry were also discovering, empathy is an act of imagination – an imaginative leap that Ron was struggling to make, as Hermione asked him to experience what it is like to be in another's shoes, or, more accurately, to understand the mind of another person.

Empathy is at the heart of what makes us social. Through empathy we can build relationships with others, giving us a sense of connection. This ability to empathize rests on an ability to understand others. When we express empathy for another, we are expressing our understanding of them. This in turn communicates to them that they are understandable. This person at least can understand me.

Simon Baron-Cohen helpfully describes empathy in terms of the way that we attend to ourselves and others.[3] A single-minded focus of attention does not lend itself to empathy, but when we move to doubled-minded focusing, empathy occurs. In double-minded attention we keep in mind someone else's mind at the same time as we think about our own mind. In other words, we can hold in mind our own current thoughts and perceptions as well as those of another.

Baron-Cohen also describes an empathy spectrum. All of us lie somewhere on this spectrum as a consequence of our genetics and our experience. The majority of people lie in the middle, experiencing a moderate degree of empathy. Research suggests that, statistically, women lie a little higher up the spectrum than men, a fact that J. K. Rowling was alluding to as she depicts Hermione's superior understanding of the feelings of another when compared to Harry and Ron.

Clearly, however, behind the statistics there are large individual differences, with some men showing high levels of empathy and some women low levels. A smaller group of people lie at the high end of the spectrum, being super-sensitive to the experiences of others. A similarly small group lie at the low end of the spectrum, struggling to empathize with others.

At the extreme end of low empathy we place people who have conditions that lead to difficulties with empathy – people on the autistic spectrum, for example. This is a genetic condition that results in compromised development of theory of mind.

Somewhere between three and four years of age, children discover the mind. They learn that they have an inner life of thoughts, feelings, beliefs and desires. They also learn that others have minds as well, and that these minds might have thoughts, feelings, beliefs and desires different from their own.

Psychologists use a particular experiment to explore theory of mind development. This is the 'Smarties task' (Smarties are similar to M&M's). A child is shown a tube of Smarties and asked what she believes to be inside. The knowledgeable youngster, especially when it comes to sweets, will confidently assert that there are Smarties inside the tube. The researcher then reveals that there are actually pencils inside rather than Smarties.

The child is then asked about her original belief. When she first saw the tube what did she believe was inside? In other words, can the child recover her original belief now that she knows what is really inside? The younger child will not be able to do this. She will state that she believed pencils to be inside. An older child will have no problem knowing that she originally believed Smarties to be inside the tube.

Individuals on the autistic spectrum struggle with this task at all ages. They find it difficult to understand the shift of perspectives before and after concealed knowledge is revealed. They struggle even more to understand the perspective of another person.

They might not know that a person entering the room would have a different belief to themselves about the now revealed contents of the Smarties tube. This makes it difficult for these people to empathize with others. The social world is a complex maze that they find hard to navigate. Often they cope by isolating themselves, hiding behind their better abilities to systematize, to see patterns in things. They are often good with computers or things that have a logic to them, preferring the predictability that these things bring compared to the unpredictability of people. The most able people with autism will use these superior abilities to make some sense of the social world and therefore to find some way of relating to others.

The other group of individuals with compromised empathy development are those described as having a disorder of personality. A combination of early environmental experience, usually stemming from early parenting, combines with a genetic sensitivity to lead to particular developmental difficulties, compromising emotional development. We will explore these difficulties in more depth later in the chapter.

There are two related parts to empathy:

1.  A cognitive part. This involves recognition, the understanding of what we feel and think and why we react as we do. This ability in turn allows us to understand people, to make sense of another's experience. As illustrated in the theory of mind experiment, it relies on our ability to understand the perspective of another, to stand in their shoes, so that we can move beyond experience to understanding. This is the part that is most difficult for people with autism.

2.  An emotional part. This is the experience part of empathy, where our responses lie. It is where our emotional reactions to people register. We feel the feelings of another person and thus understand, at least emotionally, what they are feeling. Those with certain disorders of personality – psychopathic difficulties, for example – are compromized in this part. They use their cognitive, perspective-taking abilities to get into the mind of another person, to understand what makes them tick. They then employ this knowledge to use the person to meet their own ends, unimpressed by the emotional impact this may have on the other.

Empathy therefore is deeply connected to our relationship with other people. More than relating to them, it determines how we relate. As illustrated in the example of people with psychopathic tendencies, without empathy people would just be objects, no different to the range of objects we encounter in our world. When a person is an object, his function is to meet the needs of the self. Only the needs of the one are met. For example, a person might be a sexual object, an object of scorn, an object of physical abuse or a money object.

Empathy allows us to experience others as subjects, with their own thoughts and feelings. People become a special type of 'thing' – a subject, capable of independent thoughts and feelings. When a person is a subject, his needs are seen and valued, on a par with the needs of the self. The two subjects then have a relationship whose goal is to meet the needs of both members, rather than just one of them.

Writing in the early 1920s, theologian Martin Buber described being in relationship with another person where the other is different from us and we are influenced by the uniqueness of that person.[4] Buber calls this the 'I–Thou' relationship. He differentiates this from an 'I–It' relationship where the other person is an object to us. In the 'I–It' relationship we use the other for his value in our life but do not discover what is unique about him and are not influenced by his presence in our life. Other than in a utilitarian way, he does not have an impact on us. Empathy is one feature of an 'I–Thou' relationship, where the other's experience does have an impact on us. We are in his shoes and we are affected by the act of truly being with him.

The ability to empathize conveys a lot of advantages for the individual, all related in some way to successful relationships. Baron-Cohen[5] suggests that empathy provides us with the ability to understand another person and the perspectives that he holds. This can aid negotiation and problem solving as the understanding of self and others facilitates the search for solutions to incompatible goals.

Similarly, it helps a person to figure out why another person acts as he does or to anticipate how that person may respond to an action of your own. In conveying empathy to another, we allow that person to experience being valued by us. He experiences his thoughts and feelings as being heard, acknowledged and respected.


## Empathic understanding

Empathy connects us with the experience that underlies behaviour. What inner wishes, thoughts, feelings, desires or beliefs have led the person to behave in a particular way?

Understanding and accepting these internal motivations can lead to deeper empathy for the person, reflecting a deeper and more connected relationship. The empathy reflects that we 'get it'; we understand and accept the internal world of the other person and we are prepared to enter that internal world and share it with him in some way.

Empathy helps us to stay with the feelings for longer, avoiding a precipitous desire to reassure, to make things better or to solve the problem. We instead share the experience, leading to a deeper relationship within which we might eventually be able to help, built on a more solid foundation of understanding and acceptance.

---

Kim was working with an eight-year-old boy, Peter, who was struggling in his relationship with his adoptive mother. Following an early experience of neglect and finally abandonment by his biological mother, and the planned-for but still painful loss of his temporary foster family, he was now finding it hard to believe that this mother would not one day be lost to him too. He protected against this fear by not letting her get too close to him. He was very rejecting of her attempts to nurture him, and very punishing of her when she provided a boundary to his behaviour.

One difficult day Peter refused to leave school to come home. Peter did not know why this had occurred. He felt cross with her, but it was difficult for him to make sense of this. In his early years, no one had helped him to make sense of his infantile experience, and now his inner beliefs, wishes and desires were a mystery to him.

Within the session Kim needed to help Peter understand his experience. Much as a parent does with her very young child, Kim needed to give him some words to match to this experience. This means that she could not stay at the surface level of behaviour. Giving him strategies to manage feeling anger and helping Mum to provide some discipline for his oppositional behaviour would not have got them very far. Peter would have felt shame about his experience. He would have shut off, as he expressed this complex emotion through blame and rage.

Instead, Kim explored with him the meaning of this behaviour. He told her that his mum had not let him take his trading cards to school. The teacher had recently banned these cards in her class because they were a source of conflict for the children. Kim helped Peter to develop a story about this experience.

They explored together his belief about why his mum had prevented him from taking the cards to school and his experience that she was a cross mum who didn't like him very much. Kim expressed sadness about this, how hard it must be to believe your mum does not like you and therefore is cross with you. Kim helped him to communicate these fears to his mum, talking for him when he could not find the words, talking about him when the experience was too intense.

This lovely mother was able to hear and feel compassion for her son. She did not try to persuade him of her love for him, that she was not a cross mum. This would have shut down his experience, only serving to show him that his mum did not yet get it. Instead, she stayed with his experience, empathizing with his beliefs about not being good enough to be liked. As Peter experienced this empathy, somewhere deep in his brain the 'empathy circuit' was coming alive. Peter was able to experience some empathy for himself, and this held the promise of further emotional development. The inner world of self, and eventually of others, would come alive for Peter.

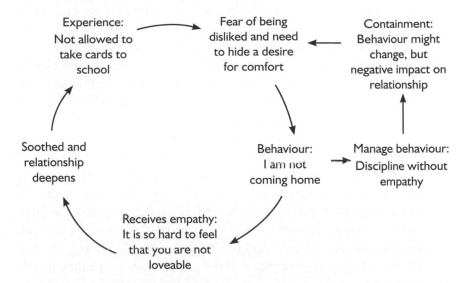

**Figure 8.1** The empathy–connection cycle

The circle in Figure 8.1 provides a visual illustration of what Peter will have been experiencing with his mother. This experience of empathy will help Peter to understand that his mother's motives are good: she wants to help him with a problem at school; she is sensitive to his distress.

To the right of the circle is the side alley of behavioural management. If discipline was used but with no empathy, the behaviour might change but the deeper connection between son and mother would not be made. In fact, when behaviour management works without empathy, this can harm the relationship; the child might comply out of a fear of the consequence or in order to achieve a consequence, but he will resent the parent's use of power to enforce the behavioural expectation.

## Empathy and love: How does empathy develop?

'We survive because we can love. And we love because we can empathize – that is, stand in another's shoes and care about what it feels like to be them' (Szalavitz and Perry).[6]

We are all born predisposed to care for others; this is part of our genetic heritage. However, for this potential to be realized we need relationship. It is out of love and connection that empathy develops. Through relationship, a child develops a curiosity about the minds of others and a capacity to experience and respond to emotional experience via empathy.

Szalavitz and Perry, a journalist and neuroscientist, joined forces to explore empathy. In *Born for Love* they highlight the absolute imperative of relationship for empathy to develop: 'Although we are genetically predisposed to care for others, the development of empathy requires a lifelong process of relational interaction.'[7]

This need for relationship is further explored in the seminal book *Ghosts from the Nursery*. The authors, American therapists Robin Karr-Morse and Meredith Wiley, are interested in the development of violence and aggression within society. The importance of relationship and connection for a healthy and peaceful society is clear. In particular, the primary bond between infant and parent is seen as critical: '...if established in a normal and healthy manner, [this bond] lays the foundation for empathy, or the sense of connection with other people as part of one's self.'[8]

Empathy develops from early innate abilities, the building blocks on which experience is written. Thus, infants are born able to experience 'emotional contagion'. This can be witnessed very easily when a number of infants are in the same room. If one of them starts to cry, the others will quickly pick up the mood and join in. This emotional contagion is part of the innate connection to the social world so essential for human young to survive. We can observe this connection when we interact with young babies. Who can resist, for example, catching a baby's attention and engaging them in a mutual tongue-poking game? The adult thrusts his tongue out, waits a moment and watches the baby imitate the same action; the magic of connection is played out in this simple game. A little older, and we delight in teaching the child to 'wave bye-bye'. We wave to the baby and are rewarded by a reciprocal wave.

By the age of 14 months, toddlers can show clear signs of empathy. This coincides with an emerging development of self and the ability to discriminate self from other. At first the toddler is unable to recognize that other people's feelings are different from her own, but with maturity the young child starts to develop the ability to understand the perspective of another and to start to respond to this. The two-year-old, for example, might recognize distress in another, and be able to offer some form of comfort – patting, hugging or maybe offering a toy. The perspective taking is rudimentary, however, and the young child is still dominated by his own experience of the world. Asked to choose a present for his father,

Kim's two-year-old son, Alex, thought a yellow fluffy duck to be the perfect present – a choice very much dominated by his own perspective rather than an understanding of the desires of his father!

Perspective taking becomes more sophisticated during the preschool years, allowing children to begin to leave their egocentricity behind and to truly respond empathically to another. At three years, Alex knew that Daddy would like a music CD for his birthday. Clinical psychologist and researcher Peter Fonagy and his colleagues, working in London, have explored the way that children learn the skill that Alex was demonstrating: to mentalize, to imagine what another person might be thinking and feeling and to make predictions based on this imagining.[9]

Early in life, therefore, children begin to mentalize their caregiver's mind. They will, however, only do this if it is safe to do so. If the mentalization involves a perception that the caregiver hates the child, or wishes she did not exist in some way, the child will experience fear or terror. These mentalizations are so uncomfortable to live with that the child switches off her developing mentalizing ability and an important foundation for empathy is lost to her.

The development of theory of mind and the ability to perspective-take and mentalize underlie the development of empathy. This development is not just maturational. Without healthy relationship experience, children will be vulnerable to switching off from understanding emotional experience, and empathy will be compromised. Szalavitz and Perry have written:

> …while we are born for love, we need to receive it in certain, specific ways early in life to benefit most from its mercy. We need to practice love as we grow through different social experiences to best be able to give it back in abundance.[10]

Consistent and sensitive interactions between a parent and child provide a foundation for healthy empathy development. This has been explored in Chapter 1. Securely attached infants develop better empathy, linked to a better developed theory of mind. The child has the experience of a parent able to accurately assess her needs, and respond to these so as to soothe over-arousal and stimulate under-arousal. In the process, the parent provides a mirror to the child, reflecting her own experience back to her in a way that helps the child to organize her own internal experience. The child experiences comfort from the parent and develops trust in him.

Relationship experience that fails to help the child understand the world around her will be a relationship that fails to nurture the development of a strong theory of mind, and perspective taking will be limited.

Alongside these emerging abilities to understand and relate to the perspectives of others is the developing experience of shame and guilt. This was explored in Chapter 4, but its importance in the development of empathy means it is worth revisiting here. As we previously considered, the development of shame and guilt is heavily influenced by the relationship the parent offers to the child. In fact, an emerging experience of shame helps the parent to teach the child what is acceptable and unacceptable in her behaviour.

It is no accident that the emotion of shame first emerges in development as a child becomes more mobile. The child becomes open to a range of behaviours, not all of which will lead to appreciation by the parent. Putting a hand on a hot stove, running into a road, treating the family pet roughly are all behaviours a parent will want to discourage or prevent. At these times the parent abruptly breaks his emotional connection or attunement with the child in order to correct or stop her behaviour. The child experiences this break as shame, a 'teaching emotion': do this and it will feel unpleasant, do that and enjoy the emotional experience. The child learns to avoid the unpleasant and behave in ways that feel good.

This is relationship-focused, not just about behaviour. The sensitive parent ends this interaction with reassurance that this experience between them has not harmed his feelings for his child. He still loves her, and no behaviour will end this love for her. Relationship repair as demonstrated through unconditional love leads to a reduction of shame and attunement is re-established.

This healthy development of shame also paves the way for the development of guilt, a sense of wrong and a desire to put things right. Remember the single- and double-minded attention we met earlier? Shame is single-minded; its focus is on the self and how badly we feel. In guilt we can hold double-minded attention: 'I feel bad and I want to make things better with you.' Without the sensitive support of a parent, the child remains single-minded, caught in shame. The experience of shame linked to re-attunement allows the double-minded attention associated with empathy. The child can experience guilt focused on the other.

Empathy develops poorly when a child experiences pervasive shame and cannot develop a strong and consistent sense of guilt when she hurts someone else.[11] Guilt is positively correlated with empathy, whereas shame is negatively correlated. Pervasive shame is commonly associated with a child's experience of ongoing abuse and neglect in her relationships with her parents. The child is seldom in the mind and heart of her parent and thus he consistently fails to meet her needs. With shame, the child's focus is primarily on protecting herself, often leading to the denial of her behaviours. She has little energy for empathy for others and the healthy experience of guilt if she hurts someone.

## Empathy and brain development

Empathy is not just about behaviour; it is a physiological process. A brief excursion into the world of brain development will demonstrate the sophistication of the development of empathy, how deeply empathy is wired into our brain and nervous system, and how empathy represents the linking of physiology between one person and another.

Empathy begets empathy. When the regions of your brain experience and express empathy for your child, this activates and develops similar regions in her brain. This enables your child to experience your empathy and prepares her brain to experience empathy for others, including her own children in the future.

Empathy requires the activation of three regions of the brain. The insula, which is crucial for emotional-cognitive integration and attunement with others, takes input from the visceral system. This nervous system connects the brain with the heart, lungs and stomach. Your heart, lungs and stomach resonate with your child's bodily expressions, and this activates the anterior cingulate cortex, providing a bridge between the emotional and the cognitive, allowing empathy. It also activates the prefrontal cortex. This allows the integration of the more cognitive regions of the brain with emotion, planning and problem solving. This allows attachment and the development of conscience. These three brain regions then stimulate special VEN cells, crucial for social-emotional communications. These VEN cells are only present in certain mammals and are closely linked to the experience of empathy. It is these that can create a heightened awareness in you of the emotions of your child.

Alongside these cells are mirror neurons. These are crucial for bodily attunement as they are in synchrony with others. They originate in the areas of the cortex associated with perceptual motor skills, the ability to integrate sensory input with motor abilities. This influences the prefrontal cortex to resonate with and make sense of your child's non-verbal communications. Together, these brain regions allow you to have a conscious awareness of your child's emotional state and the meaning of this state. As you express this awareness through your own matched non-verbal expressions, your child senses that you 'get it' and that she is safe with your non-judgemental awareness and empathic response.

Thus, experiencing empathy requires the activation of various regions of the brain that are involved in both emotions and cognition. This explains why empathy contains an understanding, 'making sense' component and an emotional 'feeling with' component.

Since expressing and being receptive to empathy require the resonating activity of similar regions in both your brain and your child's brain, this also explains why her experience of your empathy will facilitate her readiness to experience empathy for others.

Paul Gilbert, a clinical psychologist from England and author of a range of books related to empathy, explores the development of the innate capacity for empathy that lies within us all.[12] He also emphasizes the importance of early experience if the child is to move from a latent capacity to the true experience of receiving and giving empathy.

Children, he says, need kindness, gentleness, warmth and compassion. With this experience, the stress hormone level in the brain will reduce and the brain can develop the capacity for kindness and empathy. The experience of safety from being loved and cared for allows the brain to develop oriented to an expression of kindness for self and others. Conversely, being raised in conditions of danger has a different effect on the brain. Now, the stress hormones are used to organize the brain to deal with threat via defensive strategies. The child experiences anxiety and learns to be aggressive as a protective mechanism.

American researcher Allan Schore is arguably the neuroscientist who has done most to help us understand the relationship between the parent–child relationship and the child's developing brain.[13] He highlights the importance, particularly, of the development of the orbital prefrontal area of the right brain. Imagine moving back into the brain through your right eye and you will arrive at this important area.

Whilst there are several interconnected areas of the brain involved in empathy, it is here that the birthplace of empathy can be found. This area of the brain has a neurochemistry and a structure that is receptive to and ultimately programmed by the emotion-based interactions between the baby and caregiver.

As mentioned earlier, another important aspect of the way the brain works in response to empathy is mirror neurons. These are not solely responsible for empathy but are an important part of the way the brain is built to respond empathically. Mirror neurons in the brain fire when we perform an action. These same neurons also fire when we see another perform an action, hence the term mirror neurons. You have probably experienced this when you have observed another person yawning. It is very hard to observe this action without yawning yourself. These neurons act as a mirror to what we observe, firing connections in our brain and thus allowing us to understand the experience of another through such observation. We do not need to experience something ourselves in order to understand an experience. These neurons show us what it is like to experience another's experience, thus equipping us with the necessary understanding to demonstrate empathy towards them. In this way we can literally experience what another person feels.

Whilst these neurons have an important part to play in the experience of empathy, they do not constitute empathy themselves. The response is a very instinctive one, hard to switch off even when you know an experience being observed isn't real. For example, when watching a simple computer game being played by a young person on a Wii console, Kim experienced this phenomenon. The game involved controlling an avatar to head footballs as they came towards it. Every so often an object appeared that had to be avoided rather than headed – a shoe, for example. Each time one of these objects hit the head of the avatar, Kim winced. She could not switch off the response governed by the mirror neurons even though she knew what she was watching was essentially a cartoon.

Whilst this experience is instinctive, to truly experience empathy for another involves a connection with that other person. The ability to make these connections, within which we experience empathy, comes out of our early relationship experience. Our brains are ready for empathy, but we need experience of attuned, responsive relationships with others, offering us the experience of receiving empathy, before we

can truly develop our capacity to empathize with the inner experience
of another person.

## Empathy and cruelty

Empathy is what makes communities thrive. With empathy, the people
living and being together experience interdependence and this, Szalavitz
and Perry suggest, leads to healthy individuals and the promotion of
creativity, intelligence and productivity.[14] Empathy provides us with
insight and self-awareness, and allows us to experience guilt and anxiety.
These combined lead us not only to understand our self and others but
also to want to respond in ways that help us and them to feel better.

The opposite of empathy might be said to be cruelty. Simon Baron-
Cohen has developed a theory of cruelty based on the idea that cruelty
represents loss of empathy.[15] A lack of empathy leads to dysfunction,
inhumanity and brutality.

Sometimes, however, the difference between empathy and cruelty is
not clear-cut. Imagine this scene. A mother visits her adult son's bedside
and injects him with a fatal dose of heroin. A clear case of cruelty?
Maybe, but if we look a bit more deeply behind this scene, we can
understand the complexity of the relationship between empathy and
cruelty. This real-life example was the basis of a radio drama broadcast
by the BBC in May 2011.[16] The son has sustained a brain injury in
a car accident and is now in a coma. He has had brain surgery to
relieve swelling on the brain and is now stable. Medics are holding out
hope for at least a partial recovery, and the young man's father and
son are holding on to this lifeline. His mother, however, sees this as a
noose rather than a lifeline. She imagines a future life of disability and
suffering. Convinced that her son is in dreadful pain and with no hope
for the future, she seeks to end his life.

So is this empathy or cruelty? Again, even with the additional
information, this is a difficult judgement to make. There are so many
shades of grey here. Is it empathic to relieve suffering or does it just
deny the individual a chance for survival? Is she motivated by her
empathy for her son's suffering and a desire to end this for him? Does
she fear a lifetime of dependency and need as her son, successfully
brought up to independence, becomes a burden to her?

In the play, this inner experience of beliefs, wishes, desires and
motives is not explored by society. The crime is viewed at face value

and the mother is imprisoned for murder. It is difficult to grapple with the complexity of human relationships, to explore what is cruel and what is empathic. Instead, our punishments mean we take the easy option, offering black-and-white solutions to problems that contain so many shades of grey.

There are different ways we might lose or fail to develop empathy. A transient loss of empathy can occur, for example, when a person is experiencing increased stress. More permanent lack of empathy can be seen in people who have developed personality disorders, a combination of vulnerable genetics combined with difficult early experience. In particular, early developmental trauma can lead to a problem with empathy development, as is seen in individuals diagnosed with personality disorders such as borderline personality disorder and narcissism.

Probably the most startling lack of empathy when we consider cruelty is in the psychopathic personality disorder. Research has revealed that psychopathic traits result from the interaction between structural and genetic difficulties, affecting brain development and capacity for empathy, combined with poor environmental experience early in life. These are therefore seen as risk factors for the development of psychopathy.

The importance of environment in the realization of such risk factors is strikingly illustrated by the research of neuroscientist Dr Jim Fallon at the University of California. His story was featured on a *Horizon* programme broadcast by the BBC in 2011.[17] In the course of his research he explored his own brain scan and genetic profile. He discovered that he has the same risk factors as found in studies of people displaying psychopathic behaviours, a heritage which might explain the high number of murderers in one line of his family! He attributes the fact that he hasn't committed murderous acts to his happy childhood.

Individuals with psychopathic traits do have elements of empathy – for example, they can perspective-take, based on a theory of mind. This means that they can mentally place themselves in the minds of other people and predict their behaviour. What they lack, however, is a capacity to connect emotionally with the other person. They don't experience compassion or caring for the other: what Szalavitz and Perry describe as the core of empathy.[18] They cannot feel for the person and therefore cannot experience empathy, the ability to feel with them. These individuals use their ability to understand the other in order to manipulate them, rather than to connect with them. Psychopathic individuals are aware that they are hurting others but are not touched by this awareness.

An example in literature of such psychopathic traits can be seen in the character of Emily Brontë's Heathcliff in the novel *Wuthering Heights*.[19] Heathcliff is the adopted child with a hidden past, presumably of cruelty and neglect. His passion for his stepsister Cathy is the central love story of the book, but in his expression of this love we witness extreme cruelty. Most telling is Heathcliff's marriage to and subsequent mistreatment of Cathy's sister-in-law, Isabella. Heathcliff objectifies Isabella as a means of punishing Cathy and in so doing demonstrates his total lack of empathy.

Lord Byron is a real-life example, and possibly the inspiration for Emily Brontë's character. Like the fictional Heathcliff, Byron had an incestuous relationship with his sister, Augusta, but married and mistreated Annabella. He also took his daughter, Allegra, from her mother, a later mistress of his. This was no fatherly devotion, however, as she spent her short life abandoned by him and lived with a variety of substitute parents before, at the age of four and half, she was placed in a convent, where she died, still a young child.[20] In the characters of Heathcliff and Byron, we see all the hallmarks of an empathy disorder. An understanding of how to hurt someone is accompanied by a complete lack of feeling for the distress they are causing.

The development of a non-empathic way of being can be seen very early in children who have experienced cruelty and neglect in their early life. Whilst these children are still developing a personality, and can in no way be described as psychopathic, their lack of empathy and the beginnings of cruelty are evident.

---

Take Hannah, for example. At four years of age she had already witnessed and experienced much cruelty. Her experience of a loving, empathic relationship was pretty much non-existent when she came into foster care. An intelligent child, she has observed the world around her and has developed some perspective-taking skills. She can read others' minds and uses this knowledge to manipulate them. Lacking an emotional understanding, she cannot, however, empathize, and this severely compromises her ability to connect with others. The world of intersubjectivity is alien to Hannah. What Hannah does know is that the world is an unsafe place. She sees danger everywhere and she uses this foresight to guide her behaviour. Failing to understand that others will keep her safe, she coerces and manipulates in order to ensure some degree of safety. This can lead to already emerging acts of cruelty. For example, she will stamp on her young brother's head when she feels jealous of the attention he is getting.

Kim observed a striking example of Hannah's fear and her ability to manipulate others when she was at the foster home for a meeting. Hannah arrived back from nursery as the meeting was ending. The foster mother went to greet her, but Hannah ignored her as she entered the room where everyone was gathered. She made a beeline for Emily, the one person in the room who was unknown to her. Without eye contact or any other means of establishing contact, Hannah cuddled up to Emily in what was a surprisingly seductive act. Emily, startled by this sudden intimacy, found it hard not to respond to what appeared to be an intense need for comfort. Hannah then left Emily without a backward glance, moved over to the foster mother and asked her who the lady was.

There were a number of surprising elements to this interaction: the speed with which she entered and scanned the room, sorting out who was the stranger, the biggest source of threat, the complete lack of an expectation that the foster mother, with whom she had lived for some six months by this stage, would keep her safe and protected; and her ability to use her behaviour in a self-reliant way to minimize any threat that this stranger might pose.

In making herself appear vulnerable and needy, Hannah coercively triggered the other's innate need to protect, but without any real connection between them. Hannah's cognitive understanding of people guided her behaviour, but her emotional blindness did not allow her to experience others on an emotional level. She could not elicit or use the empathy that was on offer from her foster parents.

She did not enter intersubjective relationships and therefore could not benefit from the connection with others that this would bring. Over the next two years the foster parents worked hard to provide Hannah with the experience that had been so lacking in her early years. They nurtured her cognitive abilities, but, more importantly, they introduced her to the world of emotion. They taught her to recognize and respond to the emotional experience of herself and others and in doing so they opened the door to true relationship for Hannah.

## Responding to cruelty in children

Perhaps one of the most difficult behaviours to respond to in our children is when they demonstrate cruelty to others, whether people or animals.

This provokes an intense response in us. We fear for the young person and what she might be capable of. We perceive failure in ourselves, believing that we have let the other person down. She would not be so cruel if we had raised her successfully. Although challenging, responding to children who display cruelty requires an empathic response. This will help them develop sensitivity and connection with others, diverting from a trajectory of misunderstanding, cruelty and non-empathic interactions.

---

An example might be helpful to understand this more fully. Torey Hayden, in her book *One Child* describes her experience as a special education teacher with an emotionally disturbed little girl.[21] This young girl was already in trouble for extreme aggression to other children. Only the lack of an available place had so far kept her out of a locked institution. She was placed in Torey's special education class.

On her first day in this class there was a troubling episode: the little girl callously poked the eyes out of all the fish in the classroom aquarium. This behaviour was likely to provoke an intense response in those who witnessed it, a confirmation perhaps that this child should be locked away from society. It took all Torey's abilities to connect, empathize and respond to a troubled child as she stayed with her, recognizing the terror behind her defiance.

In order to empathize with the little girl, Torey first had to deal with her own strong response to the episode. She had to cope with the anger she was feeling in order to stay regulated and be in a position to understand what lay underneath the horrific behaviour. Torey needed to experience empathy for the deeply scared child rather than stay angry with the violence that was an expression of this fear. As she understood the fear and terror that the child was experiencing, her own feelings of anger reduced, she could express empathy and the child's intense feelings could also subside.

If Torey had stayed angry, she would not have understood the experience of the child. Without understanding, empathy isn't experienced. Attempts might be made to stop the behaviour in some way: consequences, discipline, punishment – all an attempt to manage a behaviour which we deem unacceptable. In managing behaviour, however, we miss opportunities to connect and empathize. The behaviour may reduce but we are making little difference to the feelings of shame and distress that led to the behaviour in the first place. The example described by Torey Hayden provides a wonderful illustration of how empathy can truly allow us to reach another person and to start the process of healing and growth.

## In conclusion

Empathy is an important part of PACE, without which we will not be able to connect and respond to children and their inner experience.

In this chapter we have explored the development of empathy and the need for relationship if the child is to make a journey of emotional growth, developing capacity for connected and reciprocal relationships. Without this early experience, a life of manipulation, coercion and sometimes cruelty can be the path in front of the child. With empathic and responsive relationships, children truly can realize their heritage and develop into wonderful, warm and empathic people in their own right.

# 9

# Joining Your Child with Empathy

Jane, mother of six-year-old Sam and seven-year-old Lynda, heard a noise outside where her children were playing with their friends, Sue and Devon, siblings from the house down the street.

Looking out the window, she was just in time to see Sam hit Lynda on the back of the head with a small stick. She heard Lynda's loud shriek as she grasped her head. Jane was outside in a flash, checking her daughter for damage, giving her a cuddle and wiping away a few tears. Sam meanwhile was on his bike in the driveway as if his mother and sister were not present. She called to him to come with her, but he ignored her.

Jane therefore escorted Sam inside, holding him gently by the arm so that he did not run away. He protested, but not too loudly. Jane thought he did not want to get too upset in front of Sue and Devon. She walked him into the kitchen for a chat so that she could understand what had happened and what she might do about it.

Jane: Sam, I saw you hit your sister with that stick.

Sam: I hate her! She's so mean and so stupid!

Jane: You really are angry with her! Really angry! So angry that you hit her!

Sam: Yeah, she's so mean! I don't care that I hit her!

Jane: Help me understand, Sam, help me! What makes you think that she's mean? Why are you that angry?

Sam: I just am! She is mean!

Jane: What did she do, Sam, that makes her seem mean to you?

Sam: She called me a baby! And Sue and Devon laughed! I'm not a baby and now they think I am! Now they won't play with me any more! I'm not a baby and she shouldn't say that!

Jane: Oh, Sam, that must have been really hard for you! Really hard! If Lynda called you a baby and your friends laughed at you, I can understand why you were angry. And you're right! You're not a baby, you're six!

Sam: She shouldn't have called me that!

Jane: I think I agree with you, Sam, if she called you that. Usually she doesn't say things like that. Why do you think she did?

Sam: I don't know. She should have agreed with me to play in the cabin. No, she wanted to play in the sand!

Jane: You wanted to play in the cabin, and she wanted to play in the sand?

Sam: Yeah, and Sue and Devon then played with her!

Jane: Ah! And you wanted them to play with you?

Sam: Yeah. But she could have played with us too.

Jane: So you were angry that they played with Lynda. So then what happened?

Sam: I kicked the road and houses that she was making in the sand. And she called me a big baby!

Jane: Ah! Now I understand why you got so angry! You really wanted to play in the cabin with your friends, and Lynda, and she didn't, and your friends did what she wanted to do.

Sam: Yeah, they always agree with her! Why don't they ever want to play with me?

Jane: Does it seem like that, Sam? That they *never* want to play what you want to do and *always* do what she wants?

Sam: Yeah. I think that they like her better than me!

Jane: Oh, Sam, if you think that, it must be so hard for you! They are your friends too, and it seems like they might want to be Lynda's friends more.

Sam: Why don't they like me?

Jane: Oh, Sam, what a worry. You think maybe they don't even like you. What a worry!

Sam: Why do they do what she wants?

Jane: Oh, Sam, I wish I knew. I wonder if sometimes they do what you want too, but right now it is hard to remember those times, because you so much wanted to play with them in the cabin today.

Sam: I don't know.

Jane: You were so disappointed! So you hit Lynda with a stick.

Sam: Yeah, that's why I hit her.

Jane: You could have hurt her, Sam.

Sam: I didn't!

Jane: You're right, Sam. It hurt when you hit her, but it didn't cause any bleeding and I don't think there will be a bruise. But I was scared until I looked her over because you are strong and that stick is big and it might have really hurt her.

Sam: I don't want to hurt her.

Jane: I know you don't, Sam. I really do. You were angry about her playing in the sand, but I don't think you wanted to hurt her. Just maybe show her how angry you were.

Sam: Yeah, that's all.

Jane: Was that a good way to show her?

Sam: No, I might have hurt her.

Jane: That's right, Sam. You might have hurt her. Now, what do you think would be a good thing to do? How can you let Lynda know that you now think you shouldn't have hit her with the stick?

Sam: I can say that I'm sorry. I can play with them in the sand.

Jane: That seems like a good plan, Sam. But if Lynda is still angry, will you be patient if she's not ready to talk to you?

Sam: I guess. I hope she will, though. I don't like her to be angry with me.

Jane: I know, Sam. You two love each other a lot I think.

Sam: Yeah, we do, Mum.

Jane might not always have the time to engage in dialogues like this one with her son. When she is able to do so, her relationship with him will become stronger. This will help Sam to develop good reflective abilities about his inner life and his behaviours. As a result, his relationship with his sister will deepen and be more satisfying. In addition, Jane still has to engage in disciplining Sam, teaching him an appropriate way to express his anger and worry. The use of empathy for Sam's experience will also make this more effective.

---

Empathy is not something that we give to our children. It is not an orange or a computer. So what is it? What is a parent's experience of empathy for her child? We have discussed it from various perspectives in the last chapter. Now we will explore how you may express your empathy in a way that your child will experience it. We will explore how your child will benefit from your empathy, as well as some of the challenges that parents may face when bringing an empathic approach to their parenting.

## Exploring what empathy is within parenting

Let's have a closer look at the example that opened this chapter. You will notice that the central activity is Jane's empathy for Sam. By understanding the context in which he hit his sister with the stick, Jane is able to experience his experience at the time. She can empathize with his uncomfortable feelings and worries that led to his angry behaviour.

This empathy precedes teaching Sam how he should have acted or thinking with him about consequences for his behaviour. By first experiencing empathy for him and his experience, she then knows how best to approach the behavioural event. In addition, working to understand his experience means that she is less likely to react to his behaviour with her own anger or frustration. Such a response would only increase Sam's defensiveness, not help him to reflect on and learn from this incident.

By experiencing empathy, Jane is also softer in her discipline. This is not leniency. Sam still learns that his behaviour is not acceptable, but it will help Sam to be more receptive to her teaching. When Sam knows that his mum understands and does not judge his motive for his action, he is more likely to work with her to change his behaviour and repair his relationship with his sister.

Empathy therefore is not permissiveness. When parents first start to think more deeply about empathy, they worry that in being more empathic they will also be letting their child get away with more. Notice in the example above how Jane is clear that her son's hitting his sister is not how he should express his anger toward her.

Expressing empathy for your child when you discipline him does not reinforce inappropriate behaviour. Rather, it helps him to deal with the emotions associated with your discipline. If he can manage these emotions better, he is more likely to remember the message that you were teaching him through discipline.

Parents can also worry that demonstrations of empathy will somehow reinforce the inappropriate behaviours. They worry that children might do these more in order to get more empathic attention from their parents. Unless a child is routinely ignored, this does not happen. When your child is already experiencing a great deal of time, reciprocal enjoyment and shared interests with you, he will not need to misbehave to get what he is already getting for free.

This example makes clear the interwoven nature of the components of PACE, though here the feature of playfulness is not evident. Playfulness is unlikely to be appropriate for a discussion of this event. Acceptance and curiosity were crucial for the dialogue and for the development of empathy. Jane clearly accepted her son's inner life which led to his aggressive act. She accepted his anger towards his sister and she accepted his thoughts that she was mean and stupid. She also accepted his statement that he did not care and had no regrets about hitting his sister. That does not mean that she agreed with these thoughts and feelings. Acceptance is not about agreeing or disagreeing. She simply accepts that these are his thoughts and feelings. She is not evaluating them, but she acknowledges that they are there, within his mind. Through acceptance is built trust. By accepting his thoughts and feelings, Sam is more likely to tell her about them. He does not have to worry that she will be angry with him or dislike him for having such thoughts and feelings.

Once Jane conveys her acceptance, she is then curious about these thoughts and feelings. Why is he angry? Why does he think his sister is mean? Why doesn't he care that he hit her? Her curiosity is also non-judgemental; when he says that she is mean because she called him a baby, she does not argue with him. Those are his reasons for his thoughts and feelings. Now she understands both them and the whole context for the hitting incident much better than she would have if she had argued with him about his thoughts and feelings or yelled, 'Just because you are angry with her gives you no right to hit her!' Such comments would have created a defensive response within Sam, as he would have experienced her as saying that his anger was simply an excuse and was not relevant. When Sam feels that his mother accepts his thoughts and feelings associated with his behaviour, he is much more likely to acknowledge on his own that hitting was not appropriate, even if his anger was. He is able to reflect that it could have hurt his sister, and that he loves her.

Jane's empathy for Sam's emotions and thoughts enabled Sam then to experience empathy for his sister, for the pain she felt when he hit her and for the possibility that she might have been hurt by his actions. This example conveys our belief, and the belief of many researchers and other therapists, that empathy begets empathy. Our children are not likely to experience empathy for others if they have not experienced our empathy for them.

## The dance of attunement

We often think of empathy in parenting as the expression of understanding and compassion for a child when he is in distress. However, it is bigger than this. It is part of a more general way that parents can experience themselves in relationship with their children. It begins at birth. When a parent and her infant are each interested in being with the other, they look, talk and move in synchrony as if they were dancing, with the body of one joining the other in harmonious expressions. This involves the whole body, especially the face, voice, arms, hands and torso. The parent and infant are focused on each other and quickly begin to show the same facial expressions, voice tones and phrasings, and bodily movements. In split seconds, the expression of one follows a similar expression to the other. This is delightful to watch and even more delightful to experience.

This same pattern of synchronized movements enables a parent to experience and communicate empathy for her child when he is manifesting some distress. The initiative comes from the child who communicates his distress verbally and non-verbally through face, voice and gestures. When the parent takes in these communications with her eyes and ears, she is openly engaged in a very receptive manner. Her brain becomes activated for empathy. As mentioned in the last chapter, aspects of her anterior insula (and its VENS cells), perceptual motor areas of the cortex (with their mirror neurons) and the prefrontal cortex (which integrates this sensory motor input and begins to make sense of it) become active and the parent begins to experience her child's experience. If she then allows herself to respond to his distress as her body wants to respond, with synchronous bodily expressions, he will experience her empathy.

The important point here is that if a parent wants to experience and then communicate empathy for her child's distress, she needs to:

- focus much more on how he is expressing himself rather than what he says

- allow herself to be receptive to her bodily tendencies to respond and not inhibit these

- hold the intention to convey empathy rather than give advice

- focus much more on how she responds to him than on what she says.

For example, in response to a daughter telling her father that she is upset, he might respond:

'That really seems to be bothering you a lot.' *(Said in a matter-of-fact monotone)*

Or

'That REALLY seems to be bothering you a LOT!' *(Said with inflections, with the whole sentence conveying a compassionate emotional tone)*

In the first response, his daughter will know that her father understands her distress but she is unlikely to know how he feels about it. She may think that he feels compassion for her, but she will not experience his compassion in a way that feels comforting and supportive. In the second response, his daughter is likely to really feel that her father 'gets it'. She experiences him as available to her in whatever way she needs. She is less likely to feel that she is dealing with this alone and she may be more confident that she can make sense of it and manage it more successfully.

### Continuous fine-tuning

When a parent responds to her infant in the attuned manner that we just described, she gets it wrong more than half the time in her first effort. Yet that does not create attachment insecurity; nor does it lead to the baby becoming discouraged and less engaged with the parent. Why is that? Because when the baby, in generally subtle ways, communicates that he does not resonate with that manner of communication, the parent then instantly changes her efforts and tries again. The second time tends to be much more successful than the first and the baby is content and continues the dialogue.

What did the baby not like? How was the parent misattuned with the baby's expressions? Often these may be small things, but they are central to parent–infant communication. The parent's vocal animation may have been a little higher than the baby's expressions. The parent's movements may have been a bit too rapid. The repetitive features of the parent's expressions may have been too rigidly the same for too long, or they may have been varying too much so that her baby did not experience the type of soothing repetitive pattern that he was hoping for. The infant's response becomes more agitated and frantic or else more passive and detached from the parent. These reactions indicate that he is not responsive to the parent's expression. They are not engaged in reciprocal communication.

Empathy works the same way. When a parent experiences and then communicates empathy for her child, she needs to immediately experience her child's response to this empathy. His response will tell her if her first expression and communication was on target or not. If she expresses empathy and he responds with withdrawal or increased agitation and frustration, most likely he did not experience her empathy. If he did not experience it, she needs to modify her expression.

The tricky bit is for a parent to begin to trust her intuition, emerging from the attuned, resonating, non-verbal communications between her and her child. This knowledge is not rational and it is often not conscious. It requires being receptive to the subtle, but clear, non-verbal expressions of her child and also her own response to these. When a parent's response conveys empathy, her child is likely to experience a calming of his distress, which is then reflected in his subsequent non-verbal response.

## Trust in empathy

A parent may often believe that her first responsibility to her child is either to give advice that will fix her child's problem or to fix the problem herself. She may give a half-hearted effort to expressing empathy before jumping into giving advice. It seems that empathy is being used as a technique to make her child more willing to accept the advice. When this occurs, it is likely that this parent does not have confidence in the power of empathy to help her child to regulate his emotions, to reflect on the source of his distress and then to know how best to manage the situation. Having confidence in empathy requires a leap of faith, especially when a parent is not used to the way the expression of empathy can help her child when in distress. A parent needs to embrace empathy all the way if it is going to be of greatest benefit to her child. With time and successful experience with empathy, a parent will be comfortable with its expression as well as with the knowledge that her empathy for her child was probably the most effective way that she could be of aid.

Dan provided treatment for a nine-year-old boy, Bryan, and his foster mother, Jean, over a period of several months. Jean was a very competent, organized and consistent parent who was very committed to the foster children placed in her care. She was clear and fair in her expectations and consequences.

However, Bryan's ongoing arguments and his refusal to follow directions and accept her rules were proving to be very frustrating to Jean. She did not understand why discipline was proving to be so ineffective. Dan had spoken to her in some detail about PACE during the early sessions, and Jean seemed to understand it and agree with its value. At one point, Dan explored with Jean how she expressed empathy for Bryan's behaviours. She replied that she told him that she knew that it was hard for him to follow the rules but that he still had to do it. Dan suggested that she might say instead, 'It seems to be so hard for you to do what I tell you to do, so hard.' Then Jean might add, with no judgement in her question, 'What do you think makes it so hard?'

Essentially, Dan was suggesting that Jean let the expression of empathy stand alone, and then follow this with curiosity in an effort to understand what make it so hard. Jean had been expressing empathy as a preliminary comment leading up to her main message, namely that he needed to do what he was told.

Jean now understood that, in expressing empathy, her intent at that moment is simply to communicate that she is experiencing his distress, nothing more. If Bryan is able to experience her empathy, then she can try understand his distress more deeply, and probably in doing this help him to understand it better as well. In subsequent sessions, Jean truly began to experience for herself the value of experiencing and expressing empathy prior to addressing any behavioural difficulties.

## Providing empathy within parenting

We have explored what empathy is and the need to trust in the power of empathy to deeply help your child and your relationship with your child. In this section we will explore ways to bring empathy into your day-to-day parenting.

## Focus on the experience, not the event or behaviour

For your empathy to be of greatest benefit to your child and your relationship with him, your gaze needs to be on his experience of an event rather than the event itself.

When you focus only on the event, you are likely to keep seeking more facts, as if a more thorough knowledge of what happened will help you to know what to do about the problem. The facts themselves may tell you more about the event, but they are not always a direct guide to your child's experience of the event. By focusing on the event, you are less likely to get a good sense of how your child experienced the event. You will not understand the nature of his distress, nor will you be able to experience and convey empathy very well. By focusing instead on how he is experiencing the event, you will be able to stand in his shoes with him. Once he has experienced your empathy, then there might be space to explore aspects of what happened. He will now be more able to reflect on the event and to gain a new sense of how to handle the situation.

---

Let us think about this through an example. Here we listen in on a father talking with his 11-year-old daughter. She is experiencing distress because of a conflict she has had with her friend. In the first part of this dialogue we meet a dad who is focused on the event rather than his daughter's experience of the event.

Dad: So what were you fighting about?

Daughter: What we're going to do this weekend.

Dad: What does she want to do?

Daughter: Go over to Joan's house.

Dad: What does she want to do over there?

Daughter: Oh, it doesn't matter, Dad. We just want to do different things.

Dad: Well, if you don't tell me what you two are fighting about, I can't help you.

Daughter: Don't worry about it, Dad. I can handle it.

This father has not got off to a good start in supporting his daughter in her distress. He is trying to understand what has happened, but by focusing on the event itself rather than his daughter's experience of the event, this dialogue is beginning to feel a bit like an interrogation. She is not feeling understood and her distress is not reducing. This is a good dad, and he is aware that this is not going too well. He therefore changes tack and starts to focus more on his daughter's experience:

Dad: *(Voice tone matching her voice)* This is bothering you a lot.

Daughter: Yeah, Dad, we hardly ever fight like this. It might be the first time.

Dad: Ah! Maybe the first time you were so upset with each other!

Daughter: Yeah, and I don't like how we yelled at each other!

Dad: She is so important to you. You've been close for years!

Daughter: Yeah, she is! I don't want to ruin our friendship over some stupid argument about what we're going to do this weekend.

Dad: You worry that a small disagreement might hurt your friendship. And you don't want that.

Daughter: I don't, Dad. I think that I'll give her a call and work it out. Thanks, Dad. I hope that she feels bad about this too. I guess I'll find out, won't I?

Dad: I'll be here when you're finished.

Now this daughter is really feeling supported by her dad; she is feeling stronger and has decided on a way to deal with the difficulty. Empathy has strengthened her relationship with her dad and given her some support with her friendship at the same time.

---

### Follow his lead as to how he wants you to sit with him in his distress

The core of empathy is attunement and the non-verbal matching of affective expressions. When your child's voice is slow and halting, your voice is slow and halting. When his voice is agitated, your voice is animated, matching the same rhythm and intensity of his voice. He will then have a fundamental sense that you understand his emotional state at that moment. From that core, the ongoing empathic discourse may have differing expressions, based on his non-verbal and verbal feedback to you as to how you can best help him.

When you want to assist your child in the process of regulating his emotions, choose words that focus on his emotional state. You can do this while conveying confidence in your voice that he can handle them no matter how intense they are.

'How hard this is for you, how hard.'

'It's so sad, so sad.'

'You wanted it so badly, and your disappointment now is so big.'

You might want to assist your child to make sense of what is happening. In this case, change the words you use a little. Choose words that focus instead on acts of understanding.

'It goes on and on. You might wonder when will it stop. When?'

'You've felt so close to him. You might think, "What is going on? Why is this happening?"'

'It hurt so much when she yelled at you? Any sense what made her so angry?'

Sometimes you will simply want to help your child to accept his current experience, no matter how hard it is. When this is your intent, sit or walk quietly with him while he struggles. The silence conveys your sense that he wants time to let his distress settle, to be with it, before starting to decide what to do with it. Acceptance, as we saw earlier, provides a good platform from which to choose a course that will be most helpful.

### Less is more: Thinking about the words you use

When you express empathy for your child, most often you will use words to convey how you experience his experience. At times, when he seems to respond to your empathic expressions, you may be tempted to keep talking, thinking that it is the words themselves that are providing relief and increased closeness with you. Of course, the words help, but as part of a bigger package. Words support the primary focus of empathy, which is non-verbal communication. Further than this, you may be tempted to treat empathy as having served its function to facilitate engagement, and now the 'real' parental assistance begins, namely giving advice. You are finding it hard to trust in empathy.

Empathy is conveyed primarily non-verbally. If you remember that, then you are likely to be aware of how your child is responding to your breathing, movement, voice modulations, rhythms and facial expressions. You will notice that your words function to carry a bit of the momentum of your being with your child and possibly a bit of emphasis here or there. If you start to use more and more words, you are likely to notice that the experience of empathy becomes lighter and your engagement with your child becomes primarily cognitive, focused on thinking rather than feeling. Thinking and reflection have their place, but if this comes too soon, it can detract from the more emotional experience of empathy.

When you do wish to help your child to reflect on his experience, it is wise to express yourself with general words first, before becoming more specific. This will give your child the opportunity to define his experience, supported by you but without you taking over. You are not telling your child what to think, but supporting your child to reflect on his experience. If your first efforts are too specific, your guess may only be partially right. This might lead your child to experience you as 'not getting it'. If that is the case, he will be less receptive to your empathic expressions. If he accepts the more general expression of empathy first, and then your more specific guess is not quite on target, he is more likely to clarify his experience for you.

For example, here are some statements which are general, and then, if this is accepted by the child, can become a little more specific:

First: 'That seems to be so hard for you!' Then: 'You seem so (sad/ worried/confused/ disappointed).'

First: 'Oh, how confusing that is!' Then: 'Oh, how confusing that you're just not sure what he wants!'

First: 'You seem to be so discouraged!' Then: 'You wanted it so badly!'

### Hold tight to the intention to simply be with, not evaluate and fix

When an infant is about six months of age, he is able to correctly read many of his parent's intentions. For example, if you point to a picture on the wall, a younger infant might look at your finger. The six-month-old will look to where you are pointing, knowing that you want him to do that. After looking at the picture, he is likely to look back to you, perhaps to confirm that you want him to look at the picture rather than the vase on the table next to the picture.

When you confirm that it is the picture you want him to look at, he will look at it again, and often acknowledge with eye contact and a happy face that he is interested in it. From this beginning in infancy, children become very proficient at understanding why you are interacting with them in a certain way. They become good at reading your motives.

In a similar way, it is likely to be obvious to your child what your intention is in expressing empathy. If your intention is simply to be with him in his experience, to share it, to comfort and support him, she will know that. If your intention, however, is to get his attention so that you can then tell him what you think about what he did and what to do, he will know that as well. The former intention will enable empathy to be experienced much more fully and meaningfully than will the latter intention.

As a result, you need simply to focus on experiencing his experience with him if it is to be effective. This is at the core of empathy. If you are going through the motions of expressing empathy but your intention to be with him, to understand and share his experience with him, is weak, then he will not experience empathy either from your comments or from your presence. He will instead experience your need for him to cooperate with you, perhaps due to your desire for him to change his behaviour.

## Remember the need for empathy when you cause him distress

Often your child is in distress because you have refused his request or you have directed him to do something that he does not want to do. This is a normal part of parenting, but the way you manage the distress can significantly strengthen the relationship you have with your child.

Expressing empathy when you are the source of your child's uncomfortable feelings can be harder than when they are due to something separate from yourself. Perhaps your child expresses his distress with anger over your discipline or directive. You may believe that it is a sign of disrespect if he expresses anger at you. Your concern with his disrespect then overrides your attention to his experience underlying the anger.

Alternatively, he may express his distress through tears and sadness, and you may feel some discomfort that you have created his unhappiness. This discomfort might lead you to try and persuade him to like your decision. You might try to reason with him to show him its value. If he still does not agree, you may become annoyed that he is being unreasonable. Finally, you may discount his distress to make yourself feel better. All these very understandable responses in you can make it more difficult to stay with empathy for your child's experience.

When distress arises out of your need to discipline or direct your child, empathy is probably even more valuable that when his unhappiness is due to something separate from you. Empathy will help him to manage his distress and to maintain a close relationship with you. A toddler often becomes very upset with his parent's limits and then he naturally turns to his parent for comfort. This empathy helps him to handle his distress and become calm. This behaviour is very helpful in enabling a toddler to realize that his parent's behavioural limitation is in his best interest. He does not like the limit, but he still trusts and is comforted by the parent who set the limit.

The same is true with older children. If you express empathy for your child after you set a limit on his behaviour, he is more likely to accept your limit and your decision to set it. This is more helpful than if you become annoyed with him or try to reason him out of his distress. Without empathy, it is most likely that your child will become angry and/or withdrawn from you. Empathy with discipline often leads to your child being closer to you than before.

---

Let us again reflect on a father–daughter conversation. Here we will listen to a father setting a limit, whilst maintaining empathy for his daughter's experience of that limit:

Dad: You won't have time to ride your bike this afternoon.

Daughter: Oh, Dad, that's not fair! I really want to go for a ride.

Dad: I can see how much you want to ride today. You're really upset.

Daughter: Yeah, Dad, I really want to ride over to Susan's house.

Dad: I can see you're unhappy about this. I wish I could let you but I can't.

Daughter: Just for an hour, Dad?

Dad: I'm sorry that you're disappointed. The answer is still no.

Daughter: Tomorrow?

Dad: I hope so, but we'll have to wait and see what is going on.

This dad sets a clear limit, but then stays focused on his daughter's experience of this limit. She is understandably unhappy. Dad is able to sympathize with this whilst maintaining the boundary that he has set for his daughter. In the next example, the mother has provided a directive to her son. Tidying bedrooms is a common source of conflict between parents and children. Again, an empathic response can help both parent and child deal with the conflict better:

Son: I don't want to clean my room now! It's fine!

Mum: Maybe for you, son, but not for me. You need to clean it now before having your free time.

Son: But then I won't have time to finish putting my model together.

Mum: And you've really been excited about that! I can see why you're upset.

Son: I just have to finish it today! I want to show it to Dad when he gets home.

Mum: And I'm saying you can show your dad your clean room. But you're not happy about that, are you? Sorry, son, the room needs to be cleaned today.

Son: Ah, Mum!

Mum: I know you're really disappointed that the model most likely won't be finished now until tomorrow.

Son: I'll clean it tomorrow, Mum!

Mum: Not tomorrow, son, today! Wish it could be different but this is important to me. It's been long overdue. I know it's hard.

Son: OK, I'll get started now and maybe I'll have time.

Mum: Great! I'll have to look at it before you get to your model. Your excitement about the model might make you overlook some things that need to be taken care of.

---

Although it is harder to convey in written dialogue, this sort of open communication includes the non-verbal components as well. Children will display how they feel through angry facial expressions and voice tone. If this is forbidden out of fear that it is disrespectful, your child is likely to begin to conceal his inner life from you. By the time he is an adolescent, you will be frustrated that he never shares his thoughts, feelings and wishes with you. This distance in your relationship is not likely to lead him to respect you more.

Allowing your child to express his disappointment and frustration about your decisions verbally and non-verbally does not diminish his respect for you. Rather, it conveys your respect for his inner life and the value you give to him speaking honestly and openly about what he thinks, feels and wants. Your child will grow up to be a young person aware of and comfortable in sharing his experience. He will feel closer to you, and respect will have grown on both sides of the relationship.


## Experiencing and expressing empathy: It's not easy!

We have tried to look at empathy from various perspectives to give you ideas for developing the habit of both experiencing and communicating empathy for your child. Our final thought may be the most important one of all: this is not easy.

We may be drawn into experiencing our child the way we were experienced by our parents when we were children. We tend to fall back, cognitively and emotionally, on aspects of our relationships with our parents. This is most likely the way that our parents related to us during the good times and bad.

If your parents did not experience your perspective when they tried to understand and guide your behaviour, you most likely did not experience their empathy for you. If you did not experience their empathy, it is harder for you consistently to experience empathy for your child. Although it is harder, you can develop your capacity to be empathic. Through repetitive usage, you can strengthen the regions of your brain associated with empathy for your child. With enough repetition, empathy can even start to become a natural way of communicating. You can be helped further by experiencing empathy from supportive relationships in your life; receiving empathy from a partner, good friend or therapist will enable you to experience empathy for your child much more readily.

But, still, it is hard to experience and communicate empathy consistently. Empathy requires that you focus on your child in his current experience. Be with him in this present moment; simply be with him. Yet, as a parent, you often find yourself living in the future. You think of the skills that he needs to develop. You imagine all the things that might go wrong with his plans. You worry about challenges that he is likely to face or accidents he may encounter, all the many things in life that you cannot predict or control. Your mind constantly jumps into the future, trying to do whatever you can to make things work out.

To give yourself some sense that you have greater control of the future than you might actually have, you are likely to find yourself reaching quickly for problem solving and advice giving, as if reasoning and thoughtful planning will win the day. When your mind is in the future for any of these reasons, you are not likely to be ready to experience empathy.

---

Dan spoke with an adoptive father a number of times about his son's habit of stealing within the home from members of the family. The father worried a great deal that at one point his son would begin to steal at school, from the neighbours or from stores. He worried about his son getting into trouble with the police and all the ways this might limit his future. The potential consequences for stealing were becoming pervasive and discouraging to both father and son. This was shutting down communication and was not helping their relationship. From his desperation about not being able to effect any changes in his son's behaviour as well as his love and commitment for him, the father was able to commit to developing and maintaining a new intention.

Dan helped him to experience his son's experience of his stealing. What did his son think and feel about it? What did he think and feel before and during his acts of stealing? Within the safety of empathy, the boy was able to express his continuing anxiety about being rejected by his parents and having to move again. His stealing represented for him an effort to hold on to his family, to have something of his family that he could keep which would never be taken away from him. The decrease in the boy's stealing behaviour was dramatic and lasting.

---

Staying with empathy can also be difficult because we so easily move into old and familiar ways of dealing with our child's distress or behaviour. After all, we may have been parenting this way for some considerable time, and, as we noted earlier, it may be the way we experienced being parented. We will consider some of the common ways that can lead us all to slip away from empathy at times.

### Reassurance

When your child is having a difficult time, it is very tempting to reassure him. Tell him that he needn't be worried, that his perceptions or fears are exaggerated or unfounded. You may be motivated out of your desire to help your child to be happy; if you can change his thoughts, maybe he will no longer experience doubts or distress. While this is tempting, it is often ineffective because his perceptions are not that easy to change. If he experiences your empathy for his perceptions, he is more likely to be able to develop a more comprehensive experience of the situation, which will make it easier for him to change his perception.

In the following example we can see how easy it is to fall into reassurance.

---

Stan thinks that his teacher does not like him and he does not want to go to school. Understandably, Mum is upset that Stan is experiencing school in this way and concerned about how she is going to get him to school. She hopes to make him feel better about his teacher and therefore to find it easier to go to school.

> Mum: Oh, Stan, of course your teacher likes you. You're such a great kid and never give him any trouble. How could you think that he doesn't?

> Stan: He just ignores me when I want some help! And he never talks to me like he does with the other kids.

> Mum: Well, he's probably just busy at times, Stan. Listen now, you are a great kid! There is no way that he doesn't like you. Trust me, Stan. You don't have anything to worry about.

> Stan: *(Sounding unsure)* I guess so.

Mum has tried hard to help Stan, but it is likely that he is unconvinced. Trying to talk him into changing his perceptions of his teacher and his perception of the teacher's behaviour towards him is very unlikely to be successful. As we have done with previous examples, we are now going to rewrite this dialogue. Let's see how it goes when Mum manages to communicate empathy for her son's experience:

> Mum: Oh, Stan, so it seems to you that your teacher does not like you. That must be hard. And I know that you like him a lot.

> Stan: He doesn't, Mum. He just ignores me when I want some help! And he never talks to me like he does with the other kids.

> Mum: So, it seems that you're not that important to him. Not like the other kids. Oh, Stan, I'm sorry about this. It must make it so difficult for you when you're in his class.

> Stan: It does, Mum. I don't feel like going sometimes.

> Mum: Do you think he knows that you don't think he likes you. What do you think he would say if he knew?

> Stan: He'd probably say that he does like me. He wouldn't admit it.

Mum: But you'd still feel that he doesn't. If you're not sure if you could believe what he says about this, can you think of anything else you might do?

Stan: I don't know.

Mum: This is hard. Do you think that the next time you ask for help and he seems to ignore this, you could mention that you're bothered that you want his help and he doesn't seem to want to help you. What might he say?

Stan: He'd probably help me. But I don't know if he'd want to.

Mum: So you still wouldn't be sure if he likes you. That would be hard to do. I wonder if you'd be closer to knowing for sure if you said something like that. Maybe he doesn't know that you do need his help sometimes even though you get good grades. Maybe he doesn't know how much you like him.

Stan: But he's the teacher, Mum. He should know that stuff.

Mum: Even though he's a grown-up, maybe he has doubts too. You handle things so well that maybe he thinks that he's not that important to you.

Stan: Well, he is.

Within this discussion based on empathy, Stan is likely to have doubts about his original perception that he is not liked by his teacher, and may be more open to exploring his doubts through his ongoing interactions with him. His mother never challenged his original belief in order to reassure him.

---

### Talking him out of it

This is a more cognitive version of reassurance. Here you may think that if you can give your child enough reasons for his perceptions being wrong, then he will change his perception. So you line up the facts that you hope will change his experience of the event. In the previous example, rather than reassuring him, Mum would have been trying to talk Stan out of it if she said:

'You get excellent grades.'

'Your behaviour in the classroom is fine.'

'The teacher has not contacted us about any concerns.'

'The teacher gives attention to the problem kids. The fact that he may ignore you suggests that he does like you for not causing him any problems.'

'All adults who know you like you. Your teacher would not be any different.'

## Problem solving

When your child expresses his distress, it is tempting to tell him what to do to solve his problems. It is possible that if he wants your advice at the time, he will try what you suggest and it will be successful. However, often when your child comes to you with distress, he is asking for your understanding and empathy, not your advice.

Giving advice when he wants empathy is likely to cause him to disengage from you and not follow the advice. He may instead sense that by telling him what to do you really 'don't get it'. He may experience your advice as you pushing his experience aside or suggesting that he should just get on and deal with it on his own. Even though you gave him advice – so in this sense he is not dealing with it on his own – he is still alone with regard to the emotional distress the situation is causing him. He might sense that you don't want to be bothered with his distress. You just want to fix it and make the problem go away. While this is probably not your intent, if you do not convey empathy for his distress, that may be how he experiences it.

## Nagging

Nagging refers to giving advice to your child and, when he does not follow your advice, you give it again and again. We often slip into nagging when we feel particularly anxious about our child's distress and want desperately to make it go away. When our first suggestion is not effective, we become increasingly animated, possibly agitated, in our efforts to eliminate the problem that the child is facing.

Nagging can be a particular problem because it greatly distracts the child from his need to fully experience his distress over a situation. He will lack the support he needs to regulate any and all emotions that are associated with his distress, and to discover the best way to manage it. The parent's distress, expressed by nagging, brings the child's focus on to the parent rather than on to the original situation.

## Minimizing

When the parent who does not express empathy is unable to make her child's problem go away through any or all of the above responses to the distress, it leaves her feeling uncomfortable. She may feel bad that her attempts to help are not meeting with success. She may even feel a sense of shame that her attempts to help are meeting with resistance. As with the shield against shame that we explored in Chapter 7, one way to deal with these horrible feelings is to try to minimize the child's experience. Here are some examples of comments that a parent might say when minimizing:

'It's not that bad.'

'It seems bad now but it won't seem so bad in the morning.'

'You're tough; you'll get through this.'

'Every cloud has a silver lining.'

'You'll have many more opportunities.'

In this section we have explored a number of challenges to providing an empathic approach to parenting. We will all recognize ourselves in these approaches to our children. It is easy to drift from empathy to these and then back to empathy again.

We hope in this chapter to have made you more aware of your parenting, more able to notice when empathy is needed and able to stay with it a bit longer. Of course, you will not be successful every time, but we believe that by being aware of the challenges you will become more empathic both for your child and for yourself. As a consequence, your relationship will strengthen to the benefit of both you and your child.

## In conclusion

Empathy involves being with your child psychologically. You are joining him in his inner life and experiencing it with him. In this way you are ready and able to sense and resonate with both his emotional and reflective states.

In so doing, you are helping him to regulate whatever emotions he is experiencing. He is not experiencing them alone. With his emotions regulated, you are also helping him to make sense of his inner life more successfully.

Experiencing and communicating empathy for your child is likely to be a central component of the emotional intimacy that you hope to attain and maintain with your child. Such intimacy brings joy and meaning to your relationship with your child throughout your lifetime. It brings strength to the relationship so that it can withstand the most intense conflicts or separations and emerge stronger. It deepens the relationship further during good times, so that sharing your days with your child becomes a treasure.

---

## STORY

### The Farmer and the Queen

There was a queen of a land that covered the best parts of the earth. Her name was Jade. She was a wise queen, just and brave. She was not content with the prosperity that she brought to her kingdom. She wanted to know how to keep her kingdom strong for years, centuries even, after her death. So she brought the wisest men and women to her throne and asked them each one question, the same one each time. 'What is the source of never-ending strength for my kingdom?' And the wise elders gave many answers:

'It is your army, your majesty.'

'It is your gold, your majesty.'

'It is the loyalty of your dukes and duchesses, your majesty.'

'It is the soil and the water, your majesty.'

'It is your hard-working people, your majesty.'

Queen Jade thought that each of the wise ones told a truth, but still she was not happy. They were missing something. What was it?

So Queen Jade travelled throughout her land. She hoped one day to find the source of the strength of her land, so that she could protect it and nurture it. Then it would flourish and her kingdom would gain in strength.

Months, even years, she travelled and she came to know her land well, but her question stayed with her as she tried to sleep at night.

One day she saw a wealthy landowner beat a farmer with a stick. She asked the landowner why he would so strike the farmer.

The landowner replied, 'Because he does not work the hours that he has committed to work for me. Because he does not give me the amounts of food that he is committed to give to me. Because he does not keep his commitments to me, your majesty, he makes it harder for me to keep my commitments to you.'

So the Queen turned to the farmer. 'Why do you not keep your commitments to the landowner?'

The farmer replied, 'Because I have a friend named George, your majesty.'

Surprised by his words, the Queen asked, 'And who is George and why would he prevent you from keeping your commitment to your landowner?'

And the farmer said, 'George is an old farmer who taught me how to plough the fields, to plant at the right time, and to care for the stock so that they are content and produce well. Now he cannot work and he has lost a foot to a rusty sickle. He has little food, no wood for the winter, and his house is falling apart and needs many repairs. So I give some of my small amount of food to him and have not enough to give the full amount to the landowner. And I give some of my time to repair his home and bring him wood and do not have enough to give what I owe to the landowner.'

The Queen was puzzled. 'And what hold does George have over you?'

And the farmer said, 'He is lonely and frightened and in pain.'

And the Queen replied, 'And what hold is that?'

Said the farmer, 'Because he is such, I too am lonely and frightened and in pain.'

'How is this so?' asked the Queen.

'I feel what he feels, your majesty,' he replied. 'There is nothing special about that. He is my friend, so I feel what he feels.'

'Do you not feel the pain of the landowner's stick?'

'Yes, your majesty, but that is the pain of the body and it will go away. My friend's pain will stay with me as long as it is with him.'

'Can't you make it go away?' asked the Queen.

'But then I would not be who I am. My heart would be truly alone and I would have little to offer my friend, my village and even your kingdom, your majesty. I will accept the beatings with the stick, and I will feel my friend's pain and loneliness. I believe this is how we are meant to be and I would not want to change it to avoid the stick.'

And Queen Jade no longer had to travel to answer the question of her kingdom's strength. And the landowner no longer beat the farmer, and the farmer and his old friend continued with their lives. It was a bit easier now, as the friend's home was repaired and there was wood for the fire. They also laughed together a great deal while telling old tales to each other.

# 10

# Bringing It All Together and an Additional Ingredient

## Parenting with PACE

We believe that parenting with PACE is a gift; it is a gift to your child and a gift to yourself.

PACE reminds you of the heart of parenting: your relationship with your child and your child's relationship with you. During and after conflicts and separations, PACE holds you together in your minds and hearts or brings you back together when you have been apart. PACE holds you to your most loving motives and your deepest dreams for your child. PACE enables you to see beneath the conflicts, the problems and the differences. PACE enables you to see the spirit of your child, the same spirit that will have been so clear and vibrant at her birth.

PACE is both simple and complex, easy and difficult. It calls on your heart to experience the full range of emotion with your child, from the lightness of playfulness to the compassion and loving kindness of empathy. PACE moves your mind in a sense of wondering, an open, ongoing curiosity about your child's inner life, helping you to understand your child's experience of you, the world and herself. And through it all PACE enables you to accept your child with full, deep, unconditional and unending acceptance, for better or for worse. This acceptance brings your child safety to express herself in her most vulnerable and her most incredible ways.

PACE does not compromise discipline; rather, it empowers discipline, your readiness and ability to guide and teach your child. PACE enables you to express a softness and understanding in your discipline even when it needs to be strong and clear. And PACE enables your child to experience your discipline in a more open and trusting manner. She has confidence that your discipline of her behaviour comes from good intentions and your belief that it is in her best interests. Finally, PACE brings you back again to your relationship with your child, a permanent, multicoloured, unique and universal relationship with her.

---

Dan recalls a foster parent, Beth, who was having difficulties with her foster son, Abe. Beth struggled with Abe's relentless challenges to her engagement with him and her efforts to provide him with the discipline that he needed from her. She struggled with PACE, lacking confidence that it provided a strong enough stand to reach a boy whose rage, mistrust and self-reliance were formidable. One day, months into his placement with her, Beth proudly said that she was able to let go of her need to control his behaviour and to elicit his compliance with her authority. She was able to embrace PACE. Dan wondered if Abe showed signs of changing. She replied that he had not, but she had changed. 'Now things are so much easier for me. I am happier. I can accept him more. I am getting the atmosphere of my home back to where it needs to be.' A month after that, she said with a quiet sense of peace and happiness, 'He seems to be becoming like me. He's happier now too. He seems to accept me more, even when I'm telling him what to do. And I never thought that I would say this, but he seems to like living with me and the rest of the family.'

---

PACE is not a miracle drug. It is simply a way to bring people together safely, while they sort out their differences, discover their strengths, and experience – truly experience – what each means to the other.

## Therapy: An additional ingredient

Henri Nouwen, a Dutch priest and internationally renowned author, provides insights into compassion that also give us insight into therapy. He writes that compassion is hard because it requires us to be with the other at their most vulnerable. To stay with them in their weakness and loneliness. Often we desire to run from or find a quick fix to the suffering. Compassion is therefore the harder journey to take with another person.[1]

Kim sits with a foster parent who is caring for a highly troubled young man with an extensive history of abuse and neglect. Kim has been supporting him in his parenting for a while now, but today he is full of despair.

'If only you would see him, Kim; that would sort him out. There is something wrong with him. He needs to be seen.'

This is a common, but sadly misguided, refrain. The belief that therapy can fix a child is an understandable hope. Therapy can be part of the journey for troubled and traumatized children, but it is a journey that is hard work, and troubling in itself. It does not 'fix the child', but it can be a part of the healing, a healing that starts with parenting, extends into the community and only then into the therapy room.

When traumatized children are supported by therapeutic parenting, when they have support in schools where their difficulties are fully understood, then they will begin to develop the security that was missing from their early life. This can provide a solid foundation for the addition of therapy. Kim wrote in a previous book that:

> too narrow a focus on individual therapy can lead to an expectation that children will adjust to a world for which they are not equipped. This therapy becomes a way of 'making children fit'. When therapy becomes part of a wider ecologically based and holistic approach, we all have a responsibility to help children to feel more comfortable and secure.[2]

In other words, we need interventions that go beyond providing individual therapy to those offering support to children within the worlds they are living in, interventions that help home, school and communities to provide therapeutic environments within which the troubled child can start to heal.

In the first chapter we described love as an essential ingredient. Love is a way of being that makes the attitude of PACE within parenting come alive. Love and PACE-led parenting will help a child heal from the early trauma of abusive, neglectful and/or disrupted parenting.

For many children, this will turn their life around and help them realize a potential that was there at the beginning, but which became jeopardized by life's circumstances. For some children, this healing is further aided by the addition of therapy. The therapy sessions add to the therapeutic healing environment in which they are living. This allows them to build further security and safety from which they can confront and come to terms with their past experience. They will learn that they are a good person to whom bad things have happened, rather than being a bad person deserving of what life has dished out. This in turn will allow them to embrace the present more fully so that they can thrive on the good things that are now being provided for them.

## Creating a therapeutic healing environment

Within this book we have explored how loving a child combined with an attitude of PACE can provide a home environment within which a child can start to heal from past trauma. Whilst the parent isn't a therapist, parenting can be therapeutic. This, alone or combined with therapy sessions, can provide the child with the experience needed for emotional growth and development.

The pyramid of need shown below (Figure 10.1) summarizes this development.

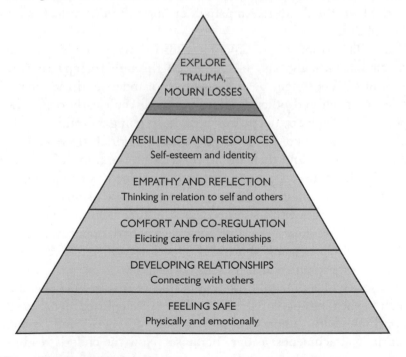

**Figure 10.1** Pyramid of need

The foundation of the pyramid is safety. Children need to feel safe at home, at school and in the community. When children can't feel safe, they rarely relax. They can easily draw the parents into this psychological world of fear and insecurity. Meeting the need for safety is a priority to help a child grow and heal. Safety within parenting and safety within therapy is the starting point for helping a child to heal.

As we have shown throughout this book, safety and relationships represent the two sides of a coin. A child will not feel safe without supportive relationships, whilst increasing the amount of positive relationship in a child's life can increase her feelings of safety and security. With safety and relationships, the capacity for regulation and reflection will develop.

As the child experiences comfort and co-regulation with a parent and with a therapist, she will experience deeper connection. This transforms negative affect into positive and builds capacity for self-regulation. The child learns that relationships can be a source of comfort and security, whilst she also develops her own inner resources to manage her emotional life. Dependency and independency become comfortable to the child, maximising her opportunities to feel safe in the face of difficulty.

The ability to reflect on experience also develops within parent–child relationships and can be enhanced through therapy sessions. This ability is dependent on the capacity to understand the internal experience of self and other. Children with difficult early experience adapt to this difficulty by not processing what is going on within people's minds. As Fonagy and his colleagues have explored, these children need help to safely 'find their mind' reflected in the mind of a caring parent.[3] Without this support, empathy development is compromised, and children will struggle to make or maintain relationships.

Helping the child with these needs will in turn help to develop her resilience and resources. Positive experience and opportunities for developing and increasing skills and capacities will build resilience, positive self-esteem and a healthy sense of identity.

This series of five highly interconnected needs are met therefore through a healing parenting environment, supported by healthy relationships with understanding school teachers and, where appropriate, attachment-sensitive therapists. Now the child is ready to face the demons of the past. Trauma and loss cannot be dealt with when there is a lack of safety. A child who does not trust others, who cannot emotionally regulate or reflect on experience, will be low in resilience and resources. This child cannot take on the added burden of understanding and coming to terms with early traumatic experience. The strength to do this will come when children live in environments that ensure that their pyramid of need is met.

For some, this will be sufficient for recovery from difficult previous experience. Others may need a period of therapy to assist in this process. This therapy is more likely to be successful if the needs highlighted in this pyramid are already met.

Whilst the pyramid represents a series of needs which build on top of each other, this is a cyclical rather than a sequential process. We all move up and down this pyramid in line with current circumstances. For example, think about a time of increased stress in your life. Your sense of safety will reduce in line with the amount of stress you are experiencing. You will also notice how you become more 'emotional' as your capacity for emotional regulation is challenged, and your thinking will become more rigid and inflexible as your capacity to reflect shuts down. As your stress outweighs your resources, past trauma and loss comes back to haunt you, adding to the current stress you are experiencing. Relationships will have increased importance to help you through this. It is at these times that you can use a friend who has an attitude of PACE towards you. With this additional support, you will live through the stress and become stronger and more resilient in the process.

A child who has never had this pyramid of need met requires help to develop emotionally, so that she can develop the internal resources to cope with increased stress and difficulty, and can learn to trust and depend on others to help her at these times. At times of distress you will notice that she returns to this earlier lack.

Parenting and therapy with PACE is an ongoing process of supporting and developing internal resources within the child, which can be drawn on in a way that increases safety and security. The two together can be greater than the sum of the parts. At times a child may have established a partial sense of both safety and successful relationships with her parents, but the traumas of her past prevent her from going further. In these situations, therapy with PACE, combined with the safety and relationship that the child has established, are sufficient to help the child address past traumas successfully. This in turn enables the sense of safety and relationships with her parents to go further. One helps the other in the context of the therapy.

In the next section we want to give you a glimpse into the therapy room. We want to help you to understand attachment-focused family therapy, which also has PACE at its heart. If you and your child decide to engage in such therapy, you will see how the important work you have put into building PACE into your parenting is an essential foundation for the next bit of the therapeutic journey.

## Attachment-focused family therapy

Attachment-focused family therapy (AFFT) was originally developed by Dan as a therapeutic intervention for families who were fostering or had adopted children with significant developmental trauma and insecurity of attachment. It was called dyadic developmental psychotherapy (DDP) to focus attention on to the importance of child and parent working with the therapist. Together they can provide the child with a corrective developmental experience that will help her to grow and heal emotionally. The broader term AFFT is used to highlight its use as a family therapy focused on improving attachment relationships, which can help all families whether foster, adoptive or biological.

This therapy is theoretically based on the models of attachment theory and intersubjectivity, which we introduced in Chapter 1. The therapist helps the family members to develop healthy patterns of relating and communicating which help them all feel safe and connected. Safety and connection will lead to a reduction in the level of fear, shame or coercion that family members experience. Through engaging in this therapeutic approach, family members learn to be open to each other's inner life, as well as the outward behaviour. This builds safety and develops reciprocal relationships within which all members of the family learn to cooperate, and shared meaning is given to the family experiences.

This emphasis on safety and healthy interactions is essential for developmentally traumatized children who often lack capacity for emotional regulation or reflective function. As these capacities are enhanced through day-to-day PACE-led parenting and within the therapy sessions, the child is enabled to respond to current experience and memories of past experience flexibly instead of through habitual, rigid and repetitive responses.

This provides a foundation to help the child, supported by her parents, to explore unhappy and painful experience in the present but also in her past. The involvement of the parent in this therapeutic work is a critical part of its success. Not least, the parent will need to support the child at home, sometimes through a period of increased distress and distressing behaviours. The old adage 'It has to get worse before it gets better' can be seen as a reality as the child copes with the intense and sometimes stressful therapeutic work of revisiting experience and giving this experience new meaning. More than this, though, by having the parents involved in the therapeutic process, the child gets her experience of safety and corrective attachment experience with the people who matter most to her. These will be long-lasting relationships able to support the child into adulthood and beyond.

---

Kim worked with a young boy who has chosen to be called Liam in this chapter. Now a thoughtful and engaging teenager, Liam has given us permission to share his therapy journey with you. A part of this journey has been illustrated in another book.[4] Here we would like to invite you into Liam's therapy over the course of two years, so that you can see both the hard work and the enormous progress a young person can make with the help of sensitive and supportive foster parents, supplemented by dyadic developmental psychotherapy.

Dan feels that it is important to stress that Kim's competence and compassion were necessary for this therapy to be effective for Liam and his family. Relationships are at the heart of parenting and of therapy. The parent and the therapist offer the child relationships from which safety, security and autonomy can all grow.

Liam and his younger sister spent their early years living in a home that featured neglect, domestic violence and, at times, physical abuse. The children were removed and placed in foster care when Liam was six years old. They were in separate placements initially but were able to live together again when placed with Jenny and Tom.

Liam was eight years old and determined not to move again. This short-term placement transformed into a long-term placement as love and commitment developed on both sides. This would be tested many times as the children brought with them into this home their hard-earned strategies to keep themselves safe in an unsafe world. Whilst these strategies no longer fitted, the children were not about to give them up to test this out! Liam was a highly self-reliant boy with a tight grip on his emotional life. Strong feelings were locked up in boxes. Liam did not give the keys up willingly.

If you are familiar with the Harry Potter films, you may remember a scene in which Harry tries to catch a key amongst a multitude of flying keys. This is how Liam envisaged the keys to his boxes. Only occasionally would his defences slip, allowing Jenny or Tom to catch a key and support him with the now revealed emotion.

Kim supported Jenny and Tom for a couple of years prior to working with Liam. They developed a therapeutic environment within which they could parent the children and begin to build the trust and security that the children badly needed. Although they did feel that they were making progress, Jenny and Tom remained troubled about Liam. They recognized his vulnerability, hidden though it was behind a confident, charming exterior. They were concerned that Liam dealt with difficult experience by entertaining or taking care of others, whilst actively resisting support or comfort for himself. This came at a cost. Reciprocal friendships were hard for Liam, and at times feelings burst from him unbidden in angry and aggressive displays of his fear and insecurity. Despite increasing trust in Jenny and Tom, this way of being was not modifying, and they feared for his future. We decided to add therapy to complement the parenting Liam was already receiving. After a period of uncertainty, Liam agreed to meet with Kim so that he could find out what we were asking him to engage with.

Kim paid a visit to the house, this time to talk with Liam rather than with Jenny and Tom. She told him what therapy would involve and what he might expect. As she anticipated, she found him to be keenly intelligent and also desperate to impress. He started, as he would continue, by keeping her at arm's length, using his intellect and honed ability to control. Nevertheless, he listened to what she had to say and quickly adopted her analogies and improved upon them. As Kim described therapy as an onion, for example, he told her that, yes, this was right. It would be scary as he needed to get through lots of layers, and sometimes, like cutting into the onion, it would make him cry. Kim would have her work cut out keeping up with him!

Liam agreed to start the work. He also agreed that Jenny would join the sessions. He wanted the therapy to help him manage his behaviour. Kim explained that her aim would be to help him do this by helping him to feel more secure with Jenny and Tom. She hoped that he would, in time, feel more comfortable sharing his feelings with them and letting them take care of him. Liam solemnly agreed whilst every fibre of his body shouted no, this would be a bad idea.

Kim and Liam decided on three aims for therapy:

1. To help Liam to feel more secure with Jenny and Tom so that he could let them take care of him.

2. To help Liam express his feelings in a straightforward way so he is in control of them rather than they being in control of him.

3. To help Liam think about his early experiences and how these impact on the way he is currently feeling, thinking and behaving.

At the end of the therapeutic work nearly two years later, Liam and Kim reviewed these aims in preparation for the final report. They looked back at the work as taking place at six levels (See Figure 10.2 below). These levels are not sequential. Whilst, to some extent, they worked at all these levels throughout the therapy, they also represent a deepening of their work together. In the early months they would be at the initial levels more of the time, the other levels becoming more open to them as they progressed.

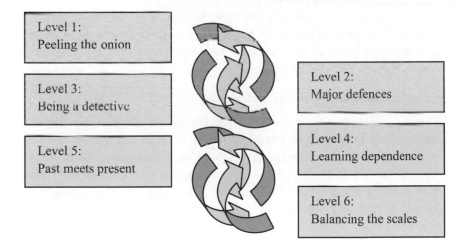

**Figure 10.2** Levels of therapy

## Level 1: Peeling the onion

This level represents the secure base that was the foundation for their work together. As they develop a therapeutic alliance based on intersubjective experiences, Liam is able to demonstrate his defences and experience acceptance of these. This acceptance helps him to feel safe and to experience emotional co-regulation. This in turn opens exploration up to them all. They enjoy the developing relationships, laugh a lot and tease each other. Level 1 is the level they can move back to when things are particularly tough.

Within this level they discover together how Liam keeps himself safe. Liam needs to feel in control. He is very uncomfortable when others try to take care of him. He uses his intellect, his cleverness, to keep people at bay. He is happier being the one who knows things and who looks after others. Always happy, always charming, always entertaining, Liam hides away the more uncomfortable negative feelings. He appears relaxed and confident. He can think about his earlier experience but does not engage emotionally with it. Like an iceberg, much of what Liam experiences is below the surface.

Kim and Liam explore together his use of boxes to store feelings: what happens as the feelings grow and 'fizz', how horrible it is as they break out of the boxes, and how hard Liam works to lock them away again. Kim introduces the idea that feelings locked away stay in charge. Liam is unconvinced, and Kim accepts his lack of conviction as they play with analogies to deepen their understanding.

Throughout this work Jenny is quietly supportive, allowing Liam to control the rhythm of the sessions, not protesting at his many distractions and demonstrating her enjoyment of her relationship with Liam. They too have a teasing, playful relationship which fits well with the DDP approach.

## Level 2: Discovering major defences

Level 2 represents a deepening of exploration as Liam is more able to trust in the alliance developed at level 1. This trust allows Kim to provide some gentle challenge alongside genuine acceptance. During this exploration she is the 'terrier', exploring and not letting things go. Liam is a jester, a big defence when the discussion gets a bit too close for comfort. They explore together the range of defences – major defences, Liam calls them – which help him to feel safe. Liam learns to notice when he entertains, distracts and controls. He says something significant and quickly passes it off as a joke. He knows everything, fearing what he does not want to know. He notices himself becoming hyperactive, silly, rude or angry when feelings get too close for comfort.

At this level, they focus on the present and Liam's current relationships. His past experience is acknowledged, but exploration of this comes as they move to a deeper level. Liam is learning how he defends against his anxieties and fears; as they move deeper, he will learn what he fears and how this connects to his early experience within his birth family.

Exploring defences is a difficult task for Liam in therapy. He struggles with fears that he will become someone else through their work together and will lose something important in the process. He enjoys being a jester and an entertainer. He does not want to let this go. Jenny and Kim help him to see that he is greater than the sum of the parts, that nothing will be lost. The difference is that he will be in charge, rather than the defences.

Kim also uses the idea of a volcano to explore how the defences have a weakness; they lead to feelings getting bigger until they eventually explode. Liam learns to recognize his impulsive, aggressive behaviour as the boxed feelings taking charge, leading to behaviour that takes him by surprise.

## Level 3: Being a detective, understanding the feelings

The exploration deepens further, alongside Liam's developing capacity for reflective function. The work at this level is to understand what lies beneath the anxiety that triggers a major defence. Readily able to recognize when he is angry, Liam learns to notice the worry, fear and sadness that underpin these angry feelings. Kim and Liam revisit day-to-day experience through guided visualization. Liam is amazed to find a whole world of feelings that had been out of awareness for so long.

Liam learns about his view of himself as not good enough in a world that is scary. As his internal working model becomes more open to him, it also becomes open to change. Liam takes some risks as he opens himself up to emotional experience, trusting that Kim and Jenny will keep him safe.

At this level, they are all detectives together as Jenny and Kim help Liam to recognize and take charge of his feelings. They use the analogy of skating. Liam recognizes how he skates towards and then away from feelings. Liam discovers that whilst he has a lot of words, he finds it much harder to have lots of feelings. He works with Jenny and Kim to be able to have both words and feelings when he needs them.

## Level 4: Learning dependence

With deeper understanding, Liam is able to stay with his feelings and begin to allow Jenny to help him with them. This is the most difficult level for Liam. They all discover how scared he is when Jenny takes care of him. He feels shame if he needs emotional support from her. He worries that she will not like an anxious or sad Liam. We also learn how scared Liam is of being unnoticed, sometimes bringing Jenny to 'pinnacle point' in order not to be forgotten. He does not trust Jenny to keep him in mind; he does not trust her not to hurt him. Locking his feelings away is his solution to these fears. Liam tells us that we are all on a boat in a pond that we need to traverse; at the centre is a whirlpool with a blade in the middle of it. Jenny and Kim can steer us through, but Liam is not sure. He tries to steer them away whenever he can.

Gradually, Liam starts to take some risks within the sessions, and later between the sessions, letting Jenny be in charge, allowing her to take care of him. Liam is learning to trust Jenny deep down inside as well as on the surface. He is learning that not only does Jenny love Liam the helper and Liam the entertainer, she also loves Liam who gets angry, is naughty or is sad or worried.

## Level 5: Discovering how the past meets the present

A backdrop to all the sessions is Liam's early experience. Within the sessions, Jenny and Liam revisit some of this experience as memories or thoughts come to the surface. At first tentative and brief, this exploration develops over time. With a developing trust in Jenny, Liam is able to stay with the memories and share his affective experience of them.

Liam learns how his past experience has taught him important things that are now contributing to the way he uses his major defences and boxes his feelings. He experiences events in the present evoking experiences from his past, and learns to notice the strong reactions that this leads to. His developing trust in Jenny facilitates this exploration as meaning is co-constructed and emotion is co-regulated.

## Level 6: Balancing the scales – putting it all together

Towards the end of therapy Liam learns to integrate all the work they have done together. He develops a coherent narrative, a way of thinking about his experience and how it impacts on him. This puts him in charge. Liam can now hold different perspectives. For example, he recognizes his view of self as not able to live up to parental expectations but can balance this with a view of parents as not able to look after him properly. This allows him to believe in his ability to live up to his foster parents' expectations of him and opens up the possibility of them being able to care for him.

Over the course of therapy Liam becomes less impulsive, less at the mercy of difficult feelings that have escaped from his boxes. Liam is learning to open and control the boxes; he is beginning to experience feelings as well as to think about things. At some point, one might even say that these boxes have faded away so that they no longer play a part in the integrated functioning of his brain. He uses his relationship with Jenny and Tom to help him with this. Liam is still very caring but now he is also able to be cared for. Liam is learning to be dependent as well as independent.

As Liam enters the teen years and the inevitable emotional roller-coaster ride that represents adolescence, he is able to use his relationship with Jenny and Tom as a secure base, a source of dependency as he takes genuine steps towards his own independence.

Alongside this more relaxed ability to live in a family and to use it as a source of support, Liam is learning to live within a peer group and to develop genuine friendships not spoilt by a need to control and dominate. This becomes a later source of the work as Kim and Liam explore Liam's perception of himself as a loner who does not like to spend too much time with friends. Liam works so hard at staying in charge within friendships that he becomes tired quickly and needs to spend time alone. He learns to understand this also in relation to his early experience: his fear of reciprocal relationships within which he opens himself up to hurt. As he learns to relax his need for control, a wider world of friendship becomes open to him. Liam dreams of a future, of a career and of a family, a future within which he can be a jester, an entertainer, an intellectual and a parent. He is comfortable being a friend and a companion, able to be sad and confused and to ask for help, but all within his own control as he takes charge of his past, present and future, with a bit of help from others.

---

## In conclusion

We all learn to parent, not instinctively, but stemming from our experience of being parented ourselves. For many of us this did not, and still does not, include an attitude of PACE.

We love our children and want the best for them. This well-meaning ambition, however, can come across as nagging, lecturing and cajoling, as we try to mould our children into the vision we have for them. The parenting that comes naturally to us is one of expectation. At our best, we provide appropriate boundaries, warmth and nurture. Our love is unconditional – we will always be there whatever may happen – but we may express this love as if it is conditional. Children mature under the weight of our expectations.

Some meet these expectations and enjoy the approval they receive, but approval earned can be lost. A nagging insecurity remains. Even when parental approval is maintained, the cost may be high. The child's efforts to please the parent can mean that her own developing autonomy is left behind. Parts of the self do not develop and dreams are not followed. Others kick against the expectations, preferring to find a different path, often leaving them with a sense of not being quite good enough, unsure of our pride in them. At its best the children grow up and develop confidence with maturity; they experience career and relationship success. They establish a new adult relationship with their parents, each reaching a new understanding of the other. The cultural expectations of parents remain the same, however. What worked for me will work for you. The children grown up have children of their own, and the cycle repeats.

Within this book we have introduced a different way of parenting. This has at its centre the attitude of PACE. Unconditional love is expressed through playfulness, acceptance, curiosity and empathy. This does not change what we want, or even expect, of our children, but it does suggest a different way of conveying this.

Stopping to be curious, accepting the inner life of the child and understanding how this influences the more externally revealed behaviour means we have a deeper level of empathy and trust in her.

We strive for connection and this produces a more emotionally resonant relationship within which it is natural to be playful; it becomes easier to add a dimension of fun to our day-to-day existence. Our parenting still provides appropriate boundaries and limits, together with warmth and nurture. The connection that PACE creates with our children, however, means that this parenting is received as fully unconditional. The children feel loved and trusted. They in turn can love and trust us.

Security is at the core of who they are and who they will become. They know that they can develop their sense of autonomy while at the same time having emotionally safe and close relationships with their parents. They continue to be influenced by our thoughts, feelings and beliefs, while being completely free to experience differences from us. They remain safe in our unconditional love.

Parenting with PACE can benefit all children, leading to stronger emotional health and greater capacity for interdependence within relationships. Whilst it can benefit all children, it is most needed for traumatized children, especially children who have experienced trauma within the family, impacting upon their development. American researcher and Trauma specialist Bessel van der Kolk describes this as 'developmental trauma'.[5]

The insecurity that these children experience means that they will struggle most with the development of attachment and the ability to be intersubjectively with another. If these children are to develop an emotionally healthy core, they will need to experience therapeutic parenting over an extended period. Parenting with PACE can provide the children with the healing environment that allows recovery from their early experience.

This is not an easy journey. We are both parents ourselves and have experienced how our own hopes, fears and expectations can at times shut down playfulness and curiosity and make acceptance and empathy thin on the ground. Fearing for our children's futures, we easily become driven by these fears, and this comes across as criticism, disapproval and doubt. At times of stress and difficulty in our lives, it is hard to hold on to core values, to stay grounded in the present and to trust in the process. PACE-led parenting is an attitude that can be cultivated and does become easier with practice, but it is hard work. We need PACE for ourselves if we are to give it to our children. Try not to be too hard on yourself if you drift from it; ensure that you have strong relationships that can provide support, rest and relaxation; and treasure the moments when you experience true connection with your child, even and especially when these moments appear only briefly. Your children will know you are trying, and their trust and security will develop from your willingness to work at this.

---

Dan recently spoke with a parent who had struggled for months in treatment with her son and still reacted to his very challenging behaviours with rage and then withdrawal – patterns from her relationships with her parents when she was a child.

In a separate meeting with Dan, she screamed that she hated her son, that he just did not appreciate all that she had done for him. Trusting in PACE, Dan replied with empathy about how hard it must be for her to be aware that she hates her son after working so very hard to be a better mother for him than her mother was for her. She then sat in silence as she cried.

Finally, as her shame lifted, she looked Dan in the eyes and said with conviction that she was a better mother than her mother was, and that she was not going to stop loving her son even if she felt hatred toward him sometimes. She was not going to give up making their relationship work. She challenged Dan to work with her. Dan had given her no advice, no behaviours to practise. He simply sat with her, experiencing and expressing PACE.

---

As we mentioned in Chapter 3, Dan has also written a book with a colleague, Jon Baylin, which describes the joys and challenges of parenting from a neuropsychological perspective.[6] Dan and Jon describe how a parent's past and present stresses can impede the integrated activity of five systems of the brain that are crucial for ongoing, effective parenting.

They describe how this process creates what they refer to as 'blocked care'. This describes how difficult it is to provide ongoing caregiving for the child when faced with these sources of stress. In their work they speak of the process of reactivating caregiving – and the brain's readiness to provide this care – and it is not surprising to note that PACE is central to the ability to begin to care again.

---

Kim follows a child who has stormed off in a rage. The child shouts at her to go away, leave her alone. Kim quickly reviews the conversation they were having.

She had asked her why she had got upset with her friend. She had felt criticized by Kim. Inside, Kim wants to scream, 'Why are you so sensitive? It makes it so hard to talk things over with you.' She takes a deep breath, crouches down next to her and says with an intensity that matches the child's: 'You thought I was blaming you. No wonder you are mad with me. I would be mad too if I thought someone thought it was my fault.'

Kim watches this child relax in front of her eyes. They have a connection. She looks at Kim with tears in her eyes and says, 'I always say the wrong thing!' Empathy is easy now. 'It is so sad that you feel like you keep saying the wrong thing; how tough to feel others blame you when things go wrong.' Kim has tears in her eyes too as she shares all this child's fears and sense of uselessness. 'I am glad you understand,' the child says. Kim tells her that she thinks she is the bravest girl she knows to keep trying despite her doubts and fears.

---

Children traumatized by their life experiences deserve to be loved, cherished and healed. Their own adaptations and defences do not always make this easy to achieve. We wish you success with your own journeys, whatever and wherever they are. We hope that this book and a deeper understanding of love and PACE will provide you with ideas so that you can help the troubled children you encounter to develop confidence and security.

# Glossary

*Attachment* In Attachment Theory the term attachment describes the special relationships a child forms with a caregiver. The attachment is an emotional bond within which the child seeks security and comfort from the adult.

*Attunement* Two people are in attunement when they are sharing an emotional experience. The attunement represents an emotional connection between them within which one person mirrors or matches the vitality and affect (biological expression of the emotion) of the other. This is not the same as sharing the same emotion. Thus, in a state of attunement a person might match the affective expression of anger, but does not become angry (emotional state) himself.

*Autonomy* This is the degree to which an individual experiences independence, able to make his own decisions without being reliant on another person.

*Co-construction* The parent helps the young child to develop a coherent autobiographical narrative about his life and experience. The child will find it difficult to make sense of his experience without first developing this understanding together with another. This shared meaning making represents the co-constructive process.

*Coherent narrative* This refers to the outcome of a process where an individual successfully makes sense of himself and his experiences. We all strive to form a coherent narrative of our life experiences.

*Co-regulation* This describes the process of a parent helping a young child to learn to regulate his affect and the emotional state that this represents. When the child is becoming dysregulated the parent matches the affect and leads the child into a regulated state. By matching the affective expression of the emotions being experienced by the child, whilst remaining regulated himself, the parent assists the child to manage this emotional experience leading to the development of self-regulation.

*Cortical structures* These refer to sections of the cerebral cortex, which is the part of the brain specialized for reasoning. It is involved with memory, attention, awareness, thought, language and consciousness. These are described as 'higher' functions of the brain because they are much less developed in animals.

*Developmental trauma* The term trauma usually refers to a single event that is traumatizing for an individual. To distinguish this from the experience of multiple traumas, researchers and clinicians sometimes use the term complex trauma. More recently the term developmental trauma has also been used to refer to people whose development has been affected by the experience of complex trauma beginning early in their life within their family.

*Dysregulation* This represents a loss of regulation of emotion. Emotional arousal has heightened to the point when an individual is unable to control and modulate this experience. The emotion overwhelms the individual and he enters a dysregulated state.

*Emotional regulation* This refers to the capacity to manage emotional arousal. As arousal increases emotional regulation allows the person to manage this emotion without losing control of it. Good emotional regulation requires that the person as an infant was cared for by a caregiver who regulated her emotion for her, and co-regulated with her as she matures towards being able to self-regulate.

*Higher brain* The rational part of our brain is sometimes referred to as the higher brain. This part of the brain is also called the cortex. It is the thinking part of the brain, helping us to attend to things, solve problems and manage the impulses driven by other parts of the brain.

*Hormones* These are chemicals released by the structure of the nervous system or the glands. They include neuropeptides – such as oxytocin and prolactin – which increase feelings of well-being, and endorphins – such as the endogenous opioids – which reduce pain sensations.

*Hyperarousal* This refers to a level of emotional arousal which has become too high and is therefore uncomfortable and difficult to manage. An individual who is hyperaroused will be jumpy and quick to react, and will find it difficult to be soothed and thus to calm down.

*Hypervigilant* This refers to an enhanced state of vigilance when an individual has become over sensitive to potential dangers within the environment. When a person is hypervigilant he will experience difficulty switching his attention away from scanning the environment for danger and will thus become inattentive to other tasks in front of him.

*Intersubjectivity* This describes a relationship within which experience is shared. It is a reciprocal relationship because the experience of each has an impact on the experience of the other. This is based on an experience of shared affective states, joint attention and congruent, complimentary intentions.

*Limbic structures* These are regions of the brain most associated with pleasure and general emotional responses.

*Protoconversation* A conversation held with an infant before speech has developed. The interaction between infant and adult has the appearance of a conversation, including turn-taking and conversational rhythm.

*Reflective function* This refers to the ability of an individual to think about his experience or the experience of others. With reflective function an individual can make sense of why things happen and why he and others behave as they do.

*Socialization* This is the process whereby an individual learns about his culture and how to live successfully within it. Children become socialized when parents model and explicitly teach them what is and is not acceptable behaviour based on cultural norms and expectations.

*Therapeutic parenting* This describes parenting which goes beyond loving and caring for a child to also helping a child to heal from past hurts and traumas.

*Unconditional acceptance* Acceptance of another person's experience without conditions.

# References

## Introduction

1. In his book *Attachment-Focused Parenting* (see note 3 below), Dan describes his earlier use of PLACE and why he now prefers to describe love as separate from the attitude of PACE.
2. Hughes, D.A. (2011) *Attachment-Focused Family Therapy: Workbook*. New York, NY: W.W. Norton & Co.
3. See Hughes, D.A. (2009) *Attachment-Focused Parenting: Effective Strategies to Care for Children*. New York, NY: W.W. Norton & Co; and Golding, K.S. (2008) *Nurturing Attachments: Supporting Children Who Are Fostered or Adopted*. London: Jessica Kingsley Publishers.
4. See www.parenting.co.uk, accessed on 17 September 2011.
5. See www.bbc.co.uk/news/uk-14899148 and www.bbc.co.uk/news/education-14898614, accessed on 17 September 2011.

## Chapter 1

1. Available at www.brainyquote.com/quotes/authors/l/lao_tzu.html, accessed on 30 August 2011.
2. Atkinson, E. (2008) *Greyfriars Bobby*. The Project Gutenberg EBook. Available at www.gutenberg.org/files/2693/2693-h/2693-h.htm, accessed on 20 December 2011.
3. de Bernières, L. (2007) *Red Dog*. London: Vintage.
4. Homer, *Odyssey* (trans. Alexander Pope). Cited in F. Addis (2010) *Opening Pandora's Box*. London: Michael O'Mara Books.
5. Available at www.brainyquote.com/quotes/quotes/a/albertelli131212.html, accessed 30 August 2011.
6. Lewis, T., Amini, F. and Lannon, R. (2000/2001) *A General Theory of Love*. New York, NY: Vintage Books.
7. Armstrong, J. (2002) *Conditions of Love: The Philosophy of Intimacy*. New York, NY: W.W. Norton & Co.
8. Winnicott, D.W. (1957/1964) *The Child, the Family, and the Outside World*. Middlesex: Penguin Books, p.27.
9. Winnicott, D.W. (1957/1964) *The Child, the Family, and the Outside World*. Middlesex: Penguin Books, p.27.
10. Winnicott, D.W. (1957/1964) *The Child, the Family, and the Outside World*. Middlesex: Penguin Books, p.85.
11. See, for example: Sluckin, W., Herbert, M. and Sluckin, A. (1983) *Maternal Bonding*. Oxford: Basil Blackwell Publishers.

12. Sunderland, M. (2006) *The Science of Parenting: Practical Guidance on Sleep, Crying, Play and Building Emotional Wellbeing for Life.* London: Dorling Kindersley, p.192.

13. Sunderland, M. (2006) *The Science of Parenting: Practical Guidance on Sleep, Crying, Play and Building Emotional Wellbeing for Life.* London: Dorling Kindersley, p.184.

14. Rowling, J.K. (2001) *Harry Potter and the Philosopher's Stone.* London: Bloomsbury Publishing.

15. Lewis, T., Amini, F. and Lannon, R. (2000/2001) *A General Theory of Love.* New York, NY: Vintage Books.

16. Descartes, R. (1637) *Discourse on the Method of Rightly Conducting the Reason, and Seeking the Truth in the Sciences,* Chapter 4. A translation by John Veitch is available at www.pinkmonkey.com/dl/library1/book0648.pdf, accessed on 20 December 2011.

17. Maclean, P.D. (2003) *The Triune Brain in Evolution: Role in Paleocerebral Functions.* New York, NY: Plenum Press.

18. Lewis, T., Amini, F. and Lannon, R. (2000/2001) *A General Theory of Love.* New York, NY: Vintage Books, p.84.

19. Lewis, T., Amini, F. and Lannon, R. (2000/2001) *A General Theory of Love.* New York, NY: Vintage Books, p.87.

20. Lewis, T., Amini, F. and Lannon, R. (2000/2001) *A General Theory of Love.* New York, NY: Vintage Books, p.144.

21. Panksepp, J. (1998) *Affective Neuroscience: The Foundations of Human and Animal Emotions.* New York, NY: Oxford University Press.

22. Bowlby, R. (2004) *Fifty Years of Attachment Theory: The Donald Winnicott Memorial Lecture.* London: Karnac Books, p.13.

23. Bowlby, R. (2007) 'Passionate about Attachments.' In K.S. Golding (ed.) *Briefing Paper: Attachment Theory into Practice.* London: Faculty for Children and Young People of the Division of Clinical Psychology, British Psychological Society, p.10.

24. Personal communication from Richard Bowlby to Dan Hughes, 2005.

25. Bowlby, J. (1953/1965) *Child Care and the Growth of Love.* Middlesex: Penguin Books.

26. Bowlby, J. (1953/1965) *Child Care and the Growth of Love.* Middlesex: Penguin Books, p.77.

27. Bowlby, J. (1953/1965) *Child Care and the Growth of Love.* Middlesex: Penguin Books, p.78.

28. Main, M. and Hesse, E. (1990) 'Parents' Unresolved Traumatic Experiences are Related to Infant Disorganized Attachment Status: Is Frightened and/or Frightening Parental Behavior the Linking Mechanism?' In M.T. Greenberg, D. Cicchetti and E.M. Cummings (eds) *Attachment in the Preschool Years: Theory, Research and Intervention.* Chicago, IL: University of Chicago Press, pp.161–182.

29. Dozier, M. (2003) 'Attachment-based treatment for vulnerable children.' *Attachment and Human Development 5,* 3, 253–257.

30. Trevarthen, C. (2001) 'Intrinsic motives for companionship in understanding: Their origin, development, and significance for infant mental health.' *Infant Mental Health Journal 22,* 1–2, 95–131.

31. Slater, L. (2004) *Opening Skinner's Box: Great Psychological Experiments of the Twentieth Century.* London: Bloomsbury Publishing.

32. This anecdote is described by Lewis *et al.* (see note 6 above) and also by Vera Fahlberg. See: Fahlberg, V. (1994) *A Child's Journey Through Placement* (UK edition). London: BAAF.

33. Lewis, T., Amini, F. and Lannon, R. (2000/2001) *A General Theory of Love.* New York, NY: Vintage Books.

34. Perry B.D. and Szalavitz, M. (2006) *The Boy Who Was Raised as a Dog. And Other Stories from a Child Psychiatrist's Notebook: What Traumatized Children Can Teach Us About Loss, Love and Healing*. New York, NY: Basic Books.

35. Perry, B.D. and Szalavitz, M. (2006) *The Boy Who Was Raised as a Dog. And Other Stories from a Child Psychiatrist's Notebook: What Traumatized Children Can Teach Us About Loss, Love and Healing*. New York, NY: Basic Books, pp.231–232.

36. Sunderland, M. (2006) *The Science of Parenting: Practical Guidance on Sleep, Crying, Play and Building Emotional Wellbeing for Life*. London: Dorling Kindersley, p.215.

37. Munsch, R. (1986/2010) *Love You Forever*. New York, NY: Firefly Books.

## Chapter 2

1.   UN Convention on the Rights of the Child. United Nations (1989), Article 31. Available at www2.ohchr.org/english/law/crc.htm, accessed on 2 November 2011.

2.   Bruner, J. (1977) 'Introduction.' In B. Tizard and D. Harvey (eds) *Biology of Play*. Suffolk: SIMP, p.v.

3.   Tizard B. (1977) 'Play: The Child's Way of Learning?' In B. Tizard and D. Harvey (eds) *Biology of Play*. Suffolk: SIMP, Chapter 14.

4.   Brown, S. (2009/2010) *Play: How It Shapes the Brain, Opens the Imagination, and Invigorates the Soul*. New York, NY: Avery/Penguin Group, p.5.

5.   Panksepp, J. (1998) *Affective Neuroscience: The Foundations of Human and Animal Emotions*. New York, NY: Oxford University Press.

6.   Panksepp, J. (1998) *Affective Neuroscience: The Foundations of Human and Animal Emotions*. New York, NY: Oxford University Press, p.280.

7.   Feitelson, D. (1977) 'Cross-Cultural Studies of Representational Play.' In B. Tizard and D. Harvey (eds) *Biology of Play*. Suffolk: SIMP, pp.6–14.

8.   Cited in: Faulkner, D. (1995) 'Play, Self and the Social World.' In P. Barnes (ed.) *Personal, Social and Emotional Development of Children*. Oxford: Blackwell Publishers/Milton Keynes: The Open University, Chapter 6.

9.   Panksepp, J. (1998) *Affective Neuroscience: The Foundations of Human and Animal Emotions*. New York, NY: Oxford University Press.

10.  Brown, S. (2009/2010) *Play: How It Shapes the Brain, Opens the Imagination, and Invigorates the Soul*. New York, NY: Avery/Penguin Group.

11.  Brown, S. (2009/2010) *Play: How It Shapes the Brain, Opens the Imagination, and Invigorates the Soul*. New York, NY: Avery/Penguin Group, p.92.

12.  Brown, S. (2009/2010) *Play: How It Shapes the Brain, Opens the Imagination, and Invigorates the Soul*. New York, NY: Avery/Penguin Group, p.87.

13.  Panksepp, J. (1998) *Affective Neuroscience: The Foundations of Human and Animal Emotions*. New York, NY: Oxford University Press, p.281.

14.  Brown, S. (2009/2010) *Play: How It Shapes the Brain, Opens the Imagination, and Invigorates the Soul*. New York, NY: Avery/Penguin Group.

15.  Brown, S. (2009/2010) *Play: How It Shapes the Brain, Opens the Imagination, and Invigorates the Soul*. New York, NY: Avery/Penguin Group.

16.  Brown, S. (2009/2010) *Play: How It Shapes the Brain, Opens the Imagination, and Invigorates the Soul*. New York, NY: Avery/Penguin Group, p.42.

17.  White, L. (1977) 'Play in Animals.' In B. Tizard and D. Harvey (eds) *Biology of Play*. Suffolk: SIMP, pp.15–32.

18.  Panksepp, J. (1998) *Affective Neuroscience: The Foundations of Human and Animal Emotions*. New York, NY: Oxford University Press.

19. Brown, S. (2009/2010) *Play: How It Shapes the Brain, Opens the Imagination, and Invigorates the Soul*. New York, NY: Avery/Penguin Group.
20. Faulkner, D. (1995) 'Play, Self and the Social World.' In P. Barnes (ed.) *Personal, Social and Emotional Development of Children*. Oxford: Blackwell Publishers/Milton Keynes: The Open University, Chapter 6.

## Chapter 3
1. Cohen, L.J. (2001) *Playful Parenting*. New York, NY: Ballantine Books, p.2.
2. Stern, D.N. (1998) *The Interpersonal World of the Infant: A View from Psychoanalysis and Developmental Psychology*. New York, NY: Basic Books.
3. Hughes, D.A. (2009) *Attachment-Focused Parenting: Effective Strategies to Care for Children*. New York, NY: W.W. Norton & Co, p.74.
4. Hughes, D. and Baylin, J. (2012) *Brain-Based Parenting: The Neuroscience of Caregiving for Healthy Attachment*. New York, NY: W.W. Norton & Co.
5. This short story has been written especially for this book. Gregory Delve is a second-year, creative writing student at Bath Spa University, Bath, England.

## Chapter 4
1. Shriver, L (2003) *We Need to Talk About Kevin*. London: Serpent's Tail.
2. Siegel, D.J. (2010) *The Mindful Therapist*. New York, NY: W.W. Norton & Co, p.xxv.
3. Brach, T. (2003) *Radical Acceptance: Embracing Your Life with the Heart of a Buddha*. New York, NY: Bantam Books, p.27.
4. Austin, J.H. (2006) *Zen-Brain Reflections*. Cambridge, MA: The MIT Press, p.237.
5. Porges, S.W. (2011) *The Polyvagal Theory: Neurophysiological Foundations of Emotions, Attachment, Communication, and Self-Regulation*. New York, NY: W.W. Norton & Co.
6. Tangney, J. and Dearing, R. (2002). *Shame and Guilt*. New York, NY: Guilford Press, p.120.

## Chapter 5
1. Austin, J.H. (2006) *Zen-Brain Reflections*. Cambridge, MA: The MIT Press, p.237.
2. Cicchetti, D., Toth, S. and Lynch, M. (1995) 'Bowlby's dream comes full circle: The application of attachment theory to risk and psychopathology.' *Advances in Clinical Child Psychology 17*, 1–75.
3. Siegel, D.J. (1999) *The Developing Mind: Toward a Neurobiology of Interpersonal Experience*. New York, NY: Guilford Press.

## Chapter 6
1. Available at www.greekmyths-greekmythology.com/pandoras-box-myth, accessed on 5 October 2011.
2. Benedict, B.M. (2001) *Curiosity: A Cultural History of Early Modern Inquiry*. Chicago, IL: University of Chicago Press, p.3.
3. White, M. and Epston, D. (1990) *Narrative Means to Therapeutic Ends*. New York, NY: W.W. Norton & Co.
4. Kashdan, T. (2009) *Curious?* New York, NY: HarperCollins Books, p.26.
5. Panksepp, J. (1998) *Affective Neuroscience: The Foundations of Human and Animal Emotions*. New York, NY: Oxford University Press.
6. Panksepp, J. (1998) *Affective Neuroscience: The Foundations of Human and Animal Emotions*. New York, NY: Oxford University Press, p.53.

7.  Siegel, D.J. (1999) *The Developing Mind: Toward a Neurobiology of Interpersonal Experience.* New York, NY: Guilford Press.
8.  Panksepp, J. (1998) *Affective Neuroscience: The Foundations of Human and Animal Emotions.* New York, NY: Oxford University Press.
9.  Panksepp, J. (1998) *Affective Neuroscience: The Foundations of Human and Animal Emotions.* New York, NY: Oxford University Press.
10. Benedict, B.M. (2001) *Curiosity: A Cultural History of Early Modern Inquiry.* Chicago, IL: University of Chicago Press.
11. Quoted in Benedict, B.M. (2001) *Curiosity: A Cultural History of Early Modern Inquiry.* Chicago, IL: University of Chicago Press, p.23.
12. Shelley, M. (2006) *Frankenstein.* London: Penguin Books. (First published 1818.)
13. Clarke, A.C. (1968) *2001: A Space Odyssey.* London: Hutchinson & Co.
14. Benedict, B.M. (2001) *Curiosity: A Cultural History of Early Modern Inquiry.* Chicago, IL: University of Chicago Press, p.2.
15. Bowlby, J. (1998) *A Secure Base: Clinical Applications of Attachment Theory.* London: Routledge. (Original work published 1988.)
16. Hughes, D.A. (2009) *Attachment-Focused Parenting: Effective Strategies to Care for Children.* New York, NY: W.W. Norton & Co, p.85.
17. Meins, E. (1997) *Security of Attachment and the Social Development of Cognition.* Hove, East Sussex: Psychology Press.
18. Kashdan, T. (2009) *Curious?* New York, NY: HarperCollins Books, p.26.
19. Kashdan, T. (2009) *Curious?* New York, NY: HarperCollins Books, p.183.
20. Panksepp, J. (1998) *Affective Neuroscience: The Foundations of Human and Animal Emotions.* New York, NY: Oxford University Press.
21. Hudson-Allez, G. (2009) *Infant Losses; Adult Searches: A Neural and Developmental Perspective on Psychopathology and Sexual Offending.* London: Karnac Books.
22. Hudson-Allez, G. (2009) *Infant Losses; Adult Searches: A Neural and Developmental Perspective on Psychopathology and Sexual Offending.* London: Karnac Books, p.42.
23. Cairns, K. (2002) *Attachment, Trauma and Resilience.* London: BAAF.

## Chapter 7

1.  Freud, S. (1909) 'Analysis of a Phobia in a Five-Year-Old Boy.' In J. Strachey (ed.) (1953–1973) *The Standard Edition of the Complete Works of Sigmund Freud* (Vol. 10). London: Hogarth, p.122.
2.  Walt Disney, as quoted at the end of the movie *Meet the Robinsons* (2007).
3.  Hughes, D.A. (2009) *Attachment-Focused Parenting: Effective Strategies to Care for Children.* New York, NY: W.W. Norton & Co, p.86.

## Chapter 8

1.  Rowling, J.K. (2003) *Harry Potter and the Order of the Phoenix.* London: Bloomsbury Publishing, pp.405–406. Copyright © J.K. Rowling 2003.
2.  Baron-Cohen, S. (2011) *Zero Degrees of Empathy: A New Theory of Human Cruelty.* London: Allen Lane, p.11.
3.  Baron-Cohen, S. (2011) *Zero Degrees of Empathy: A New Theory of Human Cruelty.* London: Allen Lane.
4.  Buber, M. (1965) *The Knowledge of Man: Selected Essays*, edited by M. Friedman. New York, NY: Harper and Row.

5.  Baron-Cohen, S. (2011) *Zero Degrees of Empathy: A New Theory of Human Cruelty*. London: Allen Lane.
6.  Szalavitz, M. and Perry, B.D. (2010) *Born for Love: Why Empathy is Essential – And Endangered*. New York, NY: HarperCollins, p.4.
7.  Szalavitz, M. and Perry, B.D. (2010) *Born for Love: Why Empathy is Essential – And Endangered*. New York, NY: HarperCollins, p.14.
8.  Karr-Morse, R. and Wiley, M.S. (1997) *Ghosts from the Nursery: Tracing the Roots of Violence*. New York, NY: Atlantic Monthly Press, p.145.
9.  Fonagy, P., Gergely, G., Jurist, E.L. and Target, M. (2002) *Affect Regulation, Mentalization, and the Development of the Self*. New York, NY: Other Press.
10. Szalavitz, M. and Perry, B.D. (2010) *Born for Love: Why Empathy is Essential – And Endangered*. New York, NY: HarperCollins, p.289.
11. See Tangney, J. and Dearing, R. (2002). *Shame and Guilt*. NY: Guilford Press.
12. Gilbert, P. (2009) *The Compassionate Mind*. London: Constable & Robinson.
13. Schore, A.N. (1994) *Affect Regulation and the Origin of the Self: The Neurobiology of Emotional Development*. New Jersey: Lawrence Erlbaum Associates.
14. Szalavitz, M. and Perry, B.D. (2010) *Born for Love: Why Empathy is Essential – And Endangered*. New York, NY: HarperCollins.
15. 'Are you good or evil?' *Horizon*. Broadcast by the BBC on 7 September 2011.
16. *The Death of Tom Inglis* by David Morley, broadcast by the BBC on 20 May 2011.
17. 'Are you good or evil?' *Horizon*. Broadcast by the BBC on 7 September 2011.
18. Szalavitz, M. and Perry, B.D. (2010) *Born for Love: Why Empathy is Essential – And Endangered*. New York, NY: HarperCollins.
19. Brontë, E. (1994) *Wuthering Heights*. London: Penguin Books. (First published 1847.)
20. O'Brien, E. (2009) *Byron in Love*. London: Orion Books.
21. Hayden, T.L. (1980) *One Child*. New York, NY: G.P. Putnam's Sons.
22. Hayden, T.L. (1980) *One Child*. New York, NY: G.P. Putnam's Sons, pp 40–41.

## Chapter 10

1.  Nouwen, J.M. (1999) *The Way of the Heart*. London: Darton, Longman and Todd.
2.  Golding, K.S. with Foulkes, J. and Courtncy, A. (2006) 'Opening the Door: How Can Therapy Help the Child and Young Person Living in Foster or Adoptive Homes?' In K.S. Golding, H.R. Dent, R. Nissim and E. Stott (eds) *Thinking Psychologically About Children Who Are Looked After and Adopted: Space For Reflection*. Chichester: John Wiley & Sons, p.306.
3.  Fonagy, P., Gergely, G., Jurist, E.L. and Target, M. (2002) *Affect Regulation, Mentalization, and the Development of the Self*. New York, NY: Other Press.
4.  Golding, K.S. (2011) 'Exploration and Integration: When Present and Past Meet.' In A. Becker-Weidman (ed.) *The Dyadic Developmental Psychotherapy Casebook*. Washington, DC: Jason Aronson, Chapter 8.
5.  van der Kolk, B.A. (2005) 'Child abuse and victimisation (Editorial).' *Psychiatric Annals 35*, 5, 374–378.
6.  Hughes, D. and Baylin, J. (2012) *Brain-Based Parenting: The Neuroscience of Caregiving for Healthy Attachment*. New York, NY: W.W. Norton & Co.

# Index

Page numbers in *italics* refer to figures.